P9-DOE-552

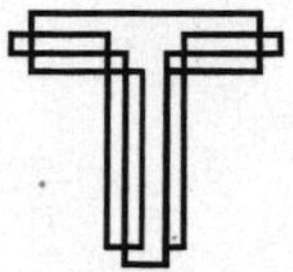

# The Gatekeeper

*Missy LeHand, FDR, and the Untold Story of the Partnership That Defined a Presidency*

Kathryn Smith

TOUCHSTONE
New York London Toronto Sydney New Delhi

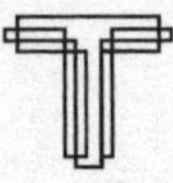

Touchstone
An Imprint of Simon & Schuster, Inc.
1230 Avenue of the Americas
New York, NY 10020



First Touchstone hardcover edition September 2016

TOUCHSTONE and colophon are registered trademarks of Simon & Schuster, Inc.

For information about special discounts for bulk purchases, please contact Simon & Schuster Special Sales at 1-866-506-1949 or business@simonandschuster.com.

The Simon & Schuster Speakers Bureau can bring authors to your live event. For more information, or to book an event, contact the Simon & Schuster Speakers Bureau at 1-866-248-3049 or visit our website at www.simonspeakers.com.

Interior design by Kyle Kabel

Manufactured in the United States of America

10 9 8 7 6 5 4 3 2 1

Library of Congress Cataloging-in-Publication Data

Names: Smith, Kathryn, 1956- author.
Title: The gatekeeper : Missy LeHand, FDR, and the untold story of the partnership that defined a presidency / by Kathryn Smith.
Description: New York : Touchstone, 2016.
Identifiers: LCCN 2016005357 | ISBN 9781501114960 (hardback) | ISBN 9781501114977 (paperback)
Subjects: LCSH: LeHand, Marguerite, 1896-1944. | Presidents—United States—Staff—Biography. | Private secretaries—United States—Biography. | Roosevelt, Franklin D. (Franklin Delano), 1882-1945—Friends and associates. | United States—Politics and government—1933-1945. | BISAC: HISTORY / United States / 20th Century. | BIOGRAPHY & AUTOBIOGRAPHY / Women. | BIOGRAPHY & AUTOBIOGRAPHY / Presidents & Heads of State.
Classification: LCC E748.L565 S65 2016 | DDC 973.917092 [B]—dc23
LC record available at https://lccn.loc.gov/2016005357

ISBN 978-1-5011-1496-0
ISBN 978-1-5011-1498-4 (ebook)

For the Original Missy Fan Club:
Barbara, Jane, and Steve

# Contents

# The Gatekeeper

PROLOGUE

# *The Daring Flight to Chicago*

On the morning of July 2, 1932, a slender, neatly dressed young woman with dark hair already threaded in silver stepped out of a car at the grass-and-gravel airport in Albany, New York. Her name was Marguerite Alice LeHand, but everyone knew her as Missy. Air travel was a new experience for the thirty-five-year-old woman, and though she had taken many other journeys with her boss, New York governor Franklin Delano Roosevelt, the stakes had never been higher than for this trip. They were flying to the Democratic National Convention in Chicago, where Roosevelt had been nominated for president of the United States the night before.

He needed Missy to help him put the finishing touches on his acceptance speech, and it had probably never occurred to her to decline making the trip with the boss she adored and called "F.D." Boarding the tiny, corrugated metal plane, she settled into a seat in the first row, where a typing table had been set up, a shiny black typewriter ready to go to work under her capable hands.

From the day in January 1921 that she first came to work for FDR as his private secretary, Missy LeHand had found herself in some very unusual places. They included a creaky houseboat meandering down the Florida coast; a tumbledown cottage in Warm Springs, Georgia; and the front seat of a Ford convertible that FDR drove at reckless speeds down country roads in Dutchess County, New York. He managed the gas and brake with hand controls, as he was paralyzed below the waist. Stricken with poliomyelitis eight months after Missy entered his employ, FDR had found his secretary integral to his rehabilitation and eventual return to public life. Now, after almost four years as governor of New York, he was ready to claim the job he had dreamed of holding since he was a young Manhattan lawyer: the presidency.

Surely Missy felt some trepidation about F.D.'s decision to fly to Chicago, although she knew that, practically speaking, it was the only way he could get to the convention before the delegates left for home. But in a larger sense, the flight was symbolic: FDR was literally launching skyward in a bold and daring gesture to show the country he was ready, willing, and fully capable of running for national office, even if he had to "run" in a wheelchair.

The announcement of FDR's planned appearance in Chicago had electrified the nation, and newsreel crews and reporters had swarmed the Albany airport. No candidate of either party had ever accepted a nomination in person, and the notion that the candidate would fly—something most Americans had never done—was almost as exotic as that of taking a rocket ship to the moon. Indeed, FDR had not flown for more than a decade, since serving the administration of Woodrow Wilson as assistant secretary of the navy during World War I, making brief sorties in open-cockpit planes in Europe.

Even though FDR's nomination had been a nip-and-tuck affair, the American Airways Ford Trimotor had been on standby at the Albany airfield for days, arrangements having been made prior to the convention to lease it with crew for $300. The crew included the pilot, a thirty-five-year-old World War I veteran named Ray D. Wonsey; a copilot; and a steward who would serve a full lunch in the tight confines of the cabin during the 783-mile journey.

Besides Missy and FDR, the party of ten passengers included his wife, Eleanor; two of their four sons, Elliott and John; speechwriter-advisor Samuel I. Rosenman; Missy's close friend and assistant, Grace Tully; and two bodyguards and a male aide, who, along with Elliott, were primarily responsible for helping FDR move around without drawing undue attention to his paralysis.

Wearing a blue summer-weight double-breasted suit and holding a Panama hat, the Democratic nominee was assisted by Elliott into the plane, FDR characteristically bantering to distract the well-wishers on hand from the sight of a fifty-year-old man who could not get out of his car unaided. The plane had been retrofitted with a wooden ramp so FDR could walk on board using a cane and Elliott's arm for support. He settled into a seat beside his pretty, blue-eyed secretary and began dictating a telegram to his elderly mother, Sara.

*This informal photo of Missy was taken around 1933, when she went to Washington as the president's private secretary.*

As the silver and blue plane roared down the runway and soared into the sky, FDR and his entourage passed around celebratory telegrams, and the steward handed out chewing gum, maps, and American Airways postcards. Eleanor knitted a baby sweater. Sam Rosenman and FDR worked on the speech, dictating a few changes for Missy to retype. The cabin, measuring a mere eighteen feet in length, soon filled with smoke as FDR puffed away on his Camels and Missy on her Lucky Strikes; both smoked two to three packs a day. However, the most hard-core practitioner of the tobacco habit in FDR's inner circle was waiting in Chicago, where he had been stationed throughout the convention. Louis McHenry Howe, the wizened former newspaperman who had orchestrated the political career of "the Boss" since his days in the New York legislature, was steadily destroying what was left of his lungs by chain-smoking a brand called Sweet Caporals. He lit one cigarette off the butt of another, and his clothing was always dusted with ash.

The acceptance speech had been drafted by FDR, Rosenman, and Raymond Moley, a pipe-smoking college professor and charter member of a new group of advisors known as the "Brain Trust." Both Rosenman and Moley would later claim authorship of the two words in the speech that became the brand of the Roosevelt era: New Deal. Neither attached much significance to them at the time.

Howe, in his sweltering Chicago hotel room, was writing his own version of the acceptance speech, convinced that launching his boss on the right foot rhetorically was as vital as getting him to the convention in the first place. Everyone in the Roosevelt camp knew that three years into the worst economic depression the country had ever seen, Americans needed hope above all things to pull themselves out of the mire. FDR, paralyzed by polio for more than a decade, was a man who knew a thing or two about hope.

The plane landed to refuel in Buffalo, where FDR welcomed a few supporters and reporters on board while the other passengers climbed off and stretched their legs. In the air again, the steward served a lunch of cold chicken, peanut butter and jelly sandwiches, salad, chocolate cake, and melting ice cream. While the steward reported that all "did full justice to the lunch," they didn't all keep it down. High winds rocked the plane and rattled the passengers. An account written by the son and granddaughter of Captain Wonsey said, "White-knuckled passengers could only cling to the upholstered arms of the aluminum chairs. In the turbulence, acceptance speech sheets slid off the desk, and the typewriter came close to pitching off the table into Miss LeHand's lap." The Roosevelts' youngest son, John, got airsick and spent most of the flight in the tail throwing up. There must have been moments when Missy wondered what in the world she was doing on that plane.

A woman of undistinguished background and an education that ended with high school, Missy had traveled far in the company of Franklin Roosevelt. She came into his orbit as a staff member for his vice presidential campaign in 1920, when he and Democratic nominee James M. Cox were soundly defeated by Warren G. Harding and his running mate, Calvin Coolidge. Invited by Eleanor to stay on for a few weeks in Hyde Park to help clean up correspondence, Missy got along so well with FDR that he asked her to become his private secretary. For the first eight months of 1921, she worked between his law office and an investment firm where he served as a Wall Street rainmaker. She was soon spellbound by the renowned Roosevelt charm.

Then, tragedy struck. In August 1921, while vacationing on Campobello Island off the coast of Maine, Roosevelt was struck by a severely disabling case of poliomyelitis, known at the time as infantile paralysis. For the next seven years he pursued treatments both conventional and outlandish in a quest to walk again, while Louis and Eleanor kept his political career alive. Though he built his upper body strength to compensate for his damaged legs, "walking" for Roosevelt required locked braces, a cane, and the arm of a strong man who sometimes went away from the experience with finger-shaped bruises. In fact, without an assistant, FDR could not rise from a chair by himself. Missy was his primary companion during this determined battle, first for long winter trips on the rickety houseboat *Larooco,* and then at the Warm Springs, Georgia, resort that FDR purchased and where he established, with Missy's help, the country's premier polio rehabilitation facility.

Much to Missy's distress, in 1928 FDR was pressured into running for governor of New York by Alfred E. Smith, the Democratic nominee for president. In doing so, he effectively abandoned his quest to walk, because the time he needed each day for therapy had to be devoted instead to campaigning and, after election, governing what was at the time the country's most populous state. Upon his election, Missy moved to Albany and Eleanor offered her a bedroom in the executive mansion. She was on call virtually around the clock, meeting and often anticipating not only the needs of the governor but also those of his busy wife.

After almost four years in Albany as an immensely popular governor, FDR was ready to run for national office. Missy, ever loyal, was his closest confidante and truest true believer—even if it meant getting on an airplane with him and flying straight into a storm.

The plane landed in Chicago at 4:30 p.m., two and a half hours behind schedule. The welcoming party included James A. Farley, FDR's floor manager at the convention; the candidate's oldest son, James; daughter Anna; and Louis Howe—along with a crowd estimated at 25,000. In the tumult, FDR's hat was knocked off his head, and his pince-nez glasses were dislodged. Louis squeezed into the car with the Boss for the trip into town and quickly scanned the speech. Soon he was complaining about it and urging his own version on FDR. "Dammit, Louis," Roosevelt exploded, "*I'm* the nominee!" However, he employed his renowned ability as what we would nowadays call a multitasker to scan Louis's speech while waving to the crowds lining the road, and decided to substitute his first page for the one Rosenman and Missy had labored over on the plane.

A few hours later, gripping the lectern at Chicago Stadium, Roosevelt delivered a speech concluding with words that would be forever linked to his name: "I pledge you, I pledge myself to a new deal for the American people."

There is no record of where Missy sat during this speech, but because she was considered "a member of the family," it's likely she was with Eleanor and the Roosevelt children. On Election Day in Hyde Park that November, the two women stood side by side on the steps of the town hall, their gloved fingers interlaced, as FDR's supporters cheered. In one telling photo of the scene, Missy beamed, while Eleanor, who dreaded becoming first lady, looked downcast.

Ensconced in the West Wing right outside the Oval Office, Missy would come to wield enormous influence and power within his administration. She was the gatekeeper to the president, while also advising him on policy and appointments, speeches and actions. FDR heeded her counsel, knowing it was based on common sense, honesty, sure instincts, and unshakable loyalty to him. Sitting in the only office adjoining his, she knew every person FDR saw and the nature of the call, and she controlled the back door that bypassed his official appointments secretary and allowed visitors to slip in unseen by the press and unrecorded by the official log. She screened his mail and decided which callers could be immediately dispatched to his phone by the White House switchboard. (Among these favored callers was Lucy Mercer Rutherfurd, the woman whose love affair with FDR had almost destroyed his marriage in 1918.)

There had never been anyone like Missy in the White House before, and it was a long time before anyone like Missy followed. The only other women—besides first ladies—who have wielded as much influence over a president since Missy were Condoleezza Rice, national security advisor and secretary of state for George W. Bush, and Barack Obama's senior advisor, Valerie Jarrett.

*Missy and FDR sit at his crowded Oval Office desk in May 1941.*

Rosenman, a member of FDR's inner circle throughout his presidency and the editor of his papers, called Missy "one of the most important people of the Roosevelt era. She sought to remain out of the limelight—and succeeded. I doubt whether her real contributions to the work of the President and to her country will ever be adequately understood except by those who personally knew her and watched her in the White House."

Rosenman's words about Missy staying out of the limelight were not exactly accurate, for in her day Missy was famous. In 1933 *Newsweek* dubbed her the "President's Super-Secretary." She appeared on the cover of Henry Luce's influential *Time* magazine in 1934 as the only female member of the White House "secretariat." During Roosevelt's second term she was named one of the seven best-dressed women in the capital, along with the French ambassador's wife. The phrase "Missy knows" was repeated over and over in an admiring profile in *The Saturday Evening Post* in 1938. *Look* magazine sent a photographer to the White House for a multipage photo spread with Missy in 1940, which gave the public a glance into her apartment on the third floor and the president's private study—well-timed publicity as Roosevelt sought an unprecedented third term.

During Missy's time, no one had heard of "glass ceilings" hindering the advancement of women, but she broke a crucial one at the same time Eleanor became the role model for the modern first lady and Frances Perkins became the first female cabinet member. Missy was the first woman to be secretary to a president at a time when "secretary" was the top staff title in the White House. In everything but name she was FDR's chief of staff—for the job title was not used by a president until Dwight Eisenhower adopted it to suit his sense of military structure.

FDR himself identified an even more significant role for her in his administration and life, saying often, "Missy is my conscience." He was a Hudson Valley blue blood who was famously described as "a traitor to his class," but Missy was a blue-collar girl from a seedy part of Boston who never let her boss forget the people he had promised to champion. Missy, wrote Washington columnist Drew Pearson, "thought about the plebes."

When a heart condition she had developed as a child led to a disabling stroke and her departure from the White House in 1941, the gaping void in FDR's inner circle was never filled. Partly paralyzed and robbed of the ability to speak, Missy predeceased her beloved F.D. by less than nine months. She disappeared from the public consciousness after her stroke, leaving only the faintest of trails.

Missy never kept a diary about the twenty-one years she spent orbiting FDR's sun, a point of pride she mentioned in every major interview, saying she had no plans to write a memoir. Her one attempt at writing an article about her work was abandoned and never published. Her friend Robert Sherwood, a noted playwright as well as one of FDR's best speechwriters, inscribed a copy of his Pulitzer Prize–winning play *Abe Lincoln in Illinois,* "For Missy LeHand, who will someday be a vitally important character in a play about the greatest President of the United States since the subject of this play." It did not happen.

In play, movie, and television scripts, she has been marginalized as a love-starved secretary or maligned as a mistress.

Research for this book has tapped a trove of letters to a man Missy loved during her time at the White House, the extensive archive kept by her family (including recently discovered home movies Missy herself shot in the 1930s), and a crucial medical document that reveals the precarious state of her health, turning almost everything previously written about Missy LeHand on its head.

What this famously discreet woman *thought* during the time she held a ringside seat on the most tumultuous years of the twentieth century will never be entirely known. What Missy knew, saw, heard, and did has never been pieced together—until now.

## CHAPTER ONE

# *When Missy Was Marguerite*

Missy LeHand's paternal grandfather escaped the shores of famine-ravaged Ireland only to die when a hatchet landed on his head in America. It is the first known instance of miserably mixed luck for the family of Franklin Delano Roosevelt's future right-hand woman.

In 1845 the Irish potato crop failed, setting off five years of unimaginable misery in a country that was viewed with the same mixture of pity, exasperation, and prejudice as Haiti and other intractably Third World countries are today. Over the next decade, Ireland's population of more than eight million fell by a third—a combination of starvation, disease, and a massive emigration that would take two million citizens away from their place of birth, most never to return. While all of Marguerite's grandparents were Irish immigrants, the LeHands were the only ones who appear to have fled to America during the famine. Her maternal grandparents, the Graffins, settled in upstate New York long before the potato crop disaster. They achieved a level of middle-class stability the LeHands didn't reach until Missy went to work for FDR and became a one-woman employment agency for her family.

The worst year for the potato crop was 1847. Those who could scrape up the passage money left Ireland, most often for England or North America. So many died on the month-long voyages to Canada and the United States on leaky, ill-provisioned vessels that they were called "coffin ships." The greed that drove the shipping companies was just one example of how the Irish were exploited, with the British government considered by many Irish as the most callous of villains. The so-called relief policies it established led to skyrocketing food prices and mass evictions of peasants by their landlords. Irish journalist and activist John Mitchell wrote in 1858, "The Almighty, indeed, sent the potato blight, but the English created the famine."

Irish memories were long and bitter. In 1937, at the start of his second term, President Roosevelt learned that Joseph P. Kennedy—the red-haired Roman Catholic grandson of a coffin ship survivor—aspired to be sent to London as ambassador to the Court of St. James's. The president's son James recalled that his father "laughed so hard he almost toppled from his wheelchair." The next year FDR appointed him anyway, and came to regret it. The outspoken Kennedy was not cut out as a diplomat, and he had an Irishman's ingrained distrust of the English.

With their common Irish, Catholic, and Boston background, Missy and Joe Kennedy became fast friends in FDR's White House orbit. No doubt he cultivated her for access to the president, but she was astute enough to realize it, and worked Kennedy for favors as well.

The wealth amassed by the Kennedys eluded the LeHands, as did the fabled Irish luck. Missy's paternal grandfather, Daniel LeHand, and grandmother Hannah, both born around 1833, escaped Ireland as young adults. They settled in Potsdam, New York, where in 1856 Daniel was working construction on a Methodist church. One day a hatchet fell from a staging platform, striking him on the head and killing him. Hannah never remarried, but raised their infant son, Daniel, alone in Potsdam. When she died at age eighty-four in 1907, her obituary said, "She possessed a fund of wit and humor peculiar to her race and her home has been for years a favorite, especially with the young people of whom she numbered many as her friends." These were traits well represented in her youngest granddaughter.

Missy's maternal grandparents were Arthur and Jane Graffin, who raised eight children on their farm in Brasher Falls, New York. Their second child, Mary Jane, and Daniel LeHand married young and had their first child, also named Daniel, in 1871 when they were just sixteen years old. Three more children followed at odd intervals: Bernard in 1883, Anna in 1894, and Marguerite in 1896.

At the time of Missy's birth, her parents were more than forty years old (and her oldest brother was nearly twenty-five years her senior). Her father, Daniel, was the coachman for a leading Potsdam family, the Clarksons, who owned a company that manufactured butter molds. She was born on September 13, 1896, at the LeHand home on the northwest corner of Cedar and Main Streets in Potsdam. Although the LeHand family moved to Somerville, Massachusetts, around 1900, they maintained close ties with their birthplaces. The local newspapers often mentioned visits to Potsdam relatives by Daniel and Mary, and Missy remained close to her New York State aunts Emma McCarthy and Nellie Graffin. A spinster who lived with her mother and other relatives throughout her life, Nellie became a frequent guest of Missy's at the White House and the Roosevelt home in Hyde Park.

An exceptional gathering of the Graffin family occurred in 1911, when Missy was fourteen. "On a most perfect summer day" in July, Missy's widowed grandmother, Jane Graffin, held a reunion at her Brasher Falls home, attended by twenty-five family members, "some of whom had not met for three decades." They gathered around tables at both a midday meal and evening supper, with dishes "perfect in quantity, quality and effect," and photographs were taken of the entire "House of Graffin" together, as well as of Jane with her grandchildren. Among them was her granddaughter from Somerville, listed in the local newspaper account as "Margaret." It was not the last time that Missy's given name would be misspelled in a newspaper.

Somerville had existed since colonial days as part of the city of Charlestown, but it became a separate town in 1842, given a "purely fanciful name" with no historical significance. In 1900, Somerville was a working-class suburb of Boston, densely populated with 62,000 residents packed into 4.2 square miles. As late as 1920, just over a third of the residents had what the U.S. Census described as "native parentage." The rest were immigrants, children of immigrants, or of "mixed" native and immigrant parentage, largely Irish and Italian. Its tonier neighbors sometimes referred to the city as "Slummerville" because of its blue-collar residents and a reputation for crime.

Among Somerville's claims to fame at the time Missy's family moved there were Mary Sawyer, the woman whose love for her pet lamb had inspired the nursery rhyme "Mary Had a Little Lamb," and McLean Asylum, a progressive hospital for the mentally ill whose patients had included the brothers of Ralph Waldo Emerson. It boasted enterprising businesspeople, too, including a young immigrant from Canada named Alfred Fuller who took a job in Somerville as a brush and mop salesman and parlayed his success into the Fuller Brush Company. Another man, Joseph Archibald Query, developed a marshmallow creme spread, which he called "fluff," and began peddling it door-to-door in 1917. He eventually sold the recipe for $500, but the product is still marketed internationally as Marshmallow Fluff. Today Somerville residents proudly claim it as their home-grown culinary creation and hold a "What the Fluff?" festival each September.

The LeHands eventually settled in a three-story house at 101 Orchard Street.

They joined St. John the Evangelist Catholic Church on Massachusetts Avenue in Cambridge and sent their younger children to the public schools. Daniel Jr., known as Dan, married a woman named Georgiana, nicknamed "Georgie," and at age thirty-nine both were living with his parents.

*The house at 101 Orchard Street had not changed much from the time Missy lived there when this photo was taken in the 1960s.*

Later in life, when Missy was profiled in national newspaper and magazine articles, she may have dressed up her background a bit. She described her father as being "in real estate," an ambiguous term that was also used in his obituary, and at least one writer got the impression she claimed French ancestry on the LeHand side. On the 1920 census, however, Daniel described himself as a gardener and landscaper. Roosevelt biographer Bernard Asbell wrote that Missy's father may have been an undependable provider because of problems with alcoholism, and that he deserted his wife and lived apart from the family until shortly before his death in 1924. The census records and repeated references to the couple in newspaper social notes, as well as Missy's interviews, call that into question. In either case, the family struggled to make ends meet, and the LeHands sometimes rented rooms to Harvard students to augment their income. In numerous interviews, Missy said her family was not poor, but that they worked for everything they had.

Throughout her life, people remarked on the manners and polish Missy displayed despite her humble background. It may be that contacts with the well-heeled young Harvard students were early contributions to her sophistication. But she was hardly living in a cultural wasteland. Then as now, the Boston area was home to dozens of colleges and universities, museums, concert halls, and theaters, and even Somerville could boast of opportunities for cultural enrichment. Beginning in 1914, live theater had a grand venue when Joseph Hobbs built the 1,200-seat Somerville Theatre on Davis Square, a few blocks from the LeHand home. With a café, meeting hall with dance floor, bowling alley, and billiard parlor, it was a popular gathering place that attracted vaudeville touring companies and up-and-coming actors who performed in its stock company, the Somerville Theatre Players. Actress Tallulah Bankhead appeared there in 1919 when she was only seventeen years old, writing to her grandfather, U.S. senator John Hollis Bankhead, that she was "nearly dead" after giving twelve performances a week. "There is nothing here at all," she complained, "but I am working very hard for the experience."

As an adult, Missy knew Tallulah, by then a Broadway and Hollywood star famous for her wild excess, who was the daughter (and often the despair) of powerful Speaker of the House William B. Bankhead. A liberal Democrat, the actress campaigned for FDR and was a frequent guest at the White House. Missy became a great theater enthusiast, making friends with playwrights and actors and attending plays in Washington and New York whenever she could escape her duties.

More accessible to those with modest incomes such as the LeHands were the movies. Pearson's Perfect Pictures, Somerville's first movie house, opened in 1904. The first offerings were short children's films, and the seven-cent admission ticket included a bag of candy per child. (Conveniently, owner Arthur Pearson was also in the candy business.) Missy was a lifelong movie buff who eventually bought her own motion picture cameras for making home movies, and visited Hollywood studios.

Missy also loved to read. Somerville built a new main library near Davis Square and two branches between 1909 and 1918, all partially funded by the foundation of steel magnate Andrew Carnegie. The main library was adjacent to Somerville High

School, where Missy continued her education after graduating from Highland Grammar School in June 1912. That same year, though, her education was rudely interrupted.

The seminal event of young Missy's life was illness. At age fifteen, she developed rheumatic fever. Almost unheard of in the United States today and now easily quelled with antibiotics, rheumatic fever was a major killer of American children in the late nineteenth and early twentieth centuries. Once the acute stage passed, the illness left its victims in an extremely weakened condition that required a lengthy recovery in bed, either at home or at a sanitarium associated with a hospital.

*Missy at eighteen near her home in Somerville, Massachusetts.*

The months of enforced rest may have contributed to Missy's love of reading; they certainly delayed the completion of her education, as she did not graduate from Somerville High until 1917, when she was twenty years old. Although Missy's symptoms abated, the heart damage was permanent. It is likely her doctors would have warned her to avoid pregnancy, as the increased stress on her compromised heart would have been detrimental to her health. She eventually became, in the jargon of the day, a "cardiac cripple," something that would strengthen the bond with her future boss after he became a "polio cripple."

By the time of Missy's graduation from high school, her sister, Anna, had married a man named Henry Farwell and had twice made her an aunt. Anna named the oldest daughter Marguerite after Missy—though she went by the nickname "Babe"—and the younger one Barbara, known within the family as "Sister." The Farwells lived next door to the LeHands, and "the girls" would be the chief objects of Missy's maternal affections for the rest of her life.

*Missy's beloved nieces, from left, Marguerite (Babe) and Barbara (Sister) Farwell, were the objects of all her maternal love.*

In 1917, Missy was tall and slim, with wavy dark brown hair and large blue eyes under dark arched brows—the classic black Irish coloring. She had a long face and a prominent jaw and nose, but a sweetness of expression that spoke of her good nature. Virtually everyone who met and wrote about her in the years to come mentioned her constant smile and her beautiful blue eyes. "Even as a high school girl, she had a certain class to her," recalled Barbara Muller Curtis, who grew up with Missy in Somerville and formed a lifelong friendship with her. "I remember one time watching her go around the corner—our houses weren't too far apart—and my mother kind of looked out the window and called my attention to her. She said, 'She certainly looks smart.' She had a dark suit on to go to high school. She stood out for having a better appearance and being smarter than most."

*Missy was twenty when she graduated from high school in 1917.*

Her sense of humor was already evident. Issues of *The Radiator,* the high school newspaper, include a senior class notes column written by Missy and another girl, full of corny jokes and harmless bits of gossip. It was the kind of sophomoric humor her future boss loved.

Missy's heart condition probably dictated her career path. Though motherhood was a poor option, nursing and teaching were traditional roles available for a working woman. However, both would daily expose her to the rowdy playgrounds of germs, which she needed to avoid whenever possible to guard her heart from further rheumatic fever attacks. Thus Missy prepared to enter the burgeoning ranks of office workers by taking a secretarial course in high school, even though secretarial jobs had only fairly recently been wrested away from men. In 1870, about the time the typewriter came into limited use, there were only seven female stenographers in the country. But by 1900 their numbers had swelled to 200,000, and in 1930 there were two million women stenographers. By that time, men held only one of every twenty-five jobs in typing.

Stenography involved taking shorthand notes during dictation and transcribing the baffling squiggles into words with a typewriter. Speed and accuracy were the hallmarks of an able stenographer. In the 1921 World's Championship Contest of the National Shorthand Reporters' Association, the winner transcribed at 215 words per minute with an accuracy rate of over 98 percent. (Alas, Missy never reached these Olympian heights. Stenography was not one of her favorite activities, and when Grace Tully joined the incoming Governor Roosevelt's staff in New York in 1928, Missy was glad to pass most of those duties on to her.)

A young woman could aim higher, however, than simply taking shorthand notes and typing, and Missy was bright and capable of so much more. "The ambition of every girl who goes into business as a stenographer—provided she has a goal and does not merely regard her position as a means of filling the interim between school and matrimony—is to become a private secretary," wrote Helen B. Gladwyn in an article in *Ladies' Home Journal* in 1916. "Certainly the ambition is a laudable one for, short of actual executive work, it is about the most agreeable and lucrative kind of position one can hold."

Romance writers fed exotic notions to young women considering secretarial careers. The 1919 novel *Miss Maitland Private Secretary* recounted the adventures of a self-effacing young woman who, by the novel's end, had helped track down a jewel thief as well as the kidnapper of her employer's granddaughter *and* attracted a proposal of marriage from the nice-looking young millionaire next door.

Working in Missy's favor when it came to finding a job was the entry of the United States into World War I on April 6, 1917, opening more opportunities for young women in the workforce as men joined the military. Missy was hired for and quit four jobs in Boston, one after just two weeks over a salary dispute, another after a few months because the owners refused to turn on the heat during the cold fall months and she feared for her health. Perhaps she felt a patriotic call to do her part, or was just ready to stretch her wings a bit. She took the civil service exam and accepted a job in Washington, D.C., working for the Ordnance Board at the Department of the Navy. She was working in the same building as the handsome young assistant secretary of the navy, Franklin Delano Roosevelt, but they did not meet.

She found the work stultifying. Because of the need for secrecy, the stenographers were given one page of notes at a time to type, all day long. One day she and a girlfriend pled illness and played hooky from work, taking a sightseeing trip to Mount Vernon. Missy told the story in an interview in the *Boston Daily Record* in 1937: "When I went back that night to my boarding house, a government nurse was waiting for me—and the things that woman said! Honestly, she made me feel that I should be shot for deserting." Missy was rescued on two counts. A medical exam was ordered and the doctor heard a heart murmur, caused by the valve damage from rheumatic fever, and prescribed rest. She also met with Charles McCarthy, secretary to FDR, who was impressed with her and gave her a government job with the

Emergency Fleet Corporation in Philadelphia. She had lasted all of three weeks in Washington.

Franklin Delano Roosevelt's time in Washington was drawing to a close, too. In the summer of 1920, he accepted the vice presidential slot on the Democratic Party ticket, running with Ohio governor James M. Cox. When Charles McCarthy agreed to serve as FDR's campaign chairman, he invited the intelligent, hardworking young woman from Somerville to join the campaign staff at headquarters in New York. She met the candidate only once, as he spent his time barnstorming the country in a futile race against Republicans Warren G. Harding and Calvin Coolidge, but it was the beginning of a relationship with FDR and his family that would continue for the rest of her life.

❁ CHAPTER TWO

# Scion of the Hudson Valley Roosevelts

Missy LeHand and Franklin Delano Roosevelt had appendectomies within a couple of years of each other, when he was thirty-three and serving as assistant secretary of the navy, and she was a seventeen-year-old high school student. It was one common experience in personal histories that could hardly have been more different: Missy was a blue-collar girl, and Franklin was a blue-blood prince.

He was born January 30, 1882, to James and Sara Delano Roosevelt. Theirs was a May-December coupling: James, a well-to-do Hudson River Valley widower with a grown son, was fifty-three when Sara, half his age, gave birth in a second-floor bedroom of Springwood, their home in Hyde Park, New York. The birth proved difficult, and mother and child almost died. From this anxious beginning, Sara became the most overbearing of mothers.

She was a proud woman. Her family name was older than the Roosevelts', and the Delanos had more money. Her father, Warren Delano, had made his fortune in China in the opium trade—though the family said it came from tea—and owned a forty-room Hudson River Valley mansion. Like Missy's family, the Delanos had come from Europe on a ship, only theirs arrived a few months after the *Mayflower,* two centuries before the potato-deprived LeHands and a few decades before the Roosevelts. Sara often proclaimed her son was a Delano rather than a Roosevelt.

Like many children of privilege, Franklin got his early

education at home from governesses and tutors. He wanted for nothing. His Delano grandparents presented him with a dapple gray rocking horse with a real hair tail and mane when he was a toddler; a live pony named Debby replaced it by the time he was four, still being dressed in skirts and wearing his hair in long blond curls. With his father, who remained in good health during his early childhood, Franklin tramped the forests and fields of the Hudson River Valley, capturing and mounting birds. James taught him to sail, launching an abiding love of boating; by age nine he owned a forty-five-foot yacht he christened the *New Moon*. For quieter times indoors, he had stamp albums that had belonged to his mother. Franklin would eventually expand the collection to 150 albums containing over a million stamps.

*Young FDR and his mother, Sara Delano Roosevelt, who smothered him with love all his life.*

Although Franklin traveled widely with his parents, including long trips to Canada, England, and Germany, he had limited exposure to other children until he entered private school in 1896, the year Missy was born. He was fourteen, Sara having delayed his departure from the home classroom by two years.

While well intentioned, Sara may have unknowingly set him up for a lifetime of illness, for his untested immune system proved no match for marauding germs. His catalogue of childhood illnesses included measles, mumps, scarlet fever, typhoid fever, sinusitis, and severe colds. In adulthood he added another bout of typhoid, influenza, double pneumonia, severe hives (on his honeymoon), and the disease that ultimately crippled him, poliomyelitis.

Long after both her husband and mother-in-law were dead, Eleanor Roosevelt wrote of Sara, "I doubt if as long as she lived she ever let him leave the house without inquiring whether he was dressed warmly enough or urging him to wear his rubbers or put on a sweater under his coat." He was not allowed to bathe by himself until he was eight and a half years old, and that was only during a visit to his grandmother Delano's house.

It's no wonder that Sara's cosseted son enjoyed only middling popularity at Groton, a Massachusetts preparatory school for boys destined for Ivy League colleges. The school's founder and headmaster was the Reverend Endicott Peabody, an Episcopal minister who believed in "muscular Christianity," achieved through cold showers, competitive athletics, prayer, and turning a blind eye to hazing. Boys grew resigned to "bootboxing"—being crammed into a footlocker—and a few had to be resuscitated after having their heads held too long under a gushing faucet, an early form of waterboarding called "pumping." Peabody was an important figure in FDR's life from his Groton days forward, officiating at his wedding and conducting private services for his inaugurations, even though he was a Republican.

Harvard was the most popular destination for graduates of Groton, and they were welcomed almost without exception. Franklin entered its halls in 1900, where he lived in a well-appointed residence hall with a Groton friend and was eventually chosen editor in chief of the student newspaper, the *Crimson*. However, he failed to reach the top rung of the social ladder at status-conscious Harvard. In his mid-thirties, FDR described as the greatest disappointment of his life that he was passed over by the socially prestigious Porcellian Club, whose members ostentatiously displayed gold pig-shaped fobs on their watch chains. Richard Whitney, a younger Grotonian who became president of the New York Stock Exchange, was still wearing his pig in 1938 when he arrived at Sing Sing to serve a term for embezzlement. By then, President Franklin Roosevelt may have taken some comfort as he ate breakfast in bed each morning gazing at the large collection of nongolden miniature "porkers" that lined his White House bedroom mantelpiece. The inspiration for the pigs, one of his many collecting hobbies, isn't known, but after he became president his family and staff delighted in finding additions to place in his Christmas stocking. Perhaps it was a private joke Franklin had with himself.

*FDR at Harvard in 1903.*

James Roosevelt had been in declining health and died after a series of heart attacks during the fall of Franklin's freshman year at Harvard. Sara, still handsome at forty-six, further tightened her focus on her son, spending her winters in a Boston apartment. Missy's mother was probably renting rooms to Harvard students by then; Franklin and Sara Roosevelt certainly had no need of such an arrangement.

Armchair psychoanalysts often attribute Roosevelt's ability to compartmentalize his life and cloak his thoughts and plans to the smothering love of his parents. It was a coping mechanism he developed to keep some part of himself hidden from a mother who could not keep her distance. He was certainly successful when it came to choosing a bride, for Sara was caught completely by surprise when her son announced plans to marry his fifth cousin once removed, Anna Eleanor Roosevelt. The two had begun courting in 1902, and Franklin proposed the next fall.

His mother pretended to be pleased but immediately set to work keeping the couple apart. Mother and son took a five-week Caribbean cruise in the spring of 1904, Franklin's college roommate on board, but Eleanor left ashore. Sara even tried to persuade an old family friend who was a diplomat in London to hire Franklin as his secretary, removing him from Eleanor's enchanting presence. Nothing worked; Franklin was not dissuaded from the willowy young woman he called "an angel." At just under six feet tall, she stood almost eye-to-eye with six-foot-two-inch Franklin. He admired her good mind, and her interest in social justice, such as the plight of immigrants in New York.

Throughout Franklin's life he spoke only of Eleanor's most attractive features: her "lovely hair and pretty eyes." Others commented also on her big blue eyes and the thick golden brown hair she usually wore Gibson Girl–style, pinned in a twist or a fat bun, or sometimes loose and held back from her face in a velvet band. (The blue eyes, slim height, and abundant hair were common features of women FDR found attractive, including Missy and Lucy Mercer Rutherfurd.) But as novelist Gerald Kolpan observed of the fictionalized Eleanor in his novel *Etta,* her face "seemed to go bad" below the nose: "Her enormous thick-lipped smile revealed teeth nearly as large of those of a horse and set in a pronounced overbite. Even this might have been a charming feature, but the face ended in a weak and receding chin that robbed her of any claim to beauty by the shallow standards of the world."

Eleanor was Theodore Roosevelt's favorite niece, but she had suffered through a childhood that could have been penned by Charles Dickens. Her father, Theodore Roosevelt's younger brother, Elliott, was a ne'er-do-well alcoholic, while her mother, Anna Hall Roosevelt, a society beauty, was disappointed in her plain and solemn oldest child. She belittled her and called her "Granny" in front of others, to Eleanor's mortification. Both parents died before she was ten, leaving Eleanor and two younger brothers in the care of their maternal grandmother. Elliott Jr. died of scarlet fever; younger brother Hall survived into late adulthood but inherited their father's alcoholism.

When Eleanor was fifteen, her grandmother sent her to the Allenswood school in England, where she found her greatest childhood happiness. The enlightened French headmistress, Mademoiselle Marie Souvestre, recognized her unusual gifts and mentored her, taking the lonely girl traveling with her on holidays. Eleanor kept Souvestre's photograph on her desk for the rest of her life. Then, lo and behold, she returned home to make her debut and caught the attention of Prince Charming.

Franklin graduated from Harvard in the spring of 1904 and presented Eleanor with an engagement ring on October 11, her twentieth birthday. He was twenty-two and had moved to New York with his mother to begin studies at Columbia Law School. The formal engagement was a brief one.

In her wedding photograph, taken two months before the March 17, 1905, ceremony, Eleanor looks steadily into the camera, full lips closed over her teeth, mummified in her satin and lace gown and court train, hands hidden by a bouquet the size of a birdcage.

*Eleanor Roosevelt in a portrait made two months before her March 17, 1905, wedding.*

No pictures were taken of the couple at their wedding, held in the New York City home of one of Eleanor's cousins. The gregarious President Theodore Roosevelt, stopping in to give away the bride between St. Patrick's Day engagements, stole the spotlight and, indeed, the show. (His daughter Alice, one of six bridesmaids, famously said her father wanted not only to be the bride at every wedding but the baby at every christening and the corpse at every funeral.) The young couple was left standing at the altar after the ceremony, ignored by most of the guests, who flocked into the library for the reception in the wake of the laughing president. It was good practice for Eleanor, who would immediately find herself thrust into the shadows by her domineering mother-in-law. While early photographs of the young couple capture a shared sense of fun and whimsy, later ones—especially after the children began arriving—often show Sara firmly planted between them, with

Eleanor looking down at a baby's downy head or staring disconsolately at the floor.

*Eleanor in 1911 with James, baby Elliott, and Anna.*

The children came fast. Eleanor returned pregnant from their European honeymoon to an apartment three blocks from Sara's, leased in their absence. (Sara later built them adjoining townhouses at 47-49 East 65th Street with a single entrance and connecting doorways on three of the six floors, allowing her twenty-four-hour access to her son.) While Franklin continued his law studies, daughter Anna arrived in 1906 and son James in 1907. Franklin Jr. was born in 1909 and died the same year, and soon afterward the grief-stricken Eleanor was pregnant with Elliott, named for her adored father. He was born in the fall of 1910. The last two boys, a second Franklin Jr. and John, were born in 1914 and 1916.

Never close to her own mother and with poor maternal

instincts, Eleanor left much of the childrearing to Sara and the servants. Her attempts at doing the best for her children were often misguided to the point of high comedy, as when she interpreted her pediatrician's instruction to give babies an "airing" several hours a day to mean hanging baby Anna in a basket out a window. Only when the wailing infant disturbed a neighbor who threatened to call the child welfare authorities did Eleanor realize she was in error. "This was a shock to me, for I thought I was being a most modern mother," she recalled.

While Eleanor was populating the Roosevelt nursery, her husband took a position in a law firm and struck out on his political career. He ran as a Democrat for a State Senate seat in 1910. (The Oyster Bay Roosevelts, as Teddy's branch of the family is called, were all Republicans.) On the campaign trail he traveled in a hired red Maxwell automobile, puttering down roads still dominated by horse-drawn buggies and wagons. His name, good looks, sincerity, and energy—"no one had ever before tried to visit every small four-corners store, every village and every town," Eleanor remembered—narrowly won the twenty-eight-year-old Franklin the election, the first Democrat to claim that Senate seat in his lifetime.

The Roosevelts took a house in Albany, giving Eleanor the opportunity to live apart from Sara. Though women would not be able to vote for another decade, she enjoyed going to the capitol and listening to speeches and debates. It was there that her husband had a fateful meeting with an odd little newspaper man named Louis McHenry Howe, who would become his most important political advisor.

It's not unusual for an attractive and charismatic politician to have a less photogenic but compelling advisor standing in the shadows—consider George W. Bush and Karl Rove or Bill Clinton and James Carville—but Howe would have seemed peculiar compared to almost any human being. Tiny and wizened, with a pockmarked face and a slash of a mouth never without its cigarette, he was called "Lousy Louis" by his fellow newshounds in

Albany because of "his really phenomenal sloppiness in dress." But appearances are ever deceiving, and Howe provides an outstanding example. He had grown up in Saratoga Springs, New York, the son of a failed newspaperman. At the time he met FDR he was forty years old, an unhappily married father of two (his wife, Grace, was the first cousin and close friend of the notorious accused ax murderess Lizzie Borden) and chronically short of funds. He latched on to the freshman senator, convinced that Roosevelt would one day become president of the United States—if he would only listen to Howe's advice.

FDR rubbed many people the wrong way in Albany. Frances Perkins, then a politically active consumer advocate, later Roosevelt's secretary of labor, recalled a self-consciously serious young man "with an unfortunate habit—so natural he was unaware of it—of throwing his head up. This, combined with his pince-nez and great height, gave him the appearance of looking down his nose at people." From his first weeks in the Senate, he butted heads with the New York Democratic Party bosses, an Irish Catholic cabal known by the name of its headquarters, Tammany Hall. He quickly joined an insurgence of progressives against the election of a corrupt Tammany politician named William "Blue-Eyed Billy" Sheehan to the U.S. Senate. (At the time, the state legislature elected U.S. senators.) Roosevelt's library served as the meeting room for the insurgents, where they filled the house to the rafters with smoke, and Sheehan's candidacy was derailed. Tammany substituted a man who wasn't much better, but FDR went along with the compromise. Many of his Democratic allies lost their seats at the next election, but Franklin's stand won him a reputation as a reformer, as well as Louis Howe's attention and loyalty.

Roosevelt was bedridden with typhoid fever when his reelection campaign began in 1912. Howe got him elected in absentia, placing newspaper ads and crisscrossing the district in the red Maxwell on Roosevelt's behalf. FDR widened his victory margin substantially, but he filled only part of the term. When

Democrat Woodrow Wilson was inaugurated president in March 1913, FDR ran into his secretary of the navy designate, Josephus Daniels, in Washington, who asked him to serve as assistant secretary. FDR was thrilled to accept the position, which had been one of Theodore Roosevelt's stepping-stones to the White House, and his knowledge of ships and oceans made him especially useful to Daniels.

The navy secretary was a shrewd North Carolina newspaper publisher who knew little about ships and even less about sailors; his ban of any beverage stronger than coffee in the onboard officers' mess was the origin of the phrase "a cup of Joe." The two had met at the Democratic convention in 1912, where Daniels admitted to having fallen in love at first sight—in a manly sort of way—with the handsome young politician. Franklin, for his part, called Daniels "the funniest looking hillbilly I had ever seen."

The Roosevelt family decamped to Washington, Louis Howe in tow as Roosevelt's special assistant. Eleanor was pleased to have again escaped her mother-in-law's controlling presence, less pleased at the constant attendance of Howe, whom she disliked. Once again, Eleanor had to learn the ways of a new city and its natives, one with as baffling a social protocol as the palace at Versailles. In addition to entertaining at home and accepting social engagements seven days a week, political wives were expected to make endless social calls to further their husbands' careers, and welcome the calls of others. Eleanor took the job seriously, averaging sixty calls each week during the first year they lived in Washington. To help her negotiate this intricate dance, in 1914 she hired a part-time social secretary, Lucy Mercer, an attractive young woman from an upper-crust family that had fallen on hard times.

Tall and slim, with large blue eyes, a winning smile, and a throaty voice—words that would later describe Missy LeHand—Lucy proved irresistible to her employer's husband. In the summer of 1916, with Eleanor and the children (including infant John) vacationing at the family compound on Campobello

Island, FDR and Lucy fell in love. They became the subject of much gossip in Washington, with Eleanor's cousin Alice conspiring to bring them together at social gatherings. (She archly commented that "Franklin deserved a good time. He was married to Eleanor.") However, it was not until the early fall of 1918, when Franklin returned from an inspection tour of World War I battlefields, that Eleanor discovered what was going on. Unpacking his luggage, she came upon a packet of love letters from Lucy and, as she put it, "the bottom dropped out of my own particular world, and I faced myself, my surroundings, my world honestly for the first time."

The couple contemplated divorce, but when Sara threatened to disinherit her son, and Louis Howe predicted the end of his political aspirations, they decided to continue their marriage. They maintained separate bedrooms for the rest of their married lives, and Franklin promised to break all contact with Lucy, a promise he violated repeatedly, including on the very day he died. Lucy accepted a post with a wealthy widower, Winthrop Rutherfurd, and eventually married him.

The Roosevelts' marriage limped on, with Eleanor distrustful and Franklin resigned. At any rate, when Franklin entered the private sector in 1921 and found himself in need of a secretary, the best candidate had Eleanor's stamp of approval: an eager-to-please young woman of undistinguished background and shrewd judgment named Marguerite Alice LeHand.

CHAPTER THREE

# *The Cuff Links Gang*

Missy was staying in the Adirondack Mountains in August 1920 when she opened a letter from Charles McCarthy, campaign chairman for the Democratic nominee for vice president. "I just received your telegram and am very glad that you are interested in this position because I think it will be a good experience for you," he wrote, offering her a secretarial job with a starting salary of $35 a week, "which can be made $40 in a week or two." She accepted the salary (equivalent to a little over $400 in current dollars) and less than a week later arrived in New York to work for the Franklin D. Roosevelt campaign at its headquarters in Grand Central Palace.

At the time the palace, located on Lexington Avenue between 46th and 47th Streets, was the city's premier exhibition hall, hosting everything from flower shows to kennel club competitions, with twelve stories of office space rising over the hall.

McCarthy had been Missy's boss at the Emergency Fleet Corporation in Philadelphia, which was established to meet the merchant shipping needs of World War I. With the last of the war business winding down, her job had ended, but McCarthy remembered her intelligence and ambition, which were needed by the badly funded and floundering Roosevelt campaign. Although presidential campaigns in those days didn't begin in earnest until Labor Day of an election year, FDR had already made one campaign trip, whistle-stopping by train through twenty states.

For President
JAMES M. COX

# HEADQUARTERS
## Franklin D. Roosevelt
GRAND CENTRAL PALACE
NEW YORK

For Vice-President
FRANKLIN D. ROOSEVELT

23, August 1920.

My dear Miss LeHand:-

I just received your telegram and am very glad that you are interested in the position because I think it will be a good experience for you. The salary is $35.00 a week, which can be made $40. within a week or two, I should say, and if you could come next Monday, August 30th, it will be fine. Please let me know by wire what you decide.

Sincerely yours,

C H McCarthy

Miss M. A. LeHand,
Saranac Inn,
New York.

*Charles McCarthy wrote to Missy in August 1920 inviting her to work for FDR's vice presidential campaign.*

Holding down the fort in New York, McCarthy felt overwhelmed and needed an energetic and even-tempered assistant in what was widely expected to be a losing battle for the Democrats.

FDR's nomination in July as the running mate of Ohio governor and newspaper publisher James Cox had been something of a surprise, but his relative youth—he was just thirty-eight—and geographic base helped balance the ticket, and his name was a major draw. After accepting, he resigned his position at the Navy Department to make the run, leaving Louis Howe behind in Washington as acting assistant secretary.

The Republicans' nominee was another Ohio newspaper publisher, the handsome but shallow Senator Warren Harding. His running mate was the famously tight-lipped governor of Massachusetts, Calvin Coolidge. (Theodore Roosevelt's sharp-tongued daughter Alice, though a die-hard Republican, once commented that Coolidge looked "as though he had been weaned on a pickle.") Harding promised voters a "return to normalcy"—coining a phrase that sounded good but whose meaning was hard to decipher. After eight years of Democratic leadership and the disillusioning experience of World War I, Americans were drawing away from the idealism and internationalism of Woodrow Wilson, who was by then partially paralyzed by a stroke and secluded at the White House under the watchful eyes of his wife and doctor. Nevertheless, Cox and Roosevelt called on the ailing leader and promised to make his fight for the United States to join the League of Nations "the chief issue of their campaign." It was, they believed, the best way to prevent another catastrophic world war.

Before Missy joined the campaign staff, FDR had given an average of seven speeches a day during his first eighteen-day train trip. Cox was setting a similarly blistering pace, while Harding campaigned for the most part by making leisurely talks from the veranda of his home in Marion, Ohio. Writer H. L. Mencken compared his bland banalities to "dogs barking idiotically through endless nights."

Missy's role at headquarters included handling correspondence and helping to schedule campaign trips, as well as coordinating with McCarthy and Steve Early, a former Associated Press reporter who had signed on as FDR's advance man. Later in the fall, Howe took a leave of absence from his job in Washington to join the campaign as its political strategist. Although Missy did not have much personal contact with the candidate, the core of his inner circle was formed in 1920, and she was counted as one of its members. Three others—Howe, Early, and Marvin McIntyre, who had been a government press agent during Roosevelt's time at the Navy Department—would with Missy form what became known as the White House secretariat. In 1920, though, they were simply charter members of what FDR dubbed the "Cuff Links Gang."

Eleanor left their vacation home in Campobello in early September to get oldest son James settled at Groton, but she joined the campaign train at FDR's behest later that month. He said he missed her, but it was also good politics to have his wife on hand for the first national election in which women could vote, the Nineteenth Amendment having gone into effect in January. She described the three-week experience in a letter to her mother-in-law as "the most killing thing for a candidate I ever knew."

It wasn't just the whistle-stopping and constant speech making that were exhausting—at which time she was expected to rivet her attention adoringly on her husband as though she had not heard his stump speech dozens of times before. Eleanor deplored the late hours kept by FDR and his cronies and the activities that accompanied them. She wholeheartedly supported another constitutional amendment, the one creating Prohibition, which had also gone into effect in 1920. Nevertheless, liquor flowed and card games flourished late into the evenings.

Eleanor did begin to appreciate Louis Howe, especially once he began seeking her out and asking for her opinion. "He did it cleverly," she recalled. "He knew that I was bewildered by some of the things expected of me as a candidate's wife." They became friends; before long they were "Eleanor" and "Louis" to each other, rather than "Mrs. Roosevelt" and "Mr. Howe." He even escorted her to Niagara Falls during a campaign stop in Buffalo, the little man standing at the elbow of the tall woman, gazing at the thundering water, while her husband was off giving his stump speech for the thousandth time.

Despite the energy and enthusiasm of the Cox-Roosevelt campaign, 1920 was a Republican year. Harding and Coolidge won over 60 percent of the popular vote and carried thirty-seven states—including the Democratic ticket's home states of New York and Ohio. "This is not a landslide," said an aide to President Wilson, "it is an earthquake."

Roosevelt pretended not to be too upset, characterizing the campaign in nautical terms as "a darned fine sail" and adding philosophically, "Every war brings after it a period of materialism and conservatism. People tire quickly of ideals and we are now repeating history." He jokingly described himself as "Ex. V.P., Canned (Erroneously reported dead)." Missy, more tactfully, characterized him later as the "very badly defeated candidate for the Vice Presidency." To thank the men who had worked so hard for him, he ordered five sets of gold cuff links from Tiffany & Co. engraved with their initials and his, and began a tradition of celebrating his birthday with a reunion of the Cuff Links Gang.

Missy was not presented with a set of cuff links—nor was Eleanor—but she got a consolation prize. Eleanor invited her to come to Hyde Park for a few weeks to deal with leftover correspondence from the campaign. It was there that Missy recalled getting her first glimpse of FDR's wife, dressed in a dark velvet gown with a white lace collar, sitting by the library fireplace reading a book aloud to her two youngest children. The boys were ages six and four then, and one or both of them gave their father's temporary assistant the name she would carry for life. In their mouths, "Miss LeHand" evolved into "Missy LeHand," and soon the only people who still called her Marguerite were her family. Eleanor must have seen something in the ever-smiling, hardworking young woman that she liked and did not find threatening. Some biographers of the Roosevelts have suggested that it was Missy's lower social class; unlike Lucy Mercer, she was not of the manor born, and though she was pretty, she was not beautiful. Eleanor never seems to have been jealous of Missy as a rival for her husband's affection, though friends said she sometimes grew impatient with the younger woman's uncritical, hero-worshipping tendencies.

With his eye on a run for the presidency in 1924, FDR decided to reenter the private sector in the interim. He became a partner with two friends in a Wall Street law firm, Emmet, Marvin & Roosevelt, but with his large family and upper-crust lifestyle, he needed more income than he could earn disinterestedly dabbling in the law. Van Lear Black, a friend who was board chairman of a security bonding firm, Fidelity & Deposit Company of Maryland, offered him the New York vice presidency, which paid $25,000 a year (more than $330,000 in current dollars), five times his navy salary. It was a rainmaker job, requiring lots of glad-handing and massaging of his social and political connections (Roosevelt's specialties), and Black was content with him working half days.

The newly minted corporate titan needed a first-rate private secretary, and he was so pleased with Missy's work that he offered her the job. She took some convincing. "I'm sorry," she told him, "but I don't want to work for a lawyer. It's too dull."

"Oh, that's all right," FDR replied. "There'll be lots besides legal briefs—consultation, mostly, and a lot of interesting things." She went home to Somerville for the Christmas holidays to mull over the offer. Whatever swayed her, Missy wrote from her family home in December that she could begin work on January 3, 1921, "if you would still like to have me." She moved into the tiny apartment of a cousin and his wife on 200th Street in the Bronx, sleeping on a sofa in the living room and commuting downtown to the financial district by subway and elevated train, a trip of more than twenty stops.

FDR split his time between his law office on Wall Street

and the nearby Fidelity & Deposit office—"the F&D," as Missy came to call it—in the Equitable Building at 120 Broadway. It was a behemoth structure covering a city block, the largest office building in the world at that time. Louis Howe remained in Washington at the Navy Department for the first few months of the new administration, planning to come to work at Fidelity & Deposit as FDR's assistant at the end of the summer.

Franklin had been right when he told Missy that she would be handling "a lot of interesting things." He plunged into charitable and civic projects, from raising money for the Boy Scouts to chairing the endowment committee of the newly established Woodrow Wilson Foundation. Soon he was spending most evenings away from home and family, making speeches or attending dinners, much to Eleanor's dismay. However, Eleanor was forging her own life in politics that spring, joining the board of the League of Women Voters and serving as a delegate to its national convention.

The other "interesting things" Franklin needed Missy's help with were financial investments. Like many people in the 1920s, he got caught up in speculative get-rich-quick schemes, some of them downright outlandish, others simply ahead of their time—live lobsters, self-adhesive postage stamps, intercontinental dirigible passenger service, a coffee substitute. He lost more than a year's salary on the lobster debacle. It was a time when tradition and prudence flew out the window.

"The decade of the nineteen twenties was at one and the same time the gaudiest, the saddest, and the most misinterpreted era in modern American history," wrote historian Bruce Catton. "It was gaudy because it was full of restless vitality burgeoning in a field where all the old rules seemed to be gone, and it was sad because it was an empty place between two eras, with old familiar certainties and hopes drifting off like mist and new ones not yet formulated."

F. Scott Fitzgerald was the scribe of the so-called Jazz Age, writing of its debutantes bobbing their hair, displaying their shapely knees, swigging bathtub gin, and smoking cigarettes in public. As a working girl on a modest salary—she accepted just $30 a week as FDR's private secretary—Missy wasn't the "flapper" sort that Fitzgerald immortalized. But while she may not have shortened her skirts to her knees, she certainly followed the trends of fashion that included the shedding of many layers of clothing. The *Journal of Commerce* in 1928 reported that the yardage required to make the typical woman's ensemble had fallen from almost twenty yards to just seven. She also adopted the popular cloche hat, perhaps an unfortunate millinery style because of her long, narrow face, but a very of-the-moment fashion choice.

At some point in the 1920s, Missy bobbed her long dark hair to chin length and took up smoking, as did many women during that decade. (Women accounted for 5 percent of cigarette sales in 1923, 17 percent by 1934.) The brand she chose was Lucky Strike, which marketed to women with slogans like "I'm a Lucky Girl," promising them that smoking would help them stay slender. The connection between smoking and cardiovascular disease was unknown; indeed, advertisements featured a kindly doctor in white jacket with the words, "20,679 physicians say, 'Luckies are less irritating.'" Missy's smoking habit was one more strike against her fragile heart—a very unlucky strike.

For Missy, the early months in FDR's employ were spent studying her new employer. In those days before fax, copy machine, and email and when the telephone was not universally used, letters were the heart of business communication. FDR was a voluminous writer of letters—an early biographer said "he was carrying on one of the largest personal correspondences in the country"—and Missy was his scribe.

"After I went to work for Mr. Roosevelt," she told *The New York Times* years later, "I read carefully all the letters he dictated. I became thoroughly acquainted with the manner in which he expressed himself. . . . In the course of time I came to know exactly how Mr. Roosevelt would answer some of his letters, how he would couch his thoughts. When he discovered that I had learned these things it took a load off his shoulders, for instead of having to dictate the answers to many letters he could just say 'yes' or 'no' and I knew what to say and how to say it."

She also learned to screen him from unnecessary annoyances, details he did not want to know, and people he did not want to see (without offending his visitors), and making sure he addressed matters, however unpleasant, that had to be decided upon. Bosses, she learned, "must be prodded to keep up with their mail; and this requires secretarial tact." The skills Missy developed in her first eight months as FDR's private secretary would serve her (and him) well for more than twenty years. But just as important was the friendship that grew between them.

Franklin Roosevelt liked to kick back and have a good time, and Missy did, too. During her years with FDR, she filled two beautiful gold charm bracelets with miniature symbols of her personal and professional life, many of them gifts from friends and family. One of the charms was a tiny pocketknife with a working blade, inscribed with the words, "Let's cut up." Cut up they did. They gossiped, they joked, they laughed—and Missy had a fine "trilling laugh" as well as the sort of "lovely, throaty voice" that assured the career of many a silent screen actress during the transition to the talkies. Grace Tully, who later became Missy's assistant, observed that Missy and FDR shared the same "sense of nonsense," something he had seldom experienced with his serious and high-minded wife.

But Missy was also a gem when the going got tough, and FDR hit a bad patch of it in the summer of 1921. In 1919, Navy Secretary Daniels—whose crusade against sin went far beyond banning wine in the officers' mess—became concerned about homosexual behavior among sailors in Newport, Rhode Island. This was almost seventy-five years before "don't ask, don't tell" became official military policy, and almost a century before being gay was removed as a barrier to military service. Then, homosexuality was a very serious offense. Daniels ordered the base commander to clean things up, and the solution he found was to set up a sting operation, using new sailors as bait. To be

*Missy chronicled her life on gold charm bracelets.*

certain the men they entrapped were indeed homosexuals, the recruits—some as young as sixteen—were allowed to submit to fellatio—and praised for their "zeal" in the investigation when they did so. As assistant secretary of the navy, FDR had signed off on the sting while Daniels was abroad, but denied knowing the sordid details.

The case erupted into scandal. When the Republican Senate took power in 1921, Roosevelt learned a report that would be extremely damaging to him was scheduled to be released. He hastened to Washington with Missy, demanding a hearing before the Senate subcommittee overseeing the sting investigation. They snagged an empty office at the Navy Department and borrowed Cuff Links Gang member Steve Early from the Associated Press, spending a long July day feverishly reading the report and writing an eighteen-page statement to refute it. Their efforts came to naught. The report was released and headlines laid the scandal at Roosevelt's feet, with the story on the front page of *The New York Times* declaring the details to be "unprintable."

Exhausted and disheartened, Missy and FDR returned by train to New York. The next day at the office, she took down a letter to Senator Henry W. Keyes, whom Roosevelt identified as the chief villain of the affair. In words dripping with gentlemanly venom, he declared that Keyes was the first graduate of Harvard he had ever met who he "believed to be personally and willfully dishonorable." He never mailed the letter, but years later when a certain senator was on his wife's guest list for dinner at the White House, FDR initially refused to come to the table. He sent Missy to convey his position to Eleanor, and Missy witnessed their ensuing showdown and recounted it to a close friend.

"Franklin," Eleanor told him, "you have forgiven almost everybody for everything they have done to you. You've kept this bitterness in your heart long enough. It's time to wash it clean."

"All right, Eleanor," he said after a moment. "I guess you're right. Roll me in and we'll wash up."

Missy said his anger was not just about what he considered the dirty politics of the affair. He blamed the senator in part for the health catastrophe that followed, feeling that the stress of the investigation had lowered his resistance to illness.

A few days after he and Missy returned to New York, FDR joined a group of Boy Scout supporters on an expedition to a camp at Bear Mountain State Park on the Hudson River. It was probably on this late July day that he was exposed to the poliomyelitis virus that would soon paralyze him. That evening, he returned home, his last night in New York before leaving to join his family at Campobello. Missy worked with him through the next morning, clearing off his desk, and then he abandoned her to the sweltering sidewalks of New York and its ovenlike subway cars. "I wish you would box up some nice cool breezes and send them our way," she wrote in a wistful postscript to a letter to him at Campobello.

Her letters were a lively mix of business, updates on law cases, theater reviews, and weather reports, with lots of exclamation points and handwritten postscripts to the typewritten words. A mouse that had been terrorizing the office had popped up again one afternoon, making her "very unhappy, otherwise things are deadly dull." Another afternoon the skies were preparing to "pour broomsticks" and he had to forgive her if, in the darkened office, she let a typo slip through. She had wasted the evening before by seeing a "terrible" play: "I never heard such perfectly awful voices from chorus girls." A letter had come to Emmet, Marvin & Roosevelt addressed to her with the suffix "Esq.," which is used for lawyers. "I love it!" she proclaimed, using one of FDR's favorite expressions, and predicting, "I am making such marvelous strides in the law work that I feel sure that you can soon turn over all your cases to me!"

In her earliest letter to Campobello, the young secretary had gotten up the nerve to ask for a considerable raise, from $30 to $40 a week. The reply to her letter came not from her boss, but from his wife. "Your letter has been so long unanswered because Mr. Roosevelt had a severe chill last Wednesday, which resulted in fever and much congestion, and I fear his return will be delayed," Eleanor wrote. She said FDR felt he could swing a raise to $35 a week, but thought he would do better if she could present her case in person once he got back to New York.

Missy's reply to Eleanor contained no gossip and jokes. She apologized profusely for bothering her boss while he was ill, adding, "I thought he looked quite tired when he left, so perhaps he will at least have a good rest." She had no idea that the reason Eleanor was replying for her husband was that he could no longer grasp a pen in his hand. He was paralyzed.

❁ CHAPTER FOUR

# Adrift

The story of FDR's polio experience was told in broad, soft-focus strokes in Dore Schary's hit play *Sunrise at Campobello,* which spawned an award-winning movie in 1960. In the film, Ralph Bellamy portrayed FDR, "the man who never forgot how to smile," and Greer Garson was Eleanor, "the woman who never forgot how to love." Hume Cronyn was the wheezing and chain-smoking Louis Howe, and Ann Shoemaker was the meddling and supercilious Sara Delano Roosevelt. The redheaded actress Jean Hagen portrayed Missy LeHand, with a cast of adorable children playing the rambunctious Roosevelt brood.

The themes and images of *Sunrise at Campobello* are enduring and stereotypical: the brave and undaunted cripple, the devoted and loving wife, the wisecracking friend, the overprotective mother, the cheerful secretary, the resilient children. Ignored were the years of drifting in an emotional wilderness that followed the crisis, when Missy LeHand was FDR's most constant companion and he saw very little of his wife, mother, and children. That was not the story Hollywood wanted to tell.

In the film as in life, polio struck FDR on August 10, 1921, after an afternoon of swimming, running, and fighting a brush fire with his family on the isolated Canadian island off the tip of Maine where they owned a rustic vacation home. He told Eleanor he felt tired and chilled, and crawled into bed without supper. By the next day, his legs refused to work, and then the paralysis crept into his back and arms so that he could not even grasp a spoon or sit up in bed. He suffered from pain, fever, and sometimes delirium. Initially he was misdiagnosed by an elderly physician who had been vacationing in the area and advised massage for a suspected blood clot on the spine. Louis and Eleanor took on this and other nursing tasks, but as Roosevelt continued to suffer and Louis Howe began to suspect a much more serious problem, a second opinion was sought. Dr. Robert Lovett of Boston, an orthopedist and polio authority, arrived at Campobello and provided the correct and terrifying diagnosis. After Roosevelt spent a few more weeks in bed, Louis outwitted the press by sneaking him onto a train for the six-hundred-mile journey back to New York.

The Hollywood film shows the Missy character at Campobello, helping out with the children, greeting Sara when she arrived, and running interference with the press. It is a fabrication. She was in New York the whole time, holding down the fort at Fidelity & Deposit and the law firm, where Howe popped in for a visit and probably confided to her the extent of the disaster that had befallen their boss. "Everyone is much excited about your coming back and much pleased," she wrote to Roosevelt in early September. "By the way—I wish I could say, 'Your Majesty.'" He returned on September 14 and went straight to Presbyterian Hospital to begin his recovery.

News of the prominent politician's polio diagnosis broke in *The New York Times* on September 16, but Howe and the doctors managed to minimize its seriousness, the first of many instances of soft-pedaling FDR's health problems to the press. The newspaper account acknowledged his paralysis but said "he definitely will not be crippled."

In our time, when a handful of cases of the Ebola virus can unleash nationwide hysteria, it is easy to imagine the tidal wave of fear that engulfed the country during a polio epidemic. In 1916, New York City was hit by one of the worst, erupting in a neighborhood of Italian immigrants called Pigtown and rapidly spreading to other locales. FDR ordered Eleanor to stay on Campobello Island with the children until it was over. By October, the national toll was a horrific 27,000 deaths and thousands more permanently paralyzed. Eighty percent of the 2,400 deaths in New York were of children under age five.

While polio primarily struck children—hence the common name "infantile paralysis"—adults contracted it, too, and the aftermath was possibly even more devastating. Turnley Walker, felled by polio as an adult, put the experience in stark terms in his 1950 book, *Rise Up and Walk*:

> The regulation hospital bed is thirty-four by seventy-four inches. In the beginning that much space is allotted to each polio—the new name you get after Infantile Paralysis slugs you. Forever after you will be known as a polio. That thirty-four-by-seventy-four inch area is a place that poliomyelitis allows you, and even though you have been a much-traveled man in the outside world, you learn to live in it.

The new "polio" at Presbyterian Hospital presented a brave face to visiting friends, grabbing his old boss Josephus Daniels in a headlock and crying, "You thought you were coming to see an invalid!" FDR spent six weeks there, during which time he recovered some strength in his arms and could sit up, just barely. His doctors encouraged his optimism, though privately doubted he would ever walk again. In late October, they sent him home to 65th Street to continue his recovery under the direction of a nurse and a physical therapist. Roosevelt came up with the idea of converting armless wooden kitchen chairs into wheelchairs so they could pass through the narrow doorways and travel in the tiny elevator.

Though there is no record of Missy's interactions with FDR during the time he was bedbound other than mentions of her coming in to take dictation, she had true empathy for his situation and probably shared those feelings with him. She, too, had been confined to her bed for months during her rheumatic fever episode. She, too, had been left with permanent damage, her weakened heart making her a "cardiac cripple," unable to run, play tennis, or engage in other exertion like most young women her age. This bond of disability that was established between boss and secretary gave them a level of understanding that was impossible for any able-bodied person to achieve. Louis Howe, who had his own heart and lung problems, could understand, and it's no wonder that he and Missy are usually cited as the people closest to FDR. Missy was still calling her boss "Mr. Roosevelt" in the letters she wrote to Campobello, but at some point in the early 1920s she began calling him "F.D." or, sometimes in writing, "Effdee." She was the only person who did this, and she continued the practice even after he became president of the United States.

During the hard winter that followed his illness, FDR underwent physical therapy in his bedroom while his mother, wife, and Howe conducted a pitched battle over his future. Howe, who had moved into the Roosevelts' townhouse, was still convinced the Boss could become president one day, while Sara insisted he needed to retire to Springwood, the family home in Hyde Park, and conserve his strength. Eleanor sided with Louis about keeping her husband actively engaged in the world, though she had private doubts about his return to politics. The final word was Franklin's, and while he had no intention of limiting his ambition, he believed that first he had to be able to walk again.

Missy was a daily visitor to the Roosevelt townhouse during the months he was homebound, ferrying documents from his offices and taking dictation for his correspondence to Democratic leaders, which continued unabated. In the summer of 1922, he moved to Hyde Park. Sara had decamped with two of his children on a European tour, and he could struggle to walk on crutches without her smothering oversight. By working out on parallel bars in the garden, he built his upper body strength so he could use his arms and shoulders to drag himself around on the floor or in the grass. However, the portrayal in *Sunrise at Campobello* of Franklin rather effortlessly hoisting himself backward into his wheelchair from a seated position on the ground—something that would require the strength of an Olympic gymnast—was another example of dramatic license. For this sort of heavy lifting, he had an African American valet, LeRoy Jones, known as Roy. To get to his upstairs bedroom, he had to haul himself hand-over-hand using the exposed ropes of a small trunk elevator.

Roosevelt liked to have company during his workouts, partly for spotting him in case he fell. He was developing the habit of nonstop talking, which his daughter, Anna, said was "an unconscious habit," that he wanted to give visitors "as good a time as possible while they were with him." John Gunther, in his biography *Roosevelt in Retrospect,* suggested that one of the reasons FDR talked so much was because he couldn't walk. "Conversation was his golf, his tennis, and his badminton," Gunther wrote. Missy and Louis were frequent companions, as were two adoring unmarried cousins who lived in the area, Margaret "Daisy" Suckley and Laura "Polly" Delano. At the summer's end he moved back to New York, having made it just once to the end of his quarter-mile driveway on crutches.

Missy organized FDR's triumphal return to the office in early October, more than a year after the polio attack. She arranged a welcome-back luncheon in a private banquet room at the Bankers Club at the Equitable Building, making sure he would have an elevator to himself, so he would not have to be seen on crutches gimping through the public dining room. His chauffeur drove him to the entrance at 120 Broadway and helped him from the car as passers-by stopped to gawk. Dripping with sweat, FDR staggered on his crutches across the sidewalk, through the doorway, and into the slippery, marble-floored lobby, heading to the elevator. Then he lost his balance and toppled over with a crash of crutches, his hat skittering across the floor. Another crowd gathered to stare. The chauffeur couldn't get him back on his feet, and FDR, laughing and talking a blue streak, appealed to a couple of young men in the crowd to lend a hand. One of them was Basil "Doc" O'Connor, a thirty-year-old lawyer with an office next door to F&D. Back on his feet, crutches under his arms, hat on his head, he resumed his triumphal return. No doubt he made light of the fall when he finally reached Missy and the other staff.

There were no more disasters that day, but he did not return to the F&D office for another two months. He also resigned from his law practice, realizing that the building where Emmet, Marvin & Roosevelt was housed was even less accessible than the Equitable Building. Besides, he was as bored by the law practice as Missy was.

The tensions at the Roosevelts' joint townhouse continued to mount, with Franklin at the center of an increasingly acrimonious tug-of-war between his wife and mother. FDR and his doctors saw little progress with the physical therapy he had been following. Finally, in the winter of 1923, Franklin had reached his limit. He announced that he was going to spend a few weeks in Florida on a leased houseboat with a crew, fishing, swimming, and enjoying the sun. The boat was called the *Weona II,* and it appeared to be just what the doctor ordered. With Roy Jones aboard helping him get around, Missy as hostess, and a changing cast of visiting friends, he spent nearly two months cruising along the Florida coast, an adventure he celebrated with a silly (though well-rhymed) poem about what he called "community life":

*You can slack off peak halyards—and eat with your knife,*
*You can dine in your shirtsleeves, and so can your wife—*
*These are some of the joys of community life!*

The poem went on to explain that the close quarters and thin walls revealed "intimate echoes of each guest's condition":

*No secrets of thought between husband and wife*
*Can safely be had in Community Life . . .*

Louis Howe came aboard for a short time, bearing paperwork from the office, and Eleanor put in a few days, but she rankled at the aimless drinking and fishing and found the night winds "eerie and menacing." Besides, she had five children at home to attend to, as well as a full plate of political causes as she encouraged other women to claim their place as voting citizens. Franklin returned to New York in March 1923 looking tan and feeling fit, and his physical therapist found noticeable improvement in his legs and back due to the exercise on the boat and in the warm Florida water. But just a few weeks of his old routines negated all his advances.

Nevertheless, FDR was convinced that he had stumbled onto a promising new treatment for paralysis, and during the summer he and a friend who had traveled on the *Weona II,* John Lawrence, bought an aging houseboat they christened the *Larooco*. The name was a contraction of Lawrence, Roosevelt and Company, whose last syllables rhymed with "cocoa." FDR called it "a great little packet," Lawrence, with a more jaundiced eye, described it as "a floating tenement." At first Eleanor objected to the plan, pointing out that their finances were already strained and could hardly bear the added expense, but she was silenced when FDR barked back, "Well, I suppose I'd better do all I can to learn to move about as much as possible. I don't want to be a useless burden to the rest of the family." She gave in, but she never set foot on the *Larooco* until its last voyage in 1926, filling her time volunteering for the Democratic Party Women's Division in New York with new friends Nancy Cook and Marion Dickerman.

In the winter of 1924, FDR with Missy and Roy set off again for the Florida Keys. Unlike Eleanor, Missy had taken to "community life"—fishing, sunbathing, drinking, and cruising around the Keys—as if she had been born to it. They joined the crew in Jacksonville: Robert Morris and his wife, Dora, who served as captain and cook, plus a mechanic to keep the engine going. Louis, whose many talents included painting, made as a parting gift for FDR a leather-bound "Log of the Houseboat *Larooco,* Being a More or Less Truthful Account of What Happened (Expurgated for the Very Young)" illustrated with watercolors. The book came with its own rules, including just what constituted a "large fish" and the stern direction that "all references to community life must be written in code." The Boss—Louis now called him the Admiral—and sometimes his guests, delighted in filling in the logbook. Missy often figured into the entries, FDR reporting that "M.A.L. ate too much" or commenting on a sunset "which was almost as poetic in coloring" as the nightgowns worn by Missy and another female passenger.

There was lots of drinking, Prohibition be damned. FDR thanked his friend Livy Davis for sending him one of the ensign flags he had designed for himself when he was assistant secretary of the navy: "I will take it south with me and some day . . . 'hist' the old rag to the mast-head and salute it with 17 rum swizzles." The potent tropical drink was a concoction of dark rum and fruit juice, shaken with ice and served in an old-fashioned glass with a garnish of cherry and an orange slice. (Not surprisingly, a miniature cocktail shaker dangled from one of Missy's gold charm bracelets.) The boat contained a "Library of the World's Worst Literature" and was well stocked with cards and board games. A favorite was Parcheesi (which FDR, inveterate lover of bad puns and corny word play, called "Ma and Pa Cheesy"), and Missy was most often the champion of long-running tournaments.

During the day, the main activities were fishing and swimming, though sharks infested the waters. When they could find a beach, the boat would pull ashore so FDR could crawl around in the sand. Guests such as Livy Davis, Henry and Frances de Rham, and a Hyde Park neighbor Maunsell Crosby—the latter an amateur ornithologist who enjoyed bird watching in the mangrove swamps—joined them for long stretches. A snapshot caught Crosby, FDR, and Missy in swimsuits sunbathing on a Florida beach. FDR's shoulders are by then massive and well defined, in sharp contrast to his shriveled legs. Missy wears a broad-brimmed hat for, despite her dark hair, she was fair-skinned and prone to sunburn. "Missy," FDR once said, "if you get any more sun today, we can use you tonight as a port running light and save some oil."

*The state of FDR's legs is evident in this never before published photo taken in 1924 with Missy and his friend Maunsell S. Crosby.*

FDR's personal appearance on the *Larooco* took on a rakish cast. He grew muttonchop sideburns, wore open-neck shirts with a scarf tied around his neck, and a white tennis hat shielding his eyes from the sun. Interestingly, Missy echoed his attire, right down to the scarf and tennis hat, and began wearing sunglasses, which would become her permanent outdoor fashion accessory.

They had separate cabins below deck, but for days and even weeks at a time, no one was aboard the boat except the crew and the two of them. Inevitably, questions arose about the nature of their relationship. Did they become lovers on the *Larooco*?

*With bobbed hair and a big smile, Missy enjoyed the winter sun in Florida on the first cruise of the* Larooco.

The first to publicly proclaim an opinion was FDR's second son, Elliott, writing about his parents in the 1973 book *An Untold Story: The Roosevelts of Hyde Park*. Although Elliott was only twelve during the first year of the winter cruises, he and his siblings sometimes came aboard for short vacations, and he noticed something "mildly" surprising: a nightgowned Missy sitting on his father's lap in the main stateroom, FDR "holding her in his sun-browned arms." He said "it was no great shock to discover that Missy shared a familial life in all aspects with Father," and claimed all his siblings and mother accepted this "as a fact of life." Eleanor Roosevelt had been dead for more than ten years by the time he made the assertion, and the other Roosevelt children disavowed the entire book. James Roosevelt wrote a book a couple of years later elaborating on his position. "Acting as his secretary, taking care of his correspondence and so forth, Missy was not, I'm convinced, father's mistress," he wrote in *My Parents: A Differing View*. "The most important part she played was probably political. She trailed only Louis and mother in the matter of convincing father he was still capable of taking an important place in the world." He allowed that his father "had a romance of sorts with Missy . . . she filled a need and made him feel a man again, which mother did not do. Missy adored father, as he adored her. I suppose you could say they came to love one another, but it was not a physical love."

Not satisfied to "smear her reputation," as James put it, with insinuations that he presented as fact, in 1984 Elliott published the first of a series of mysteries with his mother as the detective solving lurid murders. There was almost always a winking mention of Missy in a nightgown in his father's bedroom, nibbling his breakfast toast or watching a movie tucked up beside him in his narrow bed after dinner. The twenty-two books were ghost-written by William Harrington, who continued penning them under Elliott's name even after his death in 1990, giving a new spin to the term "ghost writer." Harrington, a prolific novelist, published a spy thriller in 1983 called *The English Lady* that included an interlude on the *Larooco*. He used Elliott's description of Missy and his father almost word for word: "Missy LeHand sat on his lap, and Frank Roosevelt clasped her to him in his big brown arms."

Biographer Bernard Asbell chimed in on the debate the same year Elliott published his memoir in a curious book that combined nonfiction research with the imagined memoir that FDR never wrote. (In fact, the two men had dueling articles about Missy in *Ladies' Home Journal* that year.) Anna, the Roosevelts' oldest child, was a major source for *The F.D.R. Memoirs*, which portrays Missy as a lovelorn secretary who experienced periodic nervous breakdowns whenever she seemed to be losing FDR's attention. In interviews with Missy's girlhood friend Barbara Muller Curtis and her husband, Egbert, who became manager of the Warm Springs resort in 1926, Asbell asked if Missy was in love with her boss. "I wouldn't be at all surprised," Mrs.

Curtis said tentatively, asking her husband, "Would you?" He replied, "I wouldn't be surprised." But speculating on a physical relationship was another thing entirely, and neither Curtis weighed in.

Asbell did the most exhaustive analysis of FDR's and Missy's whereabouts during his years adrift. For the 208 weeks between 1924 and 1928, FDR was away from his home and family for 116 weeks. His companion during four of those weeks was Eleanor, for two it was his mother, and for 110 it was Missy. "Thus Missy is the sole adult 'member of the family' to share an aggregate of more than two years of the most trying and self-searching four years of Roosevelt's life," Asbell wrote.

On the *Larooco* and at Warm Springs from 1924 to 1928, Missy and FDR had three of the ingredients needed for an illicit sexual relationship: he was physically capable in that he was not impotent, he and Missy found each other attractive, and they had plenty of privacy. They also availed themselves of the inhibition-lowering lubricant of alcohol on a daily basis. On the other hand, she was a single woman, living in an age when birth control was undependable and an out-of-wedlock pregnancy shameful, and was an observant Roman Catholic whose church banned birth control and considered adultery a mortal sin. Because of her heart condition, she also was aware that pregnancy in her case might prove fatal. Finally, she was devoted to Eleanor Roosevelt. All of these factors argued against sexual intimacy with her married boss.

As far as evidence goes, there is not a single written account of anyone seeing them in a compromising position, despite the hundreds of servants, bodyguards, Secret Service agents, staff members, political cronies, family members, and friends who traipsed through FDR's bedrooms—which he used as an auxiliary office—during their twenty-one years together. And certainly these two very discreet and private people never shared such a secret with anyone. For that matter, in all the interviews Missy gave, she never once mentioned the *Larooco*.

Did they? Didn't they? Missy's great-niece Jane Scarbrough is often asked, and her answer is the most honest one: "We have no reason to believe they did, but we don't know." What is without question is that FDR and Missy were devoted and affectionate companions, enjoyed each other's company immensely, and had an intimate understanding of each other's minds.

What did Eleanor Roosevelt make of her husband's growing connection with the young woman she had handpicked as his secretary? For the most part, she appears to have been relieved that she was not obligated to accompany him on his travels or serve as his full-time hostess once he reentered public life. Missy stepped up to cover the gaps, but was always careful not to put a toe over the invisible boundaries Eleanor drew. Anna described her mother as "jealous," not of how another woman might interest her husband romantically—she was over that—but of anyone who might usurp her position as the mother, hostess, governor's wife, or first lady of the land. "And I don't think Missy ever did this," Anna told Bernard Asbell. "You see, this is where Missy was a very, very astute little gal." In an occasional letter to a close friend, Eleanor would send a dart Missy's way, but these small lapses were more than compensated for by her many kindnesses to the younger woman, especially when Missy had her own woes.

As pleasant as times were on the *Larooco,* the winter of 1924 brought its crises, too. The boat had barely been launched when Missy received a telegram saying her father had died. FDR got her a berth on a northbound train so she could attend the funeral in Somerville, and to keep himself occupied in her absence he ambitiously began writing a history of the United States in longhand. He churned out fourteen pages on yellow legal paper, but abandoned the project when Missy returned. The boat's engine often sputtered to a stop, and foul weather sometimes confined the passengers below deck for days at a time, reading bad books and playing games. One evening the two were returning from a day of fishing on a skiff when they were caught in a driving storm. Missy climbed onto the houseboat, but Franklin fell back on the skiff's deck, badly twisting his leg. It took a day for Missy to locate a doctor to diagnose what turned out to be torn ligaments.

Missy then took on the additional role of orthopedic nurse, and also became a counselor to the man who seldom let anyone look behind what she called his "lighthearted facade." Years later, she tearfully confessed to Frances Perkins, FDR's secretary of labor, that some days it was noon before he could drag himself out of the bed where depression pinned him and greet his guests with a grin and a laugh. The fictional Missy of *Sunrise at Campobello* was never called upon to shoulder such duties; it depicted Eleanor as his emotional shoulder to cry on. The voyages of the *Larooco* were not part of the script.

Roosevelt was hardly getting away from it all during his *Larooco* cruises, for he took trips into Florida to call on old political colleagues, supporters, and players, including Democratic Party lion William Jennings Bryan and department store magnate J. C. Penney. During the voyage in 1924, FDR and Missy hosted his former running mate, James Cox, for tea. (After his defeat Cox had purchased the *Miami Daily News* and would later buy the *Atlanta Constitution*.) The subject of FDR chairing New York governor Alfred E. Smith's campaign for the Democratic nomination for president was raised over the cups of tea (or whatever the cups held). Smith, a Tammany Hall insider, was also an Irish American Catholic and opposed Prohibition, strikes against him in the minds of many voters, but FDR believed he was the best Democrat for the ticket. He accepted the chairmanship.

With the cruise finished and the *Larooco* docked, Missy and FDR returned to New York. Following some behind-the-scenes maneuvering by Louis, Al Smith asked FDR to give his nominating speech at the June convention at Madison Square Garden, and Louis, Eleanor, and Missy working together convinced him to agree. One weekend at Hyde Park, Sara Roosevelt's farm manager, Moses Smith, came upon FDR and Missy sitting on a blanket in the sun, brainstorming over a pad of paper. "Mose, what do you think I'm doing?" he called out. "I am writing a speech to nominate Al Smith for president!" But he had to do more than write a speech. This would be FDR's first major public appearance in almost three years, and he was determined to "walk" to the lectern. The plan was to walk partway with a crutch under one arm, the other gripping the arm of sixteen-year-old James. Then he would stop, trade James's arm for the other crutch, and make it the rest of the way alone. They practiced over and over again at the 65th Street townhouse.

On June 26, as Missy, Eleanor, the other children, and Eleanor's friends Nancy Cook and Marion Dickerman looked on from the gallery, he successfully struggled to the lectern and delivered a speech that was a triumph. It was not the one he and Missy had written together—Smith's campaign substituted one that concluded with words from a Wordsworth poem describing Smith as "the 'Happy Warrior' of the political battlefield." The audience erupted into applause, blowing klaxon horns, dancing, and shouting. The orchestra played Smith's theme song, "The Sidewalks of New York," but he was almost an afterthought. Many people watching and cheering felt the words "Happy Warrior" better applied to the speaker than the man he was nominating. Dripping in sweat and physically shaky, FDR nonetheless basked in the applause, flashing his huge grin, until he could stand no more and signaled to James to bring his wheelchair. While Smith lost the nomination to a compromise candidate and the deeply divided Democratic Party emerged from the convention in shreds, it was a triumphant comeback for FDR.

This is how the movie *Sunrise at Campobello* concludes, with a hall of people hoisting red, white, and blue banners and campaign posters, cheering lustily for the resurgent FDR. But something else happened at the convention that was equally important. He ran into an old friend and supporter, George Foster Peabody, who had purchased half interest in a run-down health spa in rural Georgia. He told FDR of a young polio patient who had regained the ability to walk by exercising in the mineral pools there. Why didn't he go see for himself? The town seventy miles south of Atlanta was called Bullochville, but it was in the process of changing its name to Warm Springs.

❀ CHAPTER FIVE

# Warm Springs

When the Southern Railway train chugged into the Bullochville, Georgia, station one evening in early October 1924, it was met by a crowd of about fifty people, almost a tenth of the town's residents. Some had walked over to the station knowing nothing more than that a "famous man" was on board. Teenager Ruth Stevens watched wide-eyed as a tall man was helped to the platform: "He was a fine-looking specimen of manhood from the waist to the tip of his head, but his legs dangled like two strings between a pair of crutches." She asked another bystander who the man was, and his reply was "Franklin D. Roosevelt of New York."

FDR arrived with a very small entourage: Eleanor, Missy, and his valet, Roy. They were met by Thomas W. Loyless, manager of George Foster Peabody's Meriwether Inn and environs, who drove them to the property a scant mile away. The inn, even with a new coat of yellow and green paint, was a three-story Victorian shamble that looked as though a spark could set it aflame faster than General Sherman ignited Atlanta. As a paraplegic, FDR was so afraid of fire that he instead rented a small cottage beside Loyless's, where the sound of squirrels scampering across the roof kept him awake his first night. Nevertheless, that October evening marked the beginning of a love affair between FDR and the small Georgia town that would last for the rest of his life, a place where Missy was ever-present, his wife an occasional and reluctant visitor.

"I sometimes wish I could find some spot on the globe where it was not essential and necessary for me to start something new—a sand bar in the ocean might answer, but I would probably start building a sea wall around it and digging for pirate treasure in the middle," FDR wrote to a friend in the spring of 1925. In truth, he soon began to see long-term possibilities for the Meriwether Inn property. After three years of wandering in the wilderness, he had found his Promised Land.

Eleanor was not thrilled, and her misgivings can be easily understood. Coming to middle Georgia in 1924 was like visiting a Third World country today. The Great Depression hit Wall Street in October 1929 with the stock market crash, but it was in full swing in Meriwether County five years before that, after the boll weevil began strangling most of the cotton crop in the field like an infant in its crib. The single cash crop agricultural economy had condemned most of Georgia's farmers to a life of unrelenting poverty, renting small farms or leasing land in return for a share of the crop as sharecroppers. Most farm families subsisted on an annual income of less than $200 per capita ($2,776 in current dollars), and Georgia's per capita tax collection was the lowest in the forty-eight states.

With cash so scarce, there was a large barter economy, and some people earned under-the-table income making illegal moonshine, a sideline that carried its own occupational hazards. Jerry Levins, whose grandfather owned a general store near Warm Springs, recalls the story of two bootleggers who got into a fight outside the store. One bit off the other's nose. The store was one of the places FDR frequented when he wanted a cold Coca-Cola, but he also developed a certain appreciation for the local brew, according to his son James.

But Franklin had come to Bullochville for another kind of liquid, the kind that flowed out of a mineral spring into the Meriwether Inn's swimming pool at 88 degrees year-round, so rich in magnesium that it was able to keep a crippled boy afloat while he exercised and helped him regain the use of his legs. Or at least that was the story FDR heard from Louis Joseph, the young man George Foster Peabody had told him about at the Democratic convention. To his excitement, Roosevelt found that the buoyancy allowed him to walk in the water that came up to his chest, almost as if he were not paralyzed. After exercising in the pool for a few days, he said he felt something that he had not felt in three years: movement in his toes.

Eleanor did not take to Bullochville, even though her paternal grandmother was a Bulloch from Georgia who had aided Confederate relatives during the Civil War. A travel guide written a few years after FDR first came to Georgia directed tourists to spots where they might see "the picturesque squalor of Negro poverty" and remarked blithely on tenant farmers who raised their numerous children as field hands. Eleanor didn't find this picturesque; she found the grinding poverty and overt racism appalling. "It was a disappointment to me to find that for many, many people life in the South was hard and poor and ugly, just as it is in parts of the North," she wrote. In addition, the distance from the hen house to the dinner table was uncomfortably short. When Missy and Eleanor traveled to nearby Manchester to buy some chickens for supper, Eleanor was disturbed to learn they had to be brought home alive, and the sight and sound of the cook wringing their necks in the yard was too much for her. By the time the local paper had announced the arrival of "Colonel Franklin Roosevelt and family, of New York," she had boarded an outgoing train, again leaving her husband in the care of Missy and Roy. Once home, she began dogging her cousin Theodore Roosevelt Jr.'s steps in his race for governor of New York. Ted, a Republican, had served in the Harding administration, and though he had no ties to the Teapot Dome oil lease scandal, Eleanor had "a framework resembling a teapot, which spouted steam" placed on top of her car and chased her cousin around the state with her friends Nancy Cook and

Marion Dickerman. He lost to Democrat Al Smith, and never forgave her.

For Missy, who had spent most of her life in major cities, arriving in rural Georgia was an experience just this side of wandering into a tribal village. The roads weren't paved. Many of the homes had outdoor toilets and no glass or even screens in the windows. Telephones were few and far between, and electricity was undependable. Years later, after the Georgia Warm Springs Foundation was established for polio patients, the physicians had to notify the power company in Manchester if they planned to use the X-ray machine. Cotton had worn out the soil, and farmers plowed with mules. Many of the programs of the New Deal, from rural electrification to agricultural reform, can trace their roots to what FDR and Missy found in Warm Springs.

They had eye-opening experiences about how the people in the county lived as they explored their new surroundings, driven about by Tom Loyless, with FDR in the front and Missy and Mrs. Loyless in the backseat. "I like him ever so much and she is nice but not broad in her interests, but she chatters away to Missy in the back seat and I hear an occasional yes or no from Missy to prove she is not sleeping," Franklin wrote to his wife. The conversation in the front seat of the car was more serious. Tom Loyless was courting Roosevelt as a buyer for the Meriwether Inn, and Roosevelt was interested in his plan for converting the property into a combination resort for the able-bodied and health spa for cripples. Soon the daily correspondence Missy typed and sent to Louis Howe at the F&D included speculation on the merits of this investment.

Meanwhile, the New York visitors were making a big splash, and not just in the Meriwether Inn's mineral springs pool. At the end of October, a banquet was given at the Tuscawilla Hotel on Bullochville's main street to mark the renaming of the town as Warm Springs. FDR was the featured speaker. The *Manchester Mercury*—which touted itself as a newspaper "Liked by Many, Cussed by Some, Read by Everybody"—published a breathless front-page account: "Mr. Roosevelt delivered the most forceful speech we have heard in many years. He is one of the great men of the country and his utterances upon the occasion stamped him as a great orator."

While this report affirmed Meriwether County's warm embrace of the newcomers, another newspaper report had a much wider impact. Shortly before FDR and Missy left for New York, a reporter from the *Atlanta Journal* came to do an interview and observed Roosevelt's agility in the pool. "So marked have the benefits been in his case, Mr. Roosevelt plans to return to Warm Springs in March or April and remain two or three months," the reporter wrote, adding that he planned "to build a cottage on the hilltop." The story, headlined "Franklin Roosevelt Will Swim to Health," was picked up by wire services and published in newspapers around the country.

When FDR and Missy returned to Warm Springs the following March, they had unexpected company. Polios from far and wide had begun arriving, inspired by the story and hoping for a cure. The formal season for the resort did not begin until May, so the dozen or so polios enjoyed a few weeks of improvised hydrotherapy under the tutelage of "Ol' Doctor Roosevelt" and his "nurse," Miss LeHand. There was no medical staff, no trained physical therapists, and one of the cottages where patients stayed was in such bad shape it was referred to as "the Wreck." But FDR employed the knowledge he had gained from his own years of therapy to teach the patients to exercise in the water, and transferred the relaxed and fun-loving social atmosphere he and Missy had created on the *Larooco* to the piney woods of rural Georgia. After exercising, there were picnics, card games, cocktails, and lots of laughing and joking. What came to be known as "the Warm Springs Spirit" was born.

By then, FDR had figured out a way to get around without depending on rides from others. He bought a decade-old Model T Ford and sketched out a system of pulleys and levers to make it drivable by hand. A local mechanic rigged the Tin Lizzy and

FDR was soon driving all over Meriwether County and beyond, Missy riding shotgun. It was the first of a series of such cars FDR had retrofitted for use in Warm Springs and Hyde Park.

One of his discoveries was a lovely overlook on Pine Mountain called Dowdell's Knob. The knob was named for a farmer who, according to local legend, brought his slaves to the site for church services prior to the Civil War. FDR became enchanted with the spot as a site for picnics, ordering a stone barbecue grill built and insisting that any patient who was depressed should be brought there for an immediate lift of spirits. With a car seat pulled out as a bench, FDR would relax among the other polios, unselfconsciously wearing his braces outside his trousers. Missy later said that she was not fond of FDR's many picnics, except at Warm Springs.

Missy graciously presided over the picnics, the dinner table, and the cocktail hour at Warm Springs. One story goes that Franklin shouted an invitation from his cottage porch one evening to Loyless, his sister, and some other friends to join them for a drink. He went inside and Missy emerged from the kitchen shortly after with a tray of cocktails for their guests. When FDR heard another knock at the door, he shouted out "Come in, come in." To their consternation, it was a Baptist minister. Missy quickly tossed a tablecloth over the tray and beat a hasty retreat into the kitchen. After the pastor left, Loyless recalled, FDR and Missy "were agonized with laughter." Other evenings were quieter. They played cards, read, and FDR built a small hanging bookshelf as a gift for his secretary.

The 1926 cruise on the *Larooco* was its last. When FDR arrived in Warm Springs in late March of that year, his plans to purchase the Meriwether Inn were firmly in place and he began seeking a buyer for the houseboat. Unfortunately, he would not have his friend Tom Loyless's help with his new project, as the manager had died shortly before of what the local paper called "organic trouble"—a euphemism for cancer. (Missy, accompanied by Anna Roosevelt, arrived in early April but the local papers did not name her, simply calling her "Mr. Roosevelt's secretary." That fall, when her name appeared in the *Mercury*'s social column for the first time, she was called "Miss LeHat.") In May, FDR purchased the cottage he had been renting from a Columbus, Georgia, couple. Meanwhile, he was negotiating with George Foster Peabody to buy the resort: the Meriwether Inn, twenty houses and buildings, the spring-fed pools, plus 1,200 acres of some of the prettiest land in Georgia.

*FDR chats with the Warm Springs medical director, Dr. Leroy Hubbard, sitting with Missy and patients by the treatment pool in 1926.*

Both Eleanor and Louis were concerned about her husband's latest business investment, both because of the cost—the $200,000 purchase price was $2.7 million in current dollars and represented the lion's share of the inheritance from his father—and in having a base of operations so far removed from New York. "Missy . . . is keen about everything here of course!" Eleanor wrote to Marion Dickerman in one of her occasional jabs at the younger woman. Nevertheless, after a long talk with her husband, she gave her support, and Louis began milking the media for publicity and corresponding with potential investors. In mid-May the *Atlanta Constitution* published a story announcing Roosevelt's purchase and detailed his ambitious plans: "a cottage colony . . . a magnificent country club building" and a sanitarium to accommodate a hundred patients. He started a new subdivision on the grounds and began building a cottage for himself that would better accommodate his physical limitations than the one he and Missy were inhabiting.

By July FDR had hired Egbert T. Curtis, "an experienced hotel man, who is making every effort to preserve the old-time atmosphere of the resort and at the same time introducing modern comfort and efficiency," according to the *Mercury*. The local papers began carrying prominent box ads for the "The Georgia Warm Springs," touting "delightful bathing pools, excellent cuisine, fine orchestra, mountain spring water." Curtis, known by the nickname "Curt," was brought into the fold by Missy: he was the fiancée of her Somerville friend Barbara Muller and had studied hotel management at Cornell.

Despite their enjoyment of their roles as an unlicensed physician and nurse, Roosevelt and Missy knew the polios needed full-time medical professionals overseeing their care. He hired Dr. Leroy W. Hubbard, an orthopedic surgeon recently retired from the New York State Board of Health, and Helena Mahoney, who had been his aide. Hubbard became medical director, Mahoney the nursing director.

The summer of 1926 was a busy one, with the elaborate society wedding of the first Roosevelt child, Anna, in June. Just twenty years old, Anna wed Curtis Dall, a Wall Street stockbroker nine years her senior, later admitting she used the marriage to escape the tensions of home. During the wedding festivities at Hyde Park, Missy stayed with Nancy Cook and Marion Dickerman, who were then living in a new cottage near Springwood called Val-Kill that Franklin had built for them and Eleanor. Unless Franklin was with her, Eleanor now stayed at Val-Kill whenever she was in Hyde Park rather than under her mother-in-law's roof, and joined with her friends in opening Val-Kill Industries, a furniture-manufacturing workshop.

For Missy, the summer brought a special treat: the Roosevelts helped send her on a trip to Europe, and Barbara Muller went as her companion. Her 1926 passport, the photo showing a serious-looking Missy in a fur collar, is stamped with stops in Italy, Spain, Portugal, France, Monaco, Sweden, and Norway.

Photograph of bearer
Marguerite A. LeHand
the seal of the Department of State is impressed thereon.

Description of bearer
Height 5 feet 7 inches
Hair dark brown
Eyes blue
Distinguishing marks or features:
Place of birth Potsdam, N.Y.
Date of birth Sept 13, 1896.
Occupation secretary
Marguerite A. LeHand
Signature of bearer

*Missy got her first passport in 1926 for a trip abroad financed by the Roosevelts.*

The young women crossed the Atlantic by ship and cruised ports on the Mediterranean and Baltic seas, as well as visiting Paris. "I loved Paris!" Missy crowed in a letter to FDR, describing a "grand shopping spree" when she bought "3 dresses & a hat & some underwear & gloves & perfume & oh just had a grand time." She may have visited the Art Nouveau boutique of the House of Guerlain on the Champs-Élysées on this trip. L'Heure Bleue ("the Blue Hour"), a perfume blended of vanilla, iris, and violet named for "the suspended moment . . . when the night has not yet found its star," became her signature fragrance. Yet she found Norway just as enthralling, and she described what she saw during a morning train ride through "the most beautiful country I ever imagined. . . . Oh I do wish you could have been along. Wonderful mountains, lakes, torents [*sic*] of water over narrow little rocks and something every minute. . . . Oh I did love it so—it just thrilled me!" She enclosed a flower she had found "beneath a glacier."

Barbara told Roosevelt biographer Bernard Asbell, "We had a good time on the trip, and she enjoyed the attention she got." On the return voyage, she confided, Missy shared a flirtation with a man who was heading home to be married. "He'd sometimes meet her early in the morning on shipboard to watch the sunrise," she said. But it was not quite *An Affair to Remember.* "She enjoyed male companionship," Barbara said, "but not enough to be interested in marrying." However, the letter Missy wrote to FDR holds a clue that their relationship was evolving. She addressed him as "Dear Father."

Missy's enthusiasm for Paris never waned. She spent several weeks in France in the summer of 1934, when she visited Paris twice, and she became a confirmed Francophile, enjoying French fashions, jewelry, history, and culture so much that many people began to believe LeHand was a French surname. Missy seems never to have disabused anyone of the notion.

That fall of 1926, Sara Roosevelt made her first trip to Warm Springs, staying at the Tuscawilla, now renamed the Hotel Warm Springs. With his own cottage under construction on the grounds of what he had dubbed the Meriwether Reserve, FDR convinced Sara to build one, and even designed it himself. She could use it when she visited, he said, and rent it out at other times.

But Franklin's dream of a resort where the revenue from wealthy pleasure seekers could underwrite the treatment of often destitute polios soon met the harsh reality that able-bodied guests were not happy mingling with cripples. Howe's courting of investors went nowhere, and FDR found himself dipping again and again into his own financial resources or borrowing from his mother. In 1927, Basil O'Connor, the young lawyer who had helped Franklin to his feet in the lobby of the Equitable Building and who had subsequently become his law partner, convinced him to turn his enterprise into a nonprofit organization. The Georgia Warm Springs Foundation was born, and some of the wealthy people who had declined to invest were willing to donate.

One of these was Edsel Ford, the able executive son of Henry Ford who is, sadly, now best remembered for the disastrous chrome-encrusted auto that bore his name. He gave $25,000 to the Foundation—more than a quarter of a million in current dollars—for the construction of an indoor swimming pool. This enabled hydrotherapy to continue year-round. Helen Lauer, a professional physiotherapist, joined the staff, and she recruited a phalanx of physical education graduates from Peabody College in Nashville. The "physios," as they were called, worked one-on-one with the patients in the pools, helping them exercise and move their moribund muscles. Attractive and outgoing, the physios over the years paired up romantically with medical staff, patients, Marines guarding the president, and other eligible males, adding to the social gaiety of Warm Springs. Fred Botts, a young man who had been one of the first polios greeting FDR on his second visit in 1925, joined the staff as registrar, an important task as more patients began arriving. Some eighty polios were present at the Thanksgiving dinner in 1927, the first of what became known as Founder's Day.

Unfortunately, many of these patients were not paying their way, and the cost of running the Foundation continued to outpace revenue. Howe's instincts for marketing led to the suggestion that FDR take before and after pictures of polios to convince benefactors that Warm Springs was reaping results. "Perhaps just one photograph showing them doing a hundred-yard dash or shoveling coal or something another after treatment, together with the statement that, when they arrived, it required two stretchers and an ambulance to get them down to the pool, might do the trick," he wrote. But instead of still photos, FDR wrote a letter to photography pioneer George Eastman of Rochester, New York, who had recently developed a home movie camera, and asked if he would donate one of the gadgets. Eastman responded with a Cine Kodak "which I have used myself somewhat but it is still in perfect condition." However, he asked Roosevelt to keep the donation confidential "as I have so many similar requests that any special treatment might prove embarrassing."

With the arrival of Eastman's camera, another love was awakened in Missy. She became devoted to home movie cameras, eventually owned two, and even traveled to Hollywood in the 1930s to tour film studios and learn more about the mechanics of moviemaking. Some of her movies, showing scenes of cookouts and social gatherings with the Roosevelts, were discovered by her great-nieces and developed for the first time seventy years after her death. One, shot poolside at Warm Springs, contains a sight so rare that there are only a handful of examples: FDR in a wheelchair.

The *Larooco* was a casualty of a hurricane in the fall of 1926, and with its destruction the Florida cruises ended. FDR and Missy arrived in Warm Springs February 11, 1927, planning to stay throughout the spring. But in March, Missy—who was not quite thirty years old—had an episode of rapid heartbeat that she later described as a "heart attack" while swimming in the pool, followed by a long and mysterious illness. A flurry of letters and telegrams passed back and forth between FDR, his wife, and Louis Howe about her condition. Louis abandoned his usually acerbic style to write, "I cannot tell you how sorry I am to learn that Missy is laid up with a bum heart. Tell her that as an expert on bum hearts, I know what an extremely uncomfortable and patience trying sort of thing it is, and I do hope by this time that she is well over it and that it was merely a temporary overstrain." A few days later, FDR sent a terse telegram to his wife, asking her to send "two tins of café des invalides," and concluding with the dire words, "Messy better live." Howe made light of the misspelling—no doubt an error at the telegram office—but Missy was indeed a mess by then.

In retrospect, Missy's "heart attack" was probably not the sort of coronary event we think of when that term is used, but rather an intermittent rapid heartbeat, or atrial fibrillation, a legacy of the heart damage caused by her childhood episode of rheumatic fever. Her heartbeat could be slowed to some degree by the drug digitalis, a derivative of the foxglove plant discovered in the late eighteenth century. It was a fairly effective treatment that is still used today. Unfortunately, a small subset of patients developed mental confusion and an agitated state of delirium that had been described in medical literature since 1874 as digitalis delirium or digitalis intoxication. This is precisely the description Missy gave when she was admitted to the hospital at the time of her 1941 health crisis at the White House: she said she had been "poisoned" by digitalis in 1927.

Biographers have uniformly labeled her illness and similar ones that followed as nervous breakdowns. Indeed, the Curtises, who were present at Warm Springs in 1927, and Grace Tully, who did not meet Missy until 1928, gave interviews to Bernard Asbell describing the illness in those terms. Eleanor Roosevelt chimed in, adding glue to the label. "Missy is very ill again," Eleanor Roosevelt wrote to her daughter Anna in 1941. "She had a heart attack & then her mind went as it does," leaving the impression for history that her husband's faithful secretary was emotionally unstable. Eleanor, like many historians who have quoted her words, did not understand the effect of digitalis intoxication on the mind.

That spring, obscure aviator Charles Lindbergh made his historic solo nonstop transatlantic flight, landing in Paris on May 21, a feat that riveted the attention of the world and turned "Lindy" into a national hero—but Missy was too sick to care. Initially looked after by physical therapist Helena Mahoney at Warm Springs, she finally became so mentally confused that she had to be sent to a hospital in New York. Her brother Bernard visited her there in early July and wrote FDR a reassuring letter. He said Missy had little memory of her first days in the hospital—"She is more or less a 'Calamity Jane'"—but had now recovered her mental capabilities. "Just herself—that's all. Looks fine. Has gained five pounds. Can read." Her care was being overseen by a Dr. Pringle, who had initially ordered all sharp objects removed from her reach, including her fountain pen, which Missy now wished returned to her as she was not allowed phone calls and was writing letters to friends and family in pencil. (None of these letters survive.) Bernard said she could leave the hospital at any time but was choosing to stay until she was sure she had "arrived." He concluded, "I am confident that you will decide to take her to Hyde Park for August."

FDR spent most of the fall of 1927 in Warm Springs, but there is no record if Missy was with him. However, she made the decision to have a cottage of her own built the following spring—not to live in, but to rent out to others for income—and by June of 1928 she was back to her old, playful self, as demonstrated in a letter she wrote from Warm Springs to "F.D." in Hyde Park detailing unexpected cost overruns. After going over a list of problems with both her cottage and the one being built for Sara Roosevelt—for which she indignantly laid the blame at the feet of Egbert Curtis—she concluded, "Much love to you even though I am much annoyed with your darned, stupid Cockney manager! . . . Call me up Mon. a.m. and I'll tell you more of my opinions!!!" (The final cost of her cottage was $3,796.77, and it rented out for $75 a month.)

But the Boss had bigger things on his mind that summer than unexpected construction costs. He had once again been invited to nominate Al Smith for president at the Democratic National Convention, and under the tutelage of Helena Mahoney he was perfecting a form of walking that he would employ in public appearances for the rest of his life. It involved a cane and the arm of a strong man.

❁ CHAPTER SIX

# *Don't You Dare*

Franklin Roosevelt was a famous man with a famous laugh. People often described him as roaring with laughter, doubled over with laughter, howling with laughter, and they prided themselves on "making" him laugh. Once Egbert Curtis said something to Missy about this "very, very characteristic" laugh, and Missy replied, "That's his political laugh." It was one of the few times she was less than discreet about her boss. "Some time later I mentioned in her presence his 'political laugh,'" Curtis remembered. "She got madder than hell. I wasn't supposed to say that."

Even Missy would not have dared characterize the method of ambulation FDR and his physical therapists devised as a "political walk," but that is exactly what it was. In 1925, writing to a friend who had urged him to consider a run for president, FDR outlined his plan of action: to walk without braces using crutches, and then switching from crutches to canes. A cane, after all, could be seen as a fashion accessory. A crutch was a medical device. He believed he had to be able to walk if he were to be able to "run."

With Helena Mahoney and Alice Plastridge, a physical therapist who worked with him at Hyde Park and later joined the staff at Warm Springs, he developed a form of walking that capitalized on the strength of his massive arms and shoulders. With his legs locked in braces under his trousers, a cane in his right hand and the left grasping the arm of a strong companion, he could stand upright and "walk" short distances, rotating his hips from the shoulders down. The ordeal was taxing for both parties. FDR's clothing would become saturated with sweat, and the chance for a fall was always there. But for the most part, it worked, the beginning of more than a decade of subterfuge when FDR was only photographed seated, or standing with artfully concealed support: a car door, a wall, a second cane behind his back. This, and the collusion of the press, is the reason many Americans were stunned when they learned the president was paralyzed below the waist. Biographer Hugh Gallagher, himself a polio survivor, called it FDR's "splendid deception."

The walk was put to the test in 1928 when Al Smith, ending his fourth term as governor of New York, again asked Roosevelt to nominate him for president at the Democratic National Convention in late June. That spring he polished his walk, determined to showcase his progress in Houston not only for political reasons, but to demonstrate what was happening at his Foundation in Warm Springs. Then there was Eleanor to consider. "I'm telling everyone you are going to Houston without crutches, so mind you stick to it," she wrote him.

Eleanor did not attend the convention to watch, but Missy did, witnessing her beloved F.D.'s triumph before fifteen thousand cheering Democrats in the steaming hot city's convention hall. (This is another instance where a movie took liberties with the facts to make it appear the Roosevelts had a close and loving marriage. The acclaimed HBO movie *Warm Springs* showed Eleanor blowing her husband a kiss from the balcony after he mouthed the words, "I love you." She was, in fact, 1,500 miles away in New York.) Elliott, by then a strapping seventeen-year-old, was his father's strong assistant as he tottered down the aisle to the platform. "There was no thought of wheelchairs and no need for crutches as he made his smiling way to the speaker's stand," Elliott recalled. "Warm Springs was working for him. With a cane and my right arm, he *walked* to the platform, no longer crippled, merely lame." The response was even greater than four years before in New York when FDR nominated the Happy Warrior Al Smith, and this time Smith got the nod on the first ballot. He would take on the Republican nominee, Herbert Hoover, a popular and able man who was President Calvin Coolidge's secretary of commerce.

Eleanor, who was busy hustling up women's votes for Smith at Democratic Party headquarters in New York, told her husband, "everyone was talking of your speech and feels you did untold good to the Governor's cause." Indeed, FDR spent the rest of the summer building support for Smith at the headquarters and later in Georgia, which was a very hard sell. Success in the Peach State meant defusing prejudice on many levels. He labored against a trio of issues known as "rum, Tammany and religion." Smith was anti-Prohibition—a "wet" in the jargon of the day—in a Bible Belt state that was mostly dry; a creature of New York's big-city political machine whose harsh accent grated on the ears of people for whom the Civil War was still a bitter memory; and, most unsettling of all, a Catholic. One woman asked FDR quite seriously if as president Smith would invalidate all non-Catholic marriages and make her children bastards. Such were FDR's personal popularity and persuasiveness in Meriwether County that the *Manchester Mercury,* which had changed its slogan to "A Progressive Newspaper Published in a Progressive Community for Progressive People," gave its endorsement to Smith.

When he wasn't campaigning for Smith, FDR concentrated on therapy and improving his "walk." He may have believed he was within reach of his dream of discarding his canes; Missy certainly did. The closest he came to success occurred the last weekend in September, at the small cottage he and Missy shared at Warm Springs. With Missy, Helena Mahoney, and Dr. Hubbard cheering him on, he managed to stagger across the living room floor, wearing his braces but without other assistance. It was the first time in seven years that he had walked without canes or crutches. According to Grace Tully, "this was one of the most thrilling moments of Missy's experience."

Describing the scene later—Tully's memory of Missy's account was the only one ever given—Missy's blue eyes swam with tears. She firmly believed that with another year or two of therapy, FDR might finally reach his goal of walking unaided. What FDR thought of the accomplishment is not known, though his actions over the next two days speak volumes. On the following Monday, Al Smith arrived in Rochester for the state Democratic convention. He and his advisors were convinced that a strong Democratic candidate for governor of the Empire State would carry the largely Republican state for him as president—crucial electoral votes he had to win—and no New York Democrat was stronger than FDR.

Smith had approached FDR earlier in the summer on the subject and been rebuffed. So had cronies from Smith's kitchen cabinet. But from a smoke-filled fifth-floor suite in the Hotel Seneca in Rochester, they launched an intense campaign by telegram and long-distance phone. FDR was evasive, giving excuses ranging from his need for more physical therapy to his concerns for the financial state of the Foundation. Smith recruited everyone he could find to convince him, including daughter Anna, who sent a telegram urging, "GO AHEAD AND TAKE IT." Her father's reply: "YOU OUGHT TO BE SPANKED." Louis Howe agreed with the Boss; he thought the timing was all wrong, with Hoover likely to surf to victory on the wave of the Coolidge prosperity, drowning Smith and FDR in the process. Missy was distraught. F.D. had come so far; how could he give up his chance to walk? Eleanor told Smith that the decision had to be her husband's.

While Smith and his cronies schemed and sweated that Monday, FDR and Missy were leisurely picnicking at Dowdell's Knob and driving around with Egbert Curtis where a phone call couldn't reach the reticent candidate. (Alcohol wasn't the only thing in short supply in Meriwether County; phones also were few and far between.) As they sat on the knob, looking at the fall golds and russets just appearing in the trees in Pine Mountain Valley, it is likely most of their conversation was about how best to resist Smith without permanently alienating him and the other Democratic Party leaders.

While FDR and Missy munched their fried chicken, Smith recruited Eleanor Roosevelt to help him make a final, desperate pitch. That evening, FDR, Missy, and Curtis arrived in Manchester, where Roosevelt had to be carried up three flights of stairs to speak at a political rally at the high school. A call was placed from Rochester to a phone booth at Manchester's City Drug Store, and someone sent word to FDR that his wife was on the line. He continued his speech, even stringing it out a half hour, but he couldn't ignore her call. When he finally answered the phone, Eleanor said a few words and handed the receiver off to Smith. Roosevelt listened to the old arguments for a few moments, and then the connection broke—or at least Roosevelt said it did. Another call came through at the phone booth from the operator, instructing him to wait for Smith's call at the Meriwether Inn.

Missy lit into her boss once they got in the car. "Don't you dare!" she said over and over as Curtis drove them through the early fall night to the Meriwether Inn, reminding him of his vow to be able to walk before he ran for office. But Smith was at his most persuasive when he got on the line at the inn, countering every argument, pushing every button.

Missy, at FDR's elbow, repeated her impassioned words, "Don't you *dare!*"

Finally Smith asked, "If those fellows nominate you tomorrow and adjourn, will you refuse to run?" For the first time, FDR hesitated, and Smith smelled victory. "All right, I won't ask any more questions," he growled, and got off the phone.

In the car, Curtis asked FDR if he really planned to run. Roosevelt turned his massive head toward him and said, "Curt, when you're in politics, you've got to play the game." He and Missy returned to their cottage; there is no record of their conversation that night, though it's tempting to imagine everything from shouting to crying to stony silence. The next day in Rochester, FDR was nominated unanimously, and accepted.

Louis was enraged ("TELL MISSY YOUR MISSUS AND MYSELF ARE JUST AS PLEASED," one of his sarcastic post-nomination wires said), but gamely began throwing a campaign together for what he was sure was a lost cause. Missy was devastated. When FDR left Warm Springs on October 5, she stayed behind at the cottage. She was ill again; some accounts describe it as an emotional breakdown. Perhaps this time it was, but it is just as likely she suffered another heart episode, as she later said her doctor told her to avoid stairs when she moved back to New York. It was FDR's only campaign until her stroke in 1941 in which she did not take an active part. Eleanor played only a small role in the gubernatorial campaign, focusing most of her attention on Smith.

FDR joyfully traveled all over New York, making speeches, shaking hands, kissing babies, and demonstrating Smith's assurances to the public that "Physically, he is as good as he ever was in his life" and "a Governor does not have to be an acrobat." Smith had been an extremely popular governor for eight years, and Roosevelt promised to continue his policies and programs. Even so, he won the election by only a whisker. Smith, however, was soundly defeated by Herbert Hoover, failing even to carry New York. It was a bitter pill that would stick in his gullet for the rest of his life and turn him incontrovertibly against the man he had begged to succeed him.

The day after the election, Eleanor told a reporter that she was not excited about her husband's victory. "If the rest of the ticket doesn't get in what does it matter?" she asked. According to Elliott Roosevelt, Missy had gotten over her initial despair over the nomination and was elated at the win. "According to her creed, once you were in a fight, you had to win it," he said. Unfortunately, she didn't get to vote herself; she had registered in Hyde Park, and absentee voting was an innovation that was still some years away.

Another of FDR's inner circle who was delighted with the outcome was his mother. Sara and Frances Perkins, who would become the state industrial commissioner, were the only ones who remained at FDR's election headquarters after it appeared he had lost—even the candidate had gone home—and they enjoyed a "quiet jubilation," Perkins recalled. Observers of Prohibition, they toasted each other with glasses of milk when the final returns pushed him over the top.

*A rare newspaper clipping sent to Missy from a friend at the Fidelity & Deposit Company after FDR was elected governor shows him taking her picture at Warm Springs.*

The *Manchester Mercury* ran post–Election Day editorials side by side on its front page: "Roosevelt Elected Governor of New York," and "Hoover Elected in Unparalleled Landslide." Incredibly, Smith *did* carry Meriwether County, and the *Mercury* was unrepentant about its endorsement: "We supported him for the reason that he has proven his metal [*sic*] and ability as an administrative officer as governor of the greatest state in the union."

When Roosevelt returned to Warm Springs on the evening of Saturday, November 10, he was greeted at the train station by a crowd estimated at three to four hundred by the *Mercury*, including "17 patients from the Warm Springs sanitorium" holding up white cards with black letters spelling out "GOVERNOR ROOSEVELT." A "college yell" followed: "One, two three, four, five, six, seven, New York State is now in Heaven." Roosevelt, "visibly moved," said a few words and then "asked to be excused to retire to his cottage for some much needed rest."

His entourage included a new secretary, another pretty blue-eyed Irish American Catholic girl, this one with deep dimples bracketing her toothy smile. Her name was Grace Tully, and she was three years younger than Missy. Grace had worked for ten years for a cardinal in New York, but had become bored with the "quietness" of taking dictation for sermons and accepted a job at the Democratic National Committee in New York to help get her idol Al Smith elected. Initially assigned to work with Eleanor Roosevelt getting out the women's vote—she suffered hand cramps from the mountain of letters Eleanor dictated the first day—Grace eventually met FDR. Like most people, she was impressed with the "vitality" of this "handsome, broad-shouldered" man, though she admitted "the first time I saw him lifted out of his wheelchair and carried by valet and chauffeur to a place in his automobile, I turned away and cried." She came to spend a great deal of time working directly with him as a stenographer and, like Missy after the 1920 election, was invited to stay on for a few weeks to help clean up the correspondence. Instead of at Hyde Park, however, the work was to be done at Warm Springs. "Georgia in November and December seemed like a preview of a New York secretary's heaven and I accepted with alacrity," Grace wrote.

> I knew that Miss Marguerite LeHand, his long-time secretary who had recently been ill, was convalescing down there until

> after voting day. . . . I had never met Missy LeHand before this 1928 trip to Warm Springs and several mutual acquaintances had cautioned me that I must be extremely tactful in recognizing her authority as FDR's secretary and her long relationship with him. It was sound enough advice in such circumstance but was completely unneeded. From the moment we met, Missy and I liked each other tremendously and our relationship from then until her death in 1944 was like that of two sisters who never quarreled. She was a magnificent person.

Apparently, Grace passed the "Missy test." When FDR and his entourage traveled to Albany to take over the Governor's Mansion, Grace was a member of Team Roosevelt. She would remain so until the end.

Another new player for Missy was Samuel I. Rosenman, a round-faced, curly-haired young attorney who had joined the campaign in New York to assist with fact-checking on Roosevelt's speeches. Rosenman was a native Texan transplanted to New York at an early age, Jewish, and served as the Democratic Party's state bill-drafting commissioner. He was so exhausted by the campaign that he slept for two days and nights after the photo-finish win, and FDR invited him to come to Warm Springs to relax. There he had his first meeting with Missy, with whom he shared 1896 as birth year. The two would become great personal friends as well as colleagues, Missy attending horse races and spending vacations with Sam and his wife, Dorothy, and she would earn his utmost respect for her "equal facility [to] be the efficient secretary, the helpful and lively participant in a policy conference, or the gracious hostess at the Roosevelt table." Soon other New York politicians were flocking to Warm Springs, as FDR hammered out his legislative agenda and chose his cabinet. He asked Sam to serve as counsel to the governor. The young attorney asked to think it over, and was still deciding when he read in a newspaper that he had accepted the job. He called Roosevelt to verify the story and the laughing governor-elect said, "Yes, I made up your mind for you."

Roosevelt, Missy, and the rest of the entourage returned to New York in early December, where FDR recruited the very able Frances Perkins as his industrial commissioner and his Hyde Park neighbor Henry Morgenthau Jr. as his chief agricultural advisor. They arrived in Albany on New Year's Eve, and FDR was sworn in at the Governor's Mansion that night. The formal inauguration was held the next day, snow falling on his inaugural parade.

Once the festivities ended, it was Roosevelt's turn to prove his "metal" (as the *Manchester Mercury* might have put it) as the chief executive of the country's most populous state—and time for Missy to prove hers as the governor's private secretary, advisor, and intimate friend.

CHAPTER SEVEN

# *The Governor's Girl Friday*

The Governor's Mansion in Albany has been called "a Victorian monstrosity of gloom." Built by a wealthy banker prior to the Civil War, it was originally a simple two-story structure in the then popular Italianate style, but over the next fifty years it was renovated, expanded, remodeled, and redecorated to encompass successive architectural and interior design fancies. Elliott Roosevelt likened it to the perfect setting for a Hollywood horror film, with "its confusion of turrets and towers, balconies and chimney stacks." This red-brick amalgam was the Roosevelt family home for four years. Missy moved in with them, the beginning of a period of cohabitation that would last for the rest of her time as FDR's girl Friday.

Missy started her Albany years living in a boardinghouse, but her doctor advised her not to climb stairs—another indicator of chronic heart trouble. Eleanor Roosevelt invited her to live at the mansion, which had an elevator, and assigned her a second-floor bedroom near FDR's large, sunny master suite. Just *how* near it was is a matter of dispute. Elliott claims the rooms adjoined, a door with a curtained window separating them, and made much again of the fact that Missy traipsed around FDR's bedroom in her nightgown. James Roosevelt said it was simply "near" his father's, and asked, that as practically a member of the family as well as an essential employee who might be needed at any hour, "was she supposed to dress to the teeth every time she was summoned at midnight?"

Both sons agreed that the domestic situation suited the three adults perfectly, and that their mother, after all, assigned the bedrooms. Eleanor took a small room farther from her husband's, a choice that was perhaps symbolic of her feelings about being his first lady. She was deeply unhappy about her new role and determined not to lose the independent life she had created for herself.

Under the affectionate coaching of Louis Howe, Eleanor had spread her wings, becoming a national political force to be reckoned with, especially in galvanizing women to vote Democratic and as an activist in liberal social causes. She was in demand as a speaker and writer, editing an influential newsletter for Democratic women, and earning substantial fees for articles in national magazines. Besides Val-Kill Industries, she, Marion Dickerman, and Nancy Cook had purchased a private girls school in Manhattan. Eleanor served as vice principal and teacher of American history and English literature at the Todhunter School, awakening the intellects of a new generation of well-to-do girls in the manner of her beloved Mademoiselle Souvestre. She loved teaching and had no intention of giving it up. That meant she spent Sunday night through Wednesday morning each week in New York during the school year, in addition to the travel she did for her other causes, family obligations, and, eventually, serving as Franklin's eyes, ears, and legs on inspection tours around the state. Often she was his nose as well, lifting the lids on cooking pots to be sure inmates of prisons and mental hospitals were getting decent food.

Having Missy on the scene meant Eleanor could depart without worries about lining up a hostess to preside over social occasions at the mansion, although she scheduled the majority of these for days when she was in Albany.

One of Missy's first tasks was to oversee an important addition at the mansion: FDR wanted a heated indoor swimming pool so he could keep up his hydrotherapy. Missy gamely accompanied him into the pool, hiding a growing distaste for exercise. "In Albany we started skating, but not very successfully—for me," she told an interviewer in 1941. "I got tired and my ankles went." As time went on and her heart condition worsened, she would find more and more excuses not to exert herself.

*Eleanor, FDR, Missy, and ER's bodyguard, Earl Miller, enjoy the Val-Kill swimming pool.*

Howe was a part-time resident of the mansion, living there on weekends. His base during the week was New York, where he could work levers on the publicity machine, tout the new governor's proposals and accomplishments, and lay the groundwork for his future run for the presidency. During the week, he and Eleanor lived in the Roosevelt townhouse, further cementing their alliance. (Years later, pictures of Eleanor far outnumbered those of FDR on Louis's White House bedroom walls, a testament to their friendship and devotion.)

Eventually Sam Rosenman and his wife, Dorothy, moved into the mansion, too, which drove Howe to distraction. He was jealous of any advisor who seemed to be getting close to the Boss, and FDR and Sam had formed a fast friendship on the campaign trail. However, Sam was far from the only advisor growing in FDR's estimation. Two Irish American Catholic political bosses, James A. Farley and Edward J. Flynn, had proved themselves invaluable in the race. Farley became chairman of the Democratic State Committee, and Flynn replaced an insider of Al Smith's as secretary of state. Two other important insiders were the strapping state police troopers, Gus Gennerich and Earl Miller, who served as bodyguards for the governor and first lady. Good-hearted Gus was essential in helping move FDR into and out of his car and up and down steps. Earl, an extremely handsome and seductive man in his mid-thirties, came to fuel the romantic imaginations of both Eleanor and Missy. It was another of the odd triangles that dominated domestic affairs in the Roosevelt extended "family."

*Cloche hats and fur collars mark the ladies in this 1930 scene in the New York governor's office. From left: Eleanor, Missy, Grace Tully, and Dorothy and Sam Rosenman. FDR is holding the Rosenmans' son on his lap.*

Earl Miller, who was a dozen years younger than Eleanor and a few years older than Missy, possessed a body builder's physique that he enjoyed showing off in bathing trunks and form-fitting riding gear. He looked very fine in his trooper's uniform, with its knee-high boots and brimmed hat. An orphan, like Eleanor, but from a social level more comparable to Missy's, his career path had included stints as a circus acrobat and stuntman, rodeo rider and judo instructor, as well as Al Smith's bodyguard. Very quickly, he and Eleanor developed an intimate friendship that puzzled her friends. What did she see in this swaggering and often gauche younger man? But they also recognized that Miller was a chivalrous fellow in the mode of a knight errant, who made Eleanor feel attractive and desirable as she had not felt since her husband's infidelity with Lucy Mercer. His jokes and silly songs made her laugh, and he teased her into smiling for photographers rather than clamping her lips over her bucked teeth, much improving her public image. He called her the "Lady." A superior horseman, Miller got Eleanor back in the saddle and taught Missy to ride, presented Eleanor with a horse named Dot, and even got FDR on horseback at Warm Springs for a few publicity photos and short films, though the governor's legs hung like limp strands of spaghetti over the horse's flanks and he could never travel at more than a placid walk.

Miller was fully aware of his attractiveness. Divorced from his first wife by the time the Roosevelts came to Albany, he had plenty of girlfriends. Around 1930, Missy became one of them. Over the years Miller told several versions of why he began dating her. One was that it gave political cover to Eleanor. Gossip had begun to spread about the unusual relationship between Miller and "his Lady," and pairing up with Missy made it possible for Miller to hang around on occasions when his presence as a bodyguard wasn't needed. Another was that he "played up" to Missy because Eleanor was hurt by the secretary's close relationship with FDR. Yet another was that he found Missy attractive and liked her. But in the end, Miller fell in love with someone else.

The woman Miller eventually married in 1932 was a cousin of his first wife, and Eleanor held the wedding at Hyde Park. (One story, told by irascible newspaperman Walter Trohan, was that in an out-of-the-mouths-of-babes moment Anna's five-year-old daughter, Eleanor "Sistie" Dall, expressed astonishment when she was introduced to Miller's teenage bride. "I thought he was going to marry Grandma!" she exclaimed.) Miller claimed Missy cried for days after she learned of his engagement, but she left no written record of her feelings. The only story her great-nieces, Barbara Jacques and Jane Scarbrough, heard about her love life was that Missy had a serious boyfriend her Catholicism prevented her from marrying because he was divorced. That description could have applied to Miller, but it could also have applied to the man she fell in love with in 1933, William Christian Bullitt, who was twice divorced. With her many duties as private secretary and backup ringmaster of the Roosevelt household three-ring circus, there were probably too many distractions to allow her to brood for long.

Even from a perspective of five tumultuous years at the White House, Missy told an interviewer in 1938 that "Albany was the hardest work I ever did." She was used to juggling FDR's varied interests and far-reaching correspondence, but now she was doing it on a huge scale and without much assistance. Grace Tully had come to Albany, but she was assigned part-time to Eleanor Roosevelt. (By then Eleanor also had as a part-time secretary, Malvina "Tommy" Thompson, who eventually worked around-the-clock for her much as Missy did for FDR.) At the capitol, FDR had settled on a strong young man named Guernsey Cross as his secretary, in part because he could help him move about. Most of Missy's workday—a loose term, as she was on call twenty-four hours a day—was spent at the mansion.

At the suggestion of Dr. Leroy Hubbard, the doctor at Warm Springs, FDR began his day with breakfast in bed and dealt with much of his early morning business there, an old sweater thrown over his pajamas to keep his shoulders warm. There Missy delivered his personal mail and took dictation for letters. Once he left for the capitol, she typed and readied the letters for his signature and planned the evening's social and business schedule, including an informal tea every afternoon. In Eleanor's absence, this included meeting with the heads of the household staff, ordering groceries, and dealing with all manner of what Missy called "oddy-endy things." One of the notations in her 1931 datebook is, "Do something about rats in Pete's cellar." Guests, usually with state business on their minds, came for tea and dinner, and then there were speeches to prepare afterward, including simple, chatty radio addresses, the precursors to his famous presidential Fireside Chats, delivered from his study in the mansion.

"I have plenty to do and I like it," Missy told a newspaper reporter in 1932 in a story headlined "Right Hand Woman for Roosevelt." "The Governor often works late, and I have worked with him up to 10:30 and nearly 11 o'clock in the evening."

According to Rosenman, some evenings lasted much longer. One example was when FDR had him invite an expert on utility regulation to come for dinner and an overnight stay so he could pick his brain. Missy was the hostess that night, and the four of them had a long dinner of small talk, followed by coffee in the study, where the governor got down to business. By 11 p.m., FDR was calling for refreshments. Since Prohibition was still in effect, Sam said he asked for a tall glass of ginger ale garnished with lemon peel, what he called a "horse's neck." (It's likely that the glass also contained whiskey, as Eleanor was away that night.) Then the discussion continued until after midnight. Sam said simply, "It was a difficult pace to keep."

Missy would certainly have seconded him. Even though she had avowed in her "Right Hand Woman" newspaper interview "I would hate to be mixed up in politics," she was absorbing knowledge about a vast array of issues. Sam developed great respect for her "sound common sense and good judgment" as well as her unwillingness to be a "yes man." Eleanor was hardly a "yes man" either, but Sam found her argumentative and aggressive manner off-putting and counterproductive, preferring Missy as a hostess because "she could sit at the table and entertain guests, lead the conversation and charm them with her gracious manner." Then she would speak her mind to FDR in private, rather than haranguing him in front of others, as Eleanor often did.

Missy also kept her eye on FDR's mood and need for diversion from matters of state. Reporters in Albany who crowded into FDR's study for press conferences became accustomed to seeing Missy seated in a corner, "peering through spectacles at a pile of letters or a stenographer's notebook," said a profile in *Newsweek*. "Missy would not intrude into the discussions, but she never missed a chance for a laugh." "On an evening when she knew a condemned man was going to the electric chair, she would ask Sam Rosenman and Grace Tully to come in and play bridge so that nothing serious would be discussed," Marion Dickerman recalled. (There were fifty-one executions under FDR's watch, which made for an awful lot of bridge.) The bridge games were a tamer version of the stag poker parties she organized in Albany and later in Washington, sometimes sitting in with "the boys," otherwise kibitzing and seeing their glasses were filled. On other evenings, a makeshift theater was set up in a hall, and guests gathered to watch first-run movies. An evening with nothing on the schedule was apparently worth noting, as Missy did on one page of her datebook: "quiet evening," she wrote.

In the first year at least, the governor's exhausting routine was broken up with a long sojourn at Warm Springs in the spring and two short ones in the fall. Even there, Missy's work continued. She typed a quick note to Grace in April 1929 bemoaning a shortage of stamps ("A new batch of mail has just come this morning") and her missing paycheck, and asked her to send a gallon of maple syrup and two cans of maple cream the governor wanted. She scrawled a PS: "Someday I'll write you a nice long letter." If she did, Grace didn't save it.

On top of the steady round of visitors and social occasions that required Missy's smiling presence, there were visits by the rambunctious Roosevelt children. When Theodore Roosevelt had served as governor of New York thirty years before, he had brought to the mansion six children ranging in age from fourteen to one, and a menagerie of animals that included twenty-two guinea pigs. Franklin and Eleanor's children were older and, except for Anna, who was married with a young daughter by then, they were either in college or boarding school. Nevertheless, a social visit when the boys were in attendance was something akin to sitting down to tea with the Mad Hatter and the March Hare, with anything likely to happen short of a dormouse being dunked in the teapot. *Liberty* magazine editor Fulton Oursler described such a tea party when Anna and the three youngest boys were home, shared with Missy, Grace, Eleanor, and Sam, "who next morning was to be sworn in as a judge." It was hardly a sober occasion for a man who would soon be donning a black robe.

"There were shouts of laughter about falls from horses and excruciating screams about a fat lady's seat, and noisy arguments about whether personal calls to Grandma could be charged to state expenses," he wrote. "In their domestic life the Roosevelts had no inhibitions whatsoever; they were all on the best and freest of terms with each other, squealed with delight at the feeblest jokes, pranced and squirmed until it all seemed to me like an unconvincing scene in a play that needed to be rewritten."

It was the first of many such occasions at the Roosevelt table for Oursler, who had met Missy the year before at the family townhouse in Manhattan. He described her as "a lovely girl whose intimate friendship was to be mine for many years. . . . The premature silver of her hair, the lovely throaty voice and the quick upturn of her face won me as no member of the Roosevelt family was ever to win me." The intimacy extended to Oursler's vivacious playwright wife, Grace, and continued until third-term politics drove them apart in 1940.

Mad tea parties aside, New York had serious issues to address in FDR's first legislative session. The assembly was Republican and recalcitrant, and the embittered Al Smith, who had hoped to remain the power behind the throne, was stirring the pot in the background even though FDR was continuing Smith's progressive agenda. Many of the proposals Roosevelt made in New York—both those that passed and those that failed—later came to fruition under the New Deal. Rosenman provided a laundry list:

> minimum wages and maximum hours, old age insurance, unemployment relief through public works and other means, unemployment insurance, regulation of public utilities, stricter regulations of banks and of the use of other people's money, improved housing through the use of public subsidies, farm relief, public development of water power, cheaper electricity especially in rural areas, greater use of state funds for education, crippled persons and the mentally and physically handicapped, repeal of prohibition laws, reforms in the administration of justice, reforestation and proper land use.

Missy and FDR had just returned from a vacation in Warm Springs when the stock market crashed on October 24, 1929, marking the start of the Great Depression. The "paper loss" that day was reported at $5 billion—equivalent to more than $79 billion today. Subsequent frenzied trading days added to the losses, smashing the gaudy Jazz Age roadster into a brick wall. Financial panics had occurred regularly in American history, and at first the seriousness of this one was not fully evident. Stocks rebounded somewhat in early 1930, reassuring people that the worst was over, but the boom was short-lived. Al Smith, then president of a development corporation, began construction on St. Patrick's Day that year of the 102-story Empire State Building. It was completed the next year, the tallest building in the world (it surpassed the new Chrysler Building because of the "raddio" tower Smith added to the top), but he had such a hard time finding tenants that the building was snidely called the "Empty State Building."

The decline in the value of stocks by mid-1932 was 89 percent—compared to the 54 percent decline reached at the bottom of the 2008 recession—and the value was not recovered until the 1950s. The other three horsemen of this financial apocalypse were high unemployment, the collapse of the banking system, and personal despair. Looking back today, scholars generally agree that misguided government action contributed mightily to the economy's crashing collapse. Interest rates were raised, making it harder for businesspeople and farmers to finance their activities; the money supply was sharply reduced just when banks needed more reserves; and Congress passed legislation that raised tariffs to record-setting levels, setting off a world trade war that sent workers away from work and into growing soup lines. The jobless rate rose from 3.2 percent in 1929 to almost 25 percent in 1933. Almost ten thousand banks failed, taking with them the savings of millions of families. There was no deposit insurance.

Across the country, families began to double up. When the 1930 census was taken in Somerville, Massachusetts, the household at 101 Orchard Street included Missy's widowed mother as well as sister Anna, now twice divorced, and her two daughters. Also living under their roof was an unrelated married couple, a cab driver and his wife. Missy wrote an apologetic letter to a Somerville neighbor, Maydelle Ramsey, whose husband, Charles, was desperate for a job. "I talked with the Governor about Mr. Ramsey, and he has wracked his brain to think of something, but nothing has happened. He has had so many of his friends who are trying to get something to do, and there just seems to be nothing. You know he has been trying to get something for Dan [Missy's brother] to do for about two years, and no success."

With Sara Roosevelt's substantial wealth and Franklin employed and housed by the state government, the Roosevelts were fairly insulated from the crash, but they were hardly immune. Anna's husband, Curtis Dall, was wiped out and lost his seat on the New York Stock Exchange and their fancy home in North Tarrytown. They moved into the Roosevelt townhouse in New York, and the stress unraveled the fragile seams of their marriage.

Yet these were the lucky people, with food to eat, decent places to live, or families to take them in. For many Americans, the deprivation caused by a seven-fold increase in unemployment would be far more serious. Weakened by malnutrition and exposure, people died of relatively minor illnesses. Men and women abandoned their families and took to riding the rails in boxcars and living in hobo villages. The birthrate dropped, and babies and children were left at orphanages or handed over to relatives. Suicide rates soared.

Dealing with the lowering boom of the Great Depression would be the major challenge of FDR's second term as governor. Herbert Hoover's failure to stem the tide practically guaranteed he would be a one-term president.

The seriousness of the Depression was becoming evident in 1930, when in a record landslide FDR was swept back into the governor's office for a second two-year term. In a private train car returning from New York to Albany, surrounded by his inner circle—Missy, Louis, Sam, Basil O'Connor, Cuff Links Gang member Tom Lynch, Grace, Eleanor, and Earl Miller—they began to talk, in a joking sort of way, about a run for president. FDR joined in the laugher but was noncommittal. Louis soon set up an organization he dubbed Friends of Roosevelt and enlisted a reporter, Ernest K. Lindley, to write a flattering biography. In the copy of *Franklin D. Roosevelt: A Career in Progressive Democracy* he presented to Missy, Lindley wrote, "To Marguerite LeHand who could have made a more stirring tale of some of these chapters." Underneath it was the postscript, "She certainly could—Franklin D Roosevelt." Lindley was one of many journalists beating a path to the governor's door. Missy's calendar book for January 30, 1931, when they were at Hyde Park for FDR's birthday, reads, "Newspaper boys arrive from Washington."

*Roosevelt "walks" into his second gubernatorial inaugural ball on the arm of son-in-law Curtis Dall. ER is on left, Missy on the right.*

Over the next two years, FDR responded to the deepening economic crisis like no other governor in the country. He pushed through the Republican-controlled legislature the nation's first unemployment relief program, funded with $20 million, and hired a young man named Harry L. Hopkins to run it. Harry would become an intimate on the level of Louis and Missy during the years to come, as well as Missy's close friend.

On top of that, FDR dealt with an erupting political scandal in New York involving the city's Tammany Hall mayor, "Gentleman Jimmy" Walker, a womanizing scoundrel who changed clothes four times a day. Through the summer of 1932, FDR kept the heat on the flamboyant mayor, hoping he would voluntarily leave office rather than have to be removed or put on trial. He knew removal would have political repercussions, and he needed Tammany's support if he were to win the nomination for president. Nevertheless, FDR presided over a judicial hearing about Walker's transgressions in late August, which led to a simple note in Missy's September 1, 1932, datebook: "Mayor resigns." Walker, in fact, left town, taking his chorus girl mistress with him on a ship bound for Europe. "Papa made me eat my spinach," he told a friend.

The last two years in the Governor's Mansion brought more illness for Missy, including a recurrence of erratic heartbeat that put her back on digitalis for a time. Eleanor, concerned about her continuing frailty, took Missy to Maine on a week-long working vacation in July 1931. She wrote to FDR that his girl Friday was eating better and smoking less and "seemed more ready to sleep tonight." They spent time at Saratoga Springs the following year, where Missy attended a horse race with the Rosenmans. She had become quite a racing fan and would remain so throughout the 1930s as she followed the exploits of Omaha, War Admiral, and Seabiscuit. At some point she added a tiny gold horse and jockey to one of her charm bracelets.

Meanwhile, FDR was building himself a new cottage at Warm Springs, a simple six-room affair of native Georgia pine. Eleanor commissioned the furniture from Val-Kill Industries, and Missy saw to such details as drapes for each of the rooms, ordering the fabric shipped from Macy's in New York. Missy traveled down a few days ahead of him in April 1932 to oversee the final details for a housewarming party on May 1.

The people of Meriwether County had quickly jumped on the presidential bandwagon. After his reelection, FDR was the guest of honor at a game supper in the county seat of Greenville given by the Meriwether Warm Springs Franklin D. Roosevelt for President Club, and the *Meriwether Vindicator* was the first newspaper in the country to endorse his candidacy.

It's no wonder that when Franklin, Missy, and Eleanor held their housewarming party at the simple white clapboard cottage, their many Georgia friends were already calling it the Little White House.

CHAPTER EIGHT

# Running for President

Fulton Oursler knocked on the front door at 49 East 65th Street in New York one December afternoon in 1931, and was seen into the Roosevelt home by a "colored butler" whose "swallow-tailed coat and iron-rimmed spectacles suggested Old Virginia rather than Dutch New York." Oursler was the editor of *Liberty,* the largest circulation weekly magazine in the country, and he was there to meet the likely Democratic nominee for president. He would never forget the experience, nor would he forget meeting for the first time the governor's private secretary. "Indeed, when I looked into the blue eyes of Marguerite LeHand, I knew somehow instantly that she would be my friend," he recalled.

The governor was closeted in his study with a delegation of South Carolina politicians, "all with luscious southern voices, alcoholic aromas and pestiferous cigars." Louis Howe, who had introduced Oursler to Missy, slipped into the study with the South Carolinians. "You might as well sit down and eavesdrop on these stuffed shirts," Missy invited. "They are here to promise the governor that they will vote for him at the convention, but they won't put it in writing." She handed him a cigar of his own, and they indeed eavesdropped on the discussion, which seemed to involve tall tales of deer hunting. The Southerners finally emerged, and Oursler was ushered in.

A few months before, *Liberty* had run the story "Is Franklin D. Roosevelt Physically Fit to Be President?" by Earle Looker, and contrary to the implication of the title, it had done much to silence the whispering campaign that insinuated FDR was not healthy enough for the job. Looker had spent weeks in the mansion observing his subject, as well as finding three doctors to give the governor a thorough examination. (Six months before that, FDR had also undergone physical examinations in order to qualify for a $560,000 "key man" insurance policy payable upon his death to the Warm Springs Foundation. It served to wipe out his personal debt to the Foundation.) The doctors agreed unanimously that FDR was physically fit to be president, although one, a Republican, made the off-the-record jest, "But remember, as far as I am concerned this doesn't go for above the neck!"

By the time of Oursler's visit, Missy was well accustomed to dealing with what she called "the newspaper boys." Just like Ernest K. Lindley, author of FDR's recent biography, they found her gracious but Sphinx-like. "The depths of Missy's discretion were plumbed as the '32 convention drew near and Washington correspondents descended in droves upon Albany to learn what manner of man it was who would surely be the next President of the United States. But Missy wouldn't talk," Doris Fleeson would later write of her in *The Saturday Evening Post*. Oursler was a different case. He became personal friends with Missy, and she confided things to him she didn't share with others. The most revealing was her devastating observation that FDR, in Oursler's words, "was really incapable of a personal friendship with anyone." Whether she included herself in this remarkable statement is unclear. Oursler valued their friendship and didn't break the confidences. His memoir, *Behold This Dreamer!*, which includes one of the most extensive profiles of Missy written by a contemporary, was published in 1964, long after his (and her) death.

A few weeks later, Oursler and his wife, Grace, were invited to dinner and an overnight stay at the mansion. They had tea with the family—the Mad Hatter affair described previously—and then changed for dinner. Oursler discovered to his horror that he had accidentally brought his teenage son's much too small dress shirt. He had to borrow a much too large one from the governor, and FDR made sure everyone at the table knew it. Dinner was just as chaotic and loud as tea, with the addition of constant ringing from telephones placed beside the plates of Eleanor and FDR. The calls were all concerned with the presidential primaries that began in late January. "I hardly remember a dozen coherent words that were spoken during the meal," Oursler wrote. "What lingers most in my mind is that Marguerite LeHand was on my right. . . . Nor shall I forget the happy gleam that Roosevelt cast in our direction. He seemed to be delighted that Marguerite was having a good time." Oursler left Albany thoroughly charmed, and with the belief that FDR's election was "a sure thing."

Other journalists were not so easily won over. Walter Lippmann of the *New York Herald Tribune* wrote a damning column about FDR, describing him as "a highly impressionistic person, without a firm grasp of public affairs and without very strong convictions. . . . He is a pleasant man who, without any important qualifications for the office, would very much like to be president." (He privately described FDR as "an amiable Boy Scout." The tag got around.) Lippmann's words stung, because there was truth in them. To get the candidate up to speed and formulate proposals for de-fanging the Depression, Sam Rosenman suggested creating an advisory circle of deep thinkers, who a newspaper correspondent later dubbed "the Brain Trust." They were Barnard College professor Raymond Moley, who had been serving as an advisor for some time, and two men he recruited from Columbia University, Rexford Tugwell and Adolf Berle. Their job was to school Roosevelt in subjects crucial to understanding and overcoming the economic crisis: agriculture, banking, railroads, foreign trade, utilities, investments. Sam and Basil O'Connor joined in, helping Moley translate the ideas FDR adopted into words for speeches. Tugwell wrote that "by June a notable weakness was transformed into an all-around competence."

Tugwell was the glamour boy of the group, a handsome man who consciously matched his shirts to his startling blue eyes. He remembered Missy as "quiet but lovely" and Grace Tully as "buxom and cheery. Their charm was pervasive." FDR, he wrote, "had an exceptionally agile mind" that sucked up everything the Brain Trust taught him, churned it around, and spewed out ideas that often ran ahead of his "teachers." As Missy sat in on discussions in the mansion office, took notes and worked on letters, speeches and position papers, she, too, was learning the language of the economic crisis that was strangling the nation's soul. "The Albany of that spring can only be described as given over to euphoria," Tugwell recalled. "The more the complexities multiplied, the more easily Franklin got through his days." Missy was ever at his side, a vital supporting player in that drama of crises, ideas, and solutions.

By the time the Brain Trust was assembled in 1932, not only had the U.S. stock market hit bottom, but the entire world was enveloped in the Depression, the first time anything of this nature had occurred. Prices and production fell, unemployment soared, and governments struggled to address the desperate needs of their people. Again, a comparison with the 2008 financial crisis is helpful. By 1932, worldwide Gross Domestic Product—the value of the goods and services produced by an economy during a certain time period—had fallen by 15 percent from its 1929 high. By the bottom of the 2008–2009 recession, global GDP had fallen less than 1 percent.

In 1932, the social safety net of unemployment insurance and many other federal, state, and local programs did not exist. Charities did what they could, but despair was growing. Homelessness skyrocketed, with hundreds of thousands of people living in squalid tent cities dubbed Hoovervilles in "honor" of the ineffectual president. (One of them popped up in New York's Central Park.) As a Depression hobo told journalist Studs Terkel, the talk was of revolution and class warfare: "You met guys ridin' the freight trains and so forth, talkin' about what they'd like to do with a machine gun. How they'd like to tear loose on the rich." The kidnapping and murder of the toddler son of aviation hero Charles Lindbergh and his wife, Anne, that spring was a shocking metaphor for the country's financial and moral crisis.

Moley brilliantly distilled the human misery into three words, "the forgotten man," used in a radio speech FDR gave from Albany in early April. He likened the financial crisis to a war and called on the country to "mobilize to meet it" by "restoring farmers' buying power," giving relief to banks so they would not have to foreclose on homeowners and farmers, and reconstructing the harmful high-tariff policy passed under Hoover that was crippling international trade. He compared Hoover to Napoleon, who lost the Battle of Waterloo because he "forgot his infantry. . . . The present administration in Washington provides a close parallel. It has either forgotten or it does not want to remember the infantry of our economic army . . . the forgotten man at the bottom of the economic pyramid."

The Forgotten Man speech was FDR's shot over the bow. Between the ideas set forth with the help of the brilliant policy wonks of the Brain Trust and the street-fighting political genius of Louis Howe and Jim Farley, Roosevelt was the front-runner on the eve of the Democratic convention. However, his nomination was far from a foregone conclusion. Al Smith, who had become FDR's implacable enemy, was making a third bid for the office he thought he deserved, and he had mobilized an impressive Stop Roosevelt movement. Howe and Farley had their hands full.

"I am terribly excited by the Democratic convention," Missy told a reporter during a trip to visit her mother in Somerville. (The article paid close attention to her attire and hairstyle—pink two-piece knitted wool dress, suntan stockings and white sport shoes, dark hair worn long and rolled in the back, pearl button earrings.) "I never was so excited over anything before. But I'm not going to Chicago though I was asked if I would like to go. I expect it will be more interesting with Governor and Mrs. Roosevelt in Albany."

Over two hot and humid days in Chicago, the Democratic delegates failed to nominate a candidate, for all of Howe's manipulations. (An example of Howe's marketing instincts was choosing "Happy Days Are Here Again" as FDR's theme song. It went on to become the top hit song of the year and a standard at Democratic Party conventions.) It was not until FDR accepted as his running mate House Speaker John Nance "Cactus Jack" Garner, a little Texan whose round face and jagged teeth resembled nothing so much as a jack-o'-lantern, that he clinched the nomination. (Garner was the author of the famous description of the vice presidency as not being worth "a bucket of warm piss.")

Missy was at the Governor's Mansion in Albany on the momentous night, July 1, with FDR and Eleanor, their sons Elliott and John, Sara Roosevelt, Grace Tully, Sam Rosenman, and other intimates. After her employer took a telephone call during dinner, Missy studied his face and remarked, "F.D., you look just like the cat that swallowed the canary." He had good reason, for the call alerted him that the California delegation under William G. McAdoo had swung its forty-four votes into his column, pushing him over the top on the fourth ballot. The official word came as they gathered around the radio in the study.

"Good old McAdoo!" exulted FDR. "The rest of the study was bedlam," Grace recalled. "Mrs. Roosevelt and Missy LeHand embraced each other. Both embraced me. John and Elliott tossed scratch paper in the air and shook hands as if they hadn't seen each other in years. The rest of the convention voting was anticlimactic. Mrs. Roosevelt [Eleanor] came down out of the clouds before the rest of us. 'I'm going to make some bacon and eggs,' she announced." It was the most successful of her limited cooking repertoire, and a family favorite.

As well-wishers flooded the mansion, FDR quickly dashed off a telegram to be read aloud by the convention chairman: "May I suggest if the Convention concurs that I come to Chicago at once for the purpose of meeting and greeting the Delegates and Attendees before they return to their homes." The rough draft of the telegram found its way into Missy's White House scrapbook, along with the state-by-state tally sheet they had kept while listening to the radio. It was inscribed with the words, "For M.A.L. with love from FDR—The Exciting Moment of the Convention!"

Missy's datebook pages for July 1 and 2 bear just a few terse words scrawled in pencil: "FDR nominated!" and "Leave by plane from [*sic*] Chicago." Plans moved ahead for the 8:30 a.m. Saturday departure from the Albany airport so that FDR could accept the nomination in person. Most of the delegates stayed for his arrival, though not Smith. No longer a "Happy Warrior," he had refused to concede his delegates and left for the train station Friday night.

The personal acceptance of the nomination at a national convention was unprecedented, as was the flight. The delirious convention goers' response to the "new deal" speech brought the Roosevelt party back to Albany—by train this time—on a tidal wave of euphoria. Missy's datebook soon filled with names of visitors, including an ominous one: Father Coughlin. Father Charles Coughlin, priest at a suburban Detroit church, had built a huge following for his radio show, *The Golden Hour of the Shrine of the Little Flower.* Initially he was an enthusiastic supporter of FDR, proclaiming, "It's either Roosevelt or ruin." Later he would become one of Roosevelt's most outspoken enemies, and Missy mobilized her Catholic connections in order to mitigate Coughlin's influence over this vital bloc of voters.

In September and October, FDR made three campaign trips on a seven-car train called the *Roosevelt Special,* traveling to the West Coast, the Midwest, the South, and to New England, covering thirteen thousand miles. Missy was part of his entourage on the first two trips, an exhilarating but exhausting journey of whistle-stopping speeches at state capitols, fairgrounds, and baseball fields, with an endless parade of local dignitaries coming aboard to pump their causes and bask in the charm of the gregarious nominee. At every stop, a band struck up "Happy

Days Are Here Again" until the song became an endless hurdy-gurdy tune playing inside every passenger's head. Roosevelt, according to Moley, "never stopped having a wonderful time." Tugwell agreed: "The calls and cheers of the crowd came up to him and he seemed to absorb the goodwill as a thirsty man drinks, capaciously and eagerly."

For the staff, though, it wasn't pure joy. Moley estimated that Marvin McIntyre, who was the trip coordinator, "must have run twenty miles a day when we were traveling"—without leaving the train. Missy was living out of a suitcase, with little privacy, spending grinding hours trying to take dictation and type as the un-air-conditioned train bumped and swayed along the tracks. There is nothing like trying to find a comfortable position in a coach seat during a long train ride to make a person feel like a piece of human origami. Getting delayed on a sightseeing trip at a stop could mean being left behind. This almost happened to Missy and another female staff member in Arizona, according to an anonymous memoir of the trip. It took "a few lusty yells" to notify the conductor to stop the train, and the two women "got on board—very hot and tired!"

Even with the long hours and hard work, the campaign train had its perks. On major stops, once the passengers disembarked, hired limousines delivered FDR and his entourage to first-class hotels and fine restaurants. Missy shared "a very palatial suite overlooking the lake" at the Colorado Springs Hotel. Considering the way most of the country was scraping by in the depths of the Depression that summer—including twelve thousand destitute World War I veterans who had camped out in Washington to demand early payment of a bonus they had been promised by Congress only to be evicted by the U.S. Army—there was no room for complaint on the *Roosevelt Special*.

One of the many people on board who would play increasing roles in Missy's life was the wealthy banker and movie mogul Joseph P. Kennedy, a fellow Irish American Catholic and Bostonian, married father of nine, and man-about-town. Kennedy was a crucial donor as well as fundraiser for Roosevelt. He got along famously with Moley, who respected his practical business experience, shared drafts of speeches he was writing, and sought his advice on policy, and he wowed the Roosevelt children. Twenty-four-year-old James recalled him as "a rather fabulous figure to a very young fellow." He would become a particular friend to Missy during FDR's first two terms. Kennedy also added to the perks of travel, arranging for a trip to the Grand Canyon, and for tickets to game three of the World Series during a stop in Chicago. The New York Yankees faced off against the hometown Cubs, and both Babe Ruth and Lou Gehrig hit two home runs, Ruth appearing to "call" one, pointing where he would hit it out of the park in the fifth inning. An exhausted Eleanor fell asleep in her seat and missed what is considered to be one of the greatest baseball games of all time.

Also on board was Associated Press reporter Lorena Hickok, the lone female journalist on the campaign beat. She became for several years Eleanor's closest friend and, some believed, her lover. A lesbian who cursed and drank like one of the boys, Lorena was forty years old; Eleanor was forty-nine. The two women got better acquainted on the train, and "Hick" would become more or less a permanent member of the household in 1933, often living in Eleanor's White House suite. While Missy almost missed boarding the train during a layover, Hick had a much worse experience. Caught at the back of a crowd when a woman fainted and unable to clamber back aboard, she hailed a taxi to drive her to the next stop. En route, the taxi was stopped and searched for an escaped convict, caught on fire, and ran out of gas. The cab driver then "calmly climbed out of the car and started down the road, leaving poor Hick a fair prey to the alleged escaped convict." However, she survived the ordeal unscathed and rejoined the train. Another reporter, John Boettiger of the *Chicago Tribune,* began romancing Anna Roosevelt Dall, though both were married to others. He would become her second husband in 1935.

Back in Albany in between train trips, former diplomat William Christian Bullitt, recently returned from a dozen years of living in Europe, arrived at the mansion for luncheon with the presidential heir presumptive. (His name appears in Missy's datebook on October 5 as "R.C. Bullitt.") FDR was impressed with the witty and urbane Philadelphian, who offered to make an under-the-radar trip to visit European leaders on his behalf to discuss unpaid war debts after he was elected president. Because presidents were still inaugurated in March rather than January—that would not change until 1937—FDR faced a long wait should he win, but dispatching a diplomat before he took office was illegal. It would have to be done carefully. Missy's first meeting with Bill Bullitt was probably a fleeting one, but he would become the love of her life in a mostly long-distance relationship that was equal parts romantic, frustrating, kind, and cruel.

For most of the campaign, Missy did not have the vital support of Grace Tully, now her full-time assistant, who was diagnosed with tuberculosis shortly after the Democratic convention. Though perceived today as an illness peculiar to impoverished countries, in the 1930s and 1940s TB cut a large swath through the U.S. population and the Roosevelt circle. Moley had suffered and recovered, and referred Grace to his specialist for treatment, but the disease claimed the lives of Marvin McIntyre and Louis Howe's secretary Margaret Durand, cut short the career of FDR's secretary of state, Cordell Hull and, many years later, was the primary cause of Eleanor Roosevelt's death.

It was Missy's persistence that got Grace to see the governor's personal physician after months of coughing; when Grace balked, Missy made an appointment for her, fetched her at her apartment in Albany, and drove her to the doctor's office for a chest X-ray. (It is unclear when Missy learned to drive, but a hand-drawn cartoon in her personal papers shows a car sending a pedestrian flying and under it a typed bit of doggerel: "Our darling Missy does I fear/Desire to copy Paul Revere./But timid ones at home should bide/When she invites them for a ride." The poem is unsigned, but has the literary hallmarks of Louis Howe.) Grace joined one of the campaign train trips for a few days, but was out of commission for long stretches in 1933 and 1934. To help fill in the gaps, Missy hired Grace's fun-loving older sister Paula, an out-of-work actress, to help during the campaign, and she later joined the White House staff. The three became the closest of friends.

Missy was again aboard when the *Roosevelt Special* chugged south, including a quick stop in Warm Springs where the residents of FDR's adopted hometown and the wheelchair-bound patients of the Foundation turned out in droves to cheer their hero. She was preparing for the final campaign trip through New England on October 27 when the unthinkable happened: her mother, Mary, had a heart attack and died; she was seventy-seven. One newspaper account went so far as to say the attack was brought on by Mary's excitement after speaking to Governor Roosevelt on the telephone. Her obituary in the *Potsdam Herald Reporter* ran next to a Republican Party ad urging readers to vote for Hoover and the rest of the GOP candidates.

Eleanor Roosevelt's nurturing instincts—so often lacking when her children were small—kicked in when an adult was hurting. Even though Franklin Jr. had broken his nose at football practice about the same time Mary died, Eleanor chose to accompany Missy home to Somerville and help the LeHands make funeral arrangements. A newspaper account described the two disembarking from the train in Boston, "Mrs. Roosevelt's arm [resting], in a gesture of maternal affection, around the shoulders of the grief-stricken young woman." The body was taken to Potsdam, and the funeral was held on October 30. It was on the trip home from Potsdam that Eleanor and Lorena Hickok, who had traveled with her as a reporter, further cemented their friendship. Now covering the candidate's wife full-time, Hick shared a drawing room with Eleanor on the train, and the two exchanged confidences about their unhappy childhoods. Hick's father had been a monster who raped her and threw her out of the house when she was just fourteen. When he died many years later and her sister sent a telegram asking for money for the funeral, Hick replied, "Send him to the glue factory."

Still mourning her adored mother, Missy climbed back on the Roosevelt roller coaster and rode it to the summit. On November 8, her face was alive with excitement in Hyde Park after she voted at the town hall. Standing with Eleanor, their gloved fingers interlaced and stylish fur neckpieces warming their necks and tickling their cheeks, they watched FDR on James's arm, cheered by their Dutchess County neighbors.

*Missy and Eleanor hold hands as FDR is hailed at the Hyde Park Town Hall on Election Day 1932.*

From there, the party journeyed to the Roosevelt townhouse in New York for a buffet dinner with close friends, and then on to the Biltmore Hotel, the official election night headquarters of the Democratic Party. Grace Tully entered the room to find her boss sitting at a large table "with telephones, radio and some 'score sheets' handy . . . Louis Howe, fairly afire with the excitement of the achievement of 'king-making.'" Ed Flynn, the Bronx political boss and New York secretary of state, remembered a very small contingent in the room: himself, Farley, Howe, Marvin McIntyre, Grace—and, of course, Missy. It was not until FDR was declared the winner that "our private party was badly broken up," he recalled. "Dozens of people began to enter the room to greet the victor."

Roosevelt won by a landslide, carrying forty-two of forty-eight states, and Democrats toppled the Republicans from the throne in Congress as well. The deer-hunting, bourbon-swilling, cigar-smoking South Carolina delegation upon whom Fulton Oursler and Missy had eavesdropped had delivered 98 percent of their state's electorate to the Roosevelt-Garner ticket. In his adopted home state, the staff of the *Atlanta Constitution* rolled a miniature brass cannon that had belonged to legendary newspaper publisher Henry W. Grady into the street, firing "a salvo that set off railroad and factory whistles all over town."

The next day, after wading through a sea of congratulatory telegrams, Team Roosevelt departed for Albany. The Associated Press dispatched a photographer to the Governor's Executive Office for a photo shoot, capturing images of a smiling Missy in a dark, silky polka-dot dress, Grace beside her in a flowered one. FDR inscribed a photo of the three of them together, "For Marguerite LeHand for her good behavior." A wire photo of Missy and Grace was sent to newspapers nationwide with the caption, "Two of the happiest young women in the country today are Miss Grace Tully and Miss Marguerite LeHand, secretaries to President-elect Franklin D. Roosevelt. It is believed that Miss LeHand will go to Washington as secretary for the new President, and if so, she will be the first woman to occupy this position."

Within a year, Missy would be the most famous private secretary in America.

## CHAPTER NINE

# *Nothing to Fear*

Missy and Grace Tully, giddy as schoolgirls, shared a car to the Capitol on the morning of Saturday, March 4, 1933, traveling with the Roosevelt motorcade from the White House up Pennsylvania Avenue. The inaugural cars were gleaming Pierce-Arrows. Their silver hood ornaments, shaped like kneeling archers poised to release their arrows, pointed the way on the cold and overcast day. The unpleasant weather was mirrored in the car FDR and Herbert Hoover shared. Their glum journey followed weeks of bitter exchanges between the men and their camps, and they had very little to say to each other. Hoover didn't even acknowledge the crowds lining the sidewalks, but once FDR had given up on his stony-faced seatmate showing any animation, he began gaily waving his top hat and smiling.

FDR had arranged for his old love Lucy Mercer Rutherfurd to have a less ostentatious car deliver her to his swearing in. This practice would continue for each of his inaugurations—no doubt with Missy's knowledge if not her assistance—Eleanor oblivious to the presence of the woman who had reduced her marriage to, as son James described it, "an armed truce."

At the Capitol, Missy's ticket admitted her to the president's platform, row C, seat 11, giving her an excellent view of her much loved F.D. taking the oath of office from white-bearded Supreme Court Chief Justice Charles Evans Hughes. His left hand rested on his family's old Dutch Bible, which was open to the 13th chapter, 13th verse of First Corinthians: "And now abideth faith, hope, charity, these three; but the greatest of these is charity."

FDR delivered the most famous words of the address—indeed, probably the most famous words he ever uttered—in his rich, ringing, tenor voice: "This great nation will endure as it has endured, will revive and will prosper. So, first of all, let me assert my firm belief that *the only thing we have to fear is fear itself*—nameless, unreasoning, unjustified terror which paralyzes needed efforts to convert retreat into advance." The speech lasted less than half an hour, and just then a beam of sunlight "broke through the gray mantle of clouds and came to rest, like a friendly hand, upon his head," a supporter wrote.

After the ceremony, Missy and Grace returned to the White House for a buffet luncheon in the State Dining Room—Missy had also gotten tickets for her family—and then watched the three-hour parade from the president's viewing stand. FDR's cousin Margaret "Daisy" Suckley recalled the first part of the parade being "dignified, the last part a sort of circus—[Hollywood cowboy actor] Tom Mix cavorting in white on a black horse—Movie actresses on a float—Bands in fantastic feather costumes, etc., etc. Democracy!" Among the marching units was the twenty-six-member F. D. Roosevelt Boy Scout Troop from Manchester, Georgia. Sixty residents of Meriwether County, including polios from the Foundation, traveled to Washington on a *Roosevelt Special* train. The trip with lower berth cost $25, "the lowest price ever for a tour to Washington, and for one of the biggest celebrations ever arranged for Georgians," promised an ad in the *Manchester Mercury*. They were among 2,482 guests for tea in the Blue Room after the parade, but there is no record if they found their old friend Missy in the throng of people juggling teacups and plates of cake. FDR, seeing to the swearing in of his cabinet in his upstairs study, nipped in toward the end of the tea to receive the remaining guests.

It is fair to say that no residents of any geographical area of the country were more excited about FDR's election than the people of his adopted home state of Georgia. When he had arrived in Warm Springs on Thanksgiving morning in 1932, Missy and his immediate family in tow, a crowd of two thousand was waiting. This wasn't just a prominent crippled man descending from the train, or the chairman of the Warm Springs Foundation, or even the governor of New York. It was the president-elect of the United States, and he was welcomed accordingly. The account in the Foundation's newsletter said, "As he passed by the Meriwether Inn, a salute of aerial bombs was fired from the campus and the patients waved in greeting." It was his first almost-presidential twenty-one-gun salute—accomplished with firecrackers.

What followed was a far cry from the slow-paced Warm Springs visits of the past. Even a simple afternoon drive with a break at the drugstore for a cold drink became a major production. Missy and bodyguard Gus Gennerich accompanied FDR and his mother on such an excursion one day, FDR parking at the curb, tooting his horn, and ordering glasses of soda water as he had dozens of times before. But by the time the drinks were delivered, a crowd of spectators was gawking at the car's passengers as if they were animals at the zoo. FDR bolted his soft drink, cranked the engine, and hastened back to the Little White House.

Even there, it must have seemed to Missy that the whole world had turned up on the doorstep to offer advice, curry favor, and demand the attention of the man who would lead the country out of its mess. FDR hunkered down beside the fireplace with Democratic bigwigs, members of Congress, and senators—including the flamboyant and dangerous Louisiana demagogue Huey Long—his Hyde Park neighbor Henry Morgenthau Jr., and Eleanor "Cissy" Patterson, the waspish publisher of the *Washington Herald,* who arrived in her private train car. Missy had her bedroom refuge, but her days were long and demands on her charm and patience were many. Somehow, she always managed to maintain her sunny smile, at least in public.

FDR's White House secretariat was firmly in place by then. Louis Howe was appointed his chief secretary. Marvin McIntyre and Steve Early were Howe's assistant secretaries, handling appointments and the press, respectively. Missy continued as FDR's private secretary, reporting directly to him, with Tully as her assistant. Missy's salary was set at $3,100—more than $56,000 in current dollars—at a time when the average annual income for an American wage earner was $1,550. Even so, she was paid only half what her male counterparts earned. Her job perks would include room, board, and maid service at the White House, as would Howe's, though Howe's wife remained at their home in Fall River, Massachusetts. Still, Missy wasn't only supporting herself. She maintained the Orchard Street house in Somerville where her sister, Anna, and her nieces lived rent-free, and she covered the cost of the girls' schooling.

Roosevelt began mulling over selections for his ten-member cabinet in December, but the appointment process played out throughout the winter. For most of this time, Raymond Moley served as a sort of one-man cabinet, fellow Brain Truster Rexford Tugwell as his top assistant. Many of the people they approached for government posts turned them down; even the faithful Sam Rosenman preferred to remain in the judiciary in New York. Eventually FDR appointed what Moley described as a "rather savorless Cabinet pudding," including Tennessee senator Cordell Hull for secretary of state, New York businessman William H. Woodin for Treasury, Chicago politician Harold L. Ickes for Interior, and Iowa agricultural newsletter editor Henry A. Wallace for Agriculture. (Woodin, Ickes, and Wallace were reconstituted Republicans.) Political boss Jim Farley, who had managed the campaign, was appointed postmaster general, then a cabinet-level post that involved handing out plum patronage jobs at post offices across the country. (One of the recipients would be Ruth Perrin, Democratic activist and close friend of Missy's Aunt Nellie. Both ladies attended the inauguration as Missy's guests. The multitalented Mrs. Perrin had nursed the ailing Grace Tully back to health at her home in Potsdam that winter.) With Eleanor's enthusiastic support, FDR recruited New York industrial commissioner Frances Perkins to head the Department of Labor, making her the first female cabinet member in U.S. history. For the crucial post of attorney general, he selected Senator Thomas J. Walsh, a much admired liberal attorney from Montana. (Walsh's chairmanships in Congress had included the Committee on the Disposition of Useless Executive Papers, a title doubtless bestowed by someone with an acute sense of irony.)

While FDR and his advisors tried to focus on the domestic New Deal, the world kept intruding. The previous year, the debtor nations in Europe had been given a one-year moratorium on repayment of loans the United States made for World War I. When the moratorium expired on December 15, France defaulted on its loan. Moley became the point man between FDR's camp and the Hoover administration, a tricky role because FDR kept changing his mind after getting advice from one corner or another. Moley did not know, for example, that Bill Bullitt had returned from his undercover travels abroad and dined with FDR in Albany, reporting on talks he had with European leaders about the war debt.

Missy's Christmas was spent in Somerville—a poignant holiday as it was the first with her mother gone—and she returned with FDR to Warm Springs in January, where he celebrated his fifty-first birthday on January 30. By then Bullitt was on a second secret trip to Europe, this time sending coded messages through Missy. (In a flirtatious letter she wrote to him more than a year later, she said she had found the "little black dictionary" she had used for translating the messages and joked she was "strongly tempted to cable a code message.")

From Warm Springs, Missy took the train back north in early February, but FDR traveled south to Florida and boarded The *Nourmahal,* the mammoth luxury yacht of his friend Vincent Astor. He was plying the waters that he and Missy had so enjoyed during his years adrift, but in much higher style with Astor, one of the richest men in the world. He had inherited the real estate fortune of his father, John Jacob Astor IV, who had gone down with the *Titanic*. With almost a quarter of the workforce unemployed and dozens of banks failing every day, the cruise raised a storm of controversy. While FDR fished and partied, Moley and Howe, feverishly working on cabinet appointments, were reduced to sending sensitive radiograms using word puzzles because the ship-to-shore radio was not secure. For example, when Henry Wallace agreed to become secretary of agriculture, the message was "CORN BELT IN THE BAG."

It took an assassination attempt to pull FDR's threatened popularity out of the fire. When the *Nourmahal* arrived in Miami in mid-February, FDR spoke briefly from his car to a crowd that included an unemployed Italian bricklayer named Giuseppe Zangara. A mentally disturbed but ambitious anarchist who had previously hoped to assassinate the king of Italy and Herbert Hoover, Zangara fired five shots before he was wrestled to the ground. FDR was unhurt, but Chicago mayor Anton Cermak, who had come to ask for federal help, took a bullet in the chest. Roosevelt ordered the mayor loaded into his car, which sped to a hospital. FDR's calm in this crisis as he held the wounded mayor in his arms, talking to keep him conscious, created a tidal wave of public adulation.

Missy joined first daughter Anna and first son Elliott Roosevelt at the train station in Philadelphia to meet FDR on his return trip. In a classic case of locking the barn door after the horse had been stolen, they were overwhelmed with security—some thousand police, detectives, and Secret Service agents surrounded and accompanied them to Hyde Park, topcoated men standing on the running boards of the president-elect's car. They spent the weeks before the inauguration at Springwood, the Roosevelt home at Hyde Park. On February 27, Moley dined with Missy, FDR, and a stenographer, and the men retired to the library to labor over the inaugural address. They worked by the fire into the wee hours, fortified by glasses of whiskey. Both later tried to claim the lion's share of the credit for the speech, but Howe, weighing in the next morning, penned the first paragraph with the line "the only thing we have to fear is fear itself" that would go down in history. Missy's hand-written corrections appear on the final draft.

The bank crisis was the most serious and immediate problem confronting FDR on the eve of his inauguration: four thousand banks would ultimately close in 1933—more than twice the number as 1932—and most of them in the first two months of the year. (The federal government did not then have regulatory power over banks, and it took Moley, Woodin, and Hoover's Treasury staff all night on March 3 to convince all forty-eight governors to temporarily close them. The last holdout was FDR's successor in New York, Herbert H. Lehman.) Hoover's Treasury men had a plan to sort out the banks that could be saved from the ones that couldn't, but the lame-duck president refused to act on it without Roosevelt taking shared responsibility.

To stop the runs on the banks that were siphoning off both cash and gold—and causing the savings of millions of Americans to evaporate—FDR's team was hoping to use an obscure law passed during World War I. It would depend on Attorney General–designate Walsh giving a legal opinion supporting use of the 1917 Trading with the Enemy Act for temporarily closing banks and placing a moratorium on the hoarding of gold and cash. This would give the fledgling government a few days to stabilize the banking system. But seventy-three-year-old Walsh, who had secretly married a much younger Cuban woman in late February, died of a heart attack on the train traveling from his honeymoon to the inauguration. (Jonathan Daniels, son of former navy secretary Josephus Daniels and later an FDR aide, snarkily said he died of "presumption beyond his powers.")

It was the first personnel crisis of his administration. FDR had no backup nominee in mind, but Missy voiced a suggestion: What about Homer Cummings? The astute Connecticut lawyer, a former Democratic National Committee chair, was slated to become governor-general of the Philippines, but he might be willing to take the attorney general's post. No one had a better suggestion, and Cummings accepted the job. He kept it until early 1939, dependably serving as "Roosevelt's legal yes-man," in the words of a contemporary journalist. It was Missy's first major personnel recommendation, but it would not be her last. In Roosevelt's second term, she successfully lobbied for the Supreme Court appointment of Harvard University Law School professor Felix Frankfurter.

Cummings and the other cabinet officers were sworn in at 6:05 p.m. Inauguration Day, and he quickly vetted the 1917 law as justification for temporarily closing all banks. While FDR conferred with his advisors, Missy and her family joined Eleanor and the Roosevelt children at the Washington Auditorium for the inaugural ball. Daisy Suckley was unimpressed: "A mass of all sorts of people in an unattractive pennanted hall—More Democracy!!" she wrote in her diary. Missy was escorted in right behind the first lady, who was regally attired in a sleeveless gown with a large corsage, a fur coat draped over her graceful, sloping shoulders. In contrast, Missy looked remarkably girlish at age thirty-six in a simple dark velvet gown with short sleeves, a triple-strand pearl necklace at her throat.

It would be the last night of revelry for some time. Although the Roosevelts went to church the next day, it was a workday like any other, with Missy setting up the office she had snagged in the West Wing—a little cubbyhole right beside the president's Oval Office. Howe, jealous of Missy's influence, had sought to place her office in the residential part of the White House, but she outmaneuvered him.

Over at the Treasury Department, Moley, Tugwell, and other advisors were slaving over the bank rescue. With the problems confronting the American people, few were paying much attention to what was happening across the ocean in Germany. There, another politician was consolidating power. Adolf Hitler had been appointed chancellor on January 30—FDR's birthday—and on FDR's first full day in office an election was held that gave Hitler's National Socialist German Workers' Party, or Nazi Party, and its coalition partner control of the country's governing body, the Reichstag. A few weeks later, the Reichstag passed an emergency law making Hitler the "temporary" dictator.

*Taken in 1934, this full-figure photo shows Missy walking from the White House to the West Wing.*

On Sunday night, Steve Early brought a few reporters into the Red Room to see the president, who asked them to refer to the four-day closing of the banks as a "holiday" rather than Hoover's funereal term "moratorium." At 11:30 p.m., FDR gave his first radio address to the nation. It was the beginning of the fabled Hundred Days, one of the most famous—or infamous, depending on one's political viewpoint—periods in American political history. Some say the "action, and action now" that FDR had promised in his inaugural address rescued America from the brink of revolution. Others see it as the beginning of the intrusion of the federal government into every aspect of Americans' lives. Both are part of the New Deal legacy, to which Missy would devote the rest of her short life. "Few ever realized how important it was to the national interest to have Missy LeHand constantly at the elbow of the President," Moley later wrote. "She had every virtue and every talent needed by the super-confidential secretary of a man in high office."

❀ CHAPTER TEN

# *Queen of the White House Staff*

The first Hundred Days of the New Deal are the most storied of any presidential administration in American history. Between March 9 and June 16, 1933, executive action and legislation addressed the turmoil in the financial, agricultural, and transportation sectors; extended emergency work relief to the desperate; and partially repealed Prohibition, enabling Americans to legally hoist a beer mug or sip a glass of wine for the first time in twelve years. An anxious Congress passed every initiative the White House proposed with barely a whimper. This did not happen by magic, but the skeleton staff manning the White House and cabinet offices indeed worked miracles.

While Missy played a supporting rather than a leading role in creating the first New Deal laws and the giant tureen of alphabet soup agencies that put them into action, she was vital to the stunning accomplishments. One admirer said she got the Oval Office working with the precision of a Swiss watch. More romantically, Grace Tully described Missy as "the Queen" of the staff that came down from Albany to the White House.

Missy left no record of her thoughts or impressions of the Hundred Days and the breakneck months that followed, as she steadfastly refused to keep a diary. It's appropriate that a tiny diary dangles from each of her gold charm bracelets, covers engraved with her name or initials but the pages inside blank. However, she flits through others' accounts: smiling, sympathetic, competent, and kind, perched in an Oval Office windowsill during FDR's first press conference, bustling into his bedroom first thing in the morning with his personal mail, sharing over cocktails an editorial page cartoon that makes him howl, horseback riding with Eleanor, giving a fond good night kiss to three-year-old Curtis "Buzzie" Dall when the Roosevelt grandchild was tucked into bed. (Buzzie thanked her by exclaiming, "Missy has a moustache!" which probably sent her running for a mirror and tweezers.)

*Missy is front and center in this 1938 photo of the White House secretarial staff. Front row, from left: Roberta Barrows, Grace Tully, Missy, Margaret "Rabbit" Durand, and Mary Eben. Second row: Paula Larrabee, Toi Bachelder, Mabel Williams, Katherine Gilligan, Prudence Shannon, Lucile Lewis, Louise Hackmeister, and Lela Stiles.*

These snapshots are telling, for while Missy was the queen of FDR's West Wing office staff, she also had a role as a lady-in-waiting and social stand-in to Eleanor Roosevelt, who ruled over the White House domicile in addition to advancing a burgeoning agenda of causes and concerns. By now, Missy was well prepared to negotiate the space between the Roosevelts represented by the long colonnade connecting the West Wing with the White House proper. It was part of her twenty-four-hour-a-day job to serve as a go-between, handing out allowance checks to Eleanor and the chronically cash-strapped adult children, smoothing hurt feelings, and delivering unpleasant messages.

The morning of Monday, March 6, was a case in point.

Eleanor gave a breathless account of the day in a letter to her increasingly intimate friend Lorena Hickok. (The letter opened effusively with "Hick darling, Oh! How good it was to hear your voice, it was so inadequate to try & tell you what it meant.") She was just finishing up breakfast when suddenly Missy appeared in her bedroom, "half asleep," to share the sad news that Chicago mayor Cermak had died as the result of the bullet he had taken for FDR in Miami. Missy stayed on for toast and coffee with the first lady, who commenced unpacking and moving furniture. In between appointments and official duties that week, the two women trotted around the residential rooms of the White House with hammer and nails, implementing the signature Roosevelt decorating style of hanging pictures on every available inch of wall space, including the doors of linen closets.

On that busy Monday, FDR continued the custom he had begun in the Governor's Mansion of having breakfast in bed. He had been up until almost 1 a.m. the night before after giving his maiden radio address—meaning Missy had been up, too—and now this first workday was packed with meetings and a luncheon for visiting governors, all anxious about his plans to solve the banking crisis. Late in the day, the new chief executive rolled into the Oval Office, transferred to his desk chair, and was left to his own devices. What happened next was either a moment of pure panic or high comedy. Some accounts say FDR felt suddenly overwhelmed by the empty expanse of mahogany and his own paralysis, and frantically pressed all his desk buzzers to summon help. In one of his jovial retellings, soon ten staffers anxiously crowded his desk. "I told them I wanted to see who was on the job!" he said. As Tully recounted, the president "frowned and said in mock seriousness: 'Here's a president with nothing to do. Hasn't anyone got something for me to do?'

"We were all too thunderstruck to say anything, until Missy turned the tables on the joke.

"'Yes, Mr. President,' she said. 'I have something for you to do—about two feet of mail. And you can start right now.'"

The two feet of mail Missy handed to F.D. was just the tip of the postal iceberg. (Her gold charm collection includes a tiny mailbox with working door and flag.) Herbert Hoover's weekly mail had averaged five thousand letters. The easy familiarity that FDR created with the public made ordinary Americans feel comfortable writing him, to the tune of fifty thousand letters a week. Initially Louis Howe's office and his secretaries Margaret "Rabbit" Durand and Lela Stiles handled the majority of mail duties, with the president's personal mail funneled to Missy. After Howe's death in early 1936, she shouldered the whole job, with the support of a flotilla of clerks and stenographers, answering every letter, using a repertoire of stock replies. A huge number of the letters—simple one- and two-paragraph affairs thanking the writer for their thoughts or regretfully informing them that the number of requests for FDR's autograph was so overwhelming that he could not provide one—went out under her signature from the first months of the Roosevelt presidency. "I have spent most of yesterday and today signing letters—such numbers of them," Missy wrote Bill Bullitt, but it is evident from the variation in Missy LeHand-writing that other people were also signing her name. Letters to people who named their babies for FDR were a special case. A Mrs. Riley in Oklahoma received a letter signed by Missy assuring her of the president's "appreciation of the compliment you have paid him in the selection of a name for your little son" accompanied by a white handkerchief embroidered with the president's signature and the words "HAPPY DAYS."

Missy's role as personal mail handler was second nature after twelve years as FDR's private secretary. In fact, Eleanor recalled that when she asked her husband if she might help with the

THE WHITE HOUSE
WASHINGTON

January 20, 1936

My dear Mr. Bridgforth:

Your letter of January eighth has been received and will be brought to the attention of the President. Meanwhile, I want to thank you for what you say concerning his address on Jackson Day.

Very sincerely yours,

M. A. Le Hand

M. A. Le Hand
PRIVATE SECRETARY

David T. Bridgforth, Esq.,
The Commodore, Apt. 202,
Wichita,
Kansas.

*Although many letters went out under Missy's signature, not all were signed by her. This one, to a supporter in Kansas, does bear her handwriting.*

mail—she was desperate to avoid the traditional first lady strait-jacket of presiding over tea tables—he looked at her "quizzically" and said that Missy might feel she was interfering. His answer temporarily thwarted his wife's intrusion into his realm, but she wouldn't be kept at bay for long. At Hick's urging, she held a press conference for female reporters on March 6, as the president's press conferences were male only (and white male at that). From there she was off and running to become the most influential—and controversial—first lady in history. Her strong social justice convictions and tremendous energy turned her into a public figure as beloved—and despised—as her husband, and soon she needed help with her *own* mail. In her first nine months as first lady, she received close to a thousand letters a week.

Louis plundered both the governor's office in Albany and the campaign headquarters for key support staff. He installed Louise Hackmeister—"tall, handsome and smartly turned out," in Tully's words, over the White House switchboard. "Hacky," who had worked at campaign headquarters, possessed a rare gift for identifying voices without the caller stating a name, as well as the ability to track down almost anyone, anywhere. FDR called her his "telephone detective." Mary Eben, who had worked with Missy at the Fidelity & Deposit offices, initially joined Eleanor Roosevelt's staff, but, as Tully put it, "she was anxious to be transferred to 'our side of the house' . . . and Missy created the post of librarian" for her. Mary, a gifted mimic whose specialty was Eleanor Roosevelt imitations, also did a lot of what Missy called the "oddy-endy things" for her, including some of her personal shopping.

Eleanor had a triumvirate of lieutenants to run the office of first lady and the domestic side of the White House. Her personal secretary was the capable Malvina "Tommy" Thompson, who was as much at Eleanor's beck and call as Missy was at FDR's, although she didn't live in the White House. Neither did Eleanor's social secretary, Edith Helm, the gently smiling widow of an admiral. Less fondly remembered by almost everyone, especially the domestic staff, was Henrietta Nesbitt, a fifty-eight-year-old, down-on-her-luck Hyde Park neighbor who had until this point struggled through the Depression by selling baked goods out of her kitchen. Eleanor plucked Mrs. Nesbitt and her unemployed husband, Henry, out of obscurity and installed them as official housekeeper and assistant. (Mrs. Nesbitt referred to her husband, whose last job had been as a whale meat salesman, as "Dad.") Determined but unqualified, she became overnight the supervisor of thirty-two maids, butlers, and cooks, sixty rooms, and everything that came out of the kitchen. In the last role she was decidedly not a success. Ernest Hemingway described his White House dinner as the worst food he had ever eaten. Mrs. Nesbitt's dull menus would be the bane of the president's existence. Missy partook of her first uninspired dinner on March 7: clear soup, broiled lamp chops, green peas, baked potatoes, fruit, and coffee. Things didn't improve. Missy's niece Barbara Farwell, writing home from a visit to the White House that November, damned the cooking with faint praise: "We had lunch with the wives of the Supreme Court Judges this noon and it didn't taste bad at all."

Despite all his grumbling, the president never made good on his threats to fire Mrs. Nesbitt. It took Harry Truman to give the housekeeper her walking papers. (The last straw was her refusal of Bess Truman's request for a stick of butter to take to a potluck luncheon.) In retirement, she wrote her memoirs—complete with secret recipes—in which she portrayed herself as a successful practitioner of home economics and domestic staff management.

FDR's daily rebellion against Mrs. Nesbitt's insipid gastronomy and Eleanor's choice of ghastly domestic wine was the cocktail ritual he dubbed the "Children's Hour," which began on March 6. The immediate staff—Missy, Grace, Louis, Marvin McIntyre, and Steve Early—gathered around his desk in his White House study while he gleefully mixed potent martinis. Missy saw to it that there were some tasty snacks to go along with the booze. Tully recalled the times fondly. "In those earlier years, when we were, in effect, on a 'shakedown cruise,' it provided all of us with a chance to talk over the smaller problems of office mechanics and to give the Boss a fill-in on office and press room gossip," she wrote. "Above all, it served to cement an intangible but deep sense of camaraderie which always existed among those who worked closely and on a personal basis with him."

Second-tier staff weren't part of the Children's Hour, but Louis's secretary Lela Stiles had a sweet memory of her early days at the executive office and Missy's effort to make her feel comfortable around the president. She invited the "girls" on staff to a small party in her apartment. "However, when we arrived, the usher met us and escorted us to the second floor and down the hall to the President's study," she recalled. "Missy had asked us to wear evening clothes and now we understood! The usher opened the door and there was the President of the United States, sitting behind his big desk, mixing cocktails!" FDR, having been briefed on Stiles's Kentucky background, teased her about her fondness for bourbon whiskey. They remained for dinner, Missy arranging for the women to take turns sitting beside the president so they could get to know him better. The little party was an example of both Missy's kindness and the skillful way she used social occasions to help the staff bond with each other and the Boss.

Missy cherished a special memento of her hours in FDR's study. Throughout his first term, F.D. wielded his martini shaker from a Chippendale ladder-back armchair with a green leather seat that had been given him by Teddy Roosevelt. In 1937, he made a gift of it to Missy, having apparently gotten a new one for his birthday that year. The brass plate on the bottom is engraved "For M.A.L.—Used by me at desk of White House study from March 4, 1933 to January 30, 1937. FDR."

Missy frequently joined FDR in another pursuit that he found relaxing—and that she pretended to—a swim in the pool that had been paid for by the public with a fundraising campaign launched by the New York *Daily News*. As in Albany, he tried to keep up his hydrotherapy with short daily swims, and though Missy privately disliked the water, she gamely donned her one-piece suit and joined him, even on days when she had gotten up early in the morning to go horseback riding with Eleanor.

The mixture of work and play continued into the evening. Besides the family suppers, Missy was a guest at every White House social event, beginning with a formal dinner honoring the Polish ambassador on March 21. (It was Mrs. Nesbitt's public debut, and she again served green peas.) British prime minister Ramsey MacDonald visited for four days in April, and he sent an autographed picture to Missy upon his return to London. She wrote his secretary an effusive thank-you letter: "I really am not at all a seeker of photographs or autographs but I fell in love with your Prime Minister immediately and really hated to see him leavc," she said.

While the evenings at 1600 Pennsylvania Avenue laid first claim on Missy's presence, invitations poured in from embassies and Washington hostesses who hoped to display the New Dealers like trophies. Missy was asked to art exhibitions, garden parties, receptions for film stars, cocktail parties, "at home" afternoons, pool parties, and a potpourri of eclectic events such as a black-tie concert by the Marimba Ensemble of the National Police of Guatemala at the Pan-American Union. She declined an invitation by the White House Correspondents' Association to attend a preview of the Joan Crawford vehicle *The Gorgeous Hussy*, a movie about "the glamorous creature who became the power behind the throne at the White House." It was the White House of Andrew Jackson, but still.

For Missy was indeed becoming glamorous. Tully observed the change in her friend, who had always been "neat as a pin—a bit fussy in her grooming but rather casual about her disinterest in smart clothes." In Washington, Missy abandoned her thrifty habits and began "to think less in terms of 'rainy day caution' and to present herself in chic and more expensive attire." She developed a weakness for evening gowns, especially in blue, the president's favorite color, which set off her lovely eyes and silver-streaked hair. By 1935 she had acquired a mink coat, an ermine cape, and a diamond wristwatch. In 1937 a newspaper syndicate named Missy one of the seven most fashionable women in the capital, describing her as "without doubt the best dressed woman behind an important Washington desk."

THE WHITE HOUSE
TO ALL GUARDS ON
DUTY AT THE WHITE HOUSE
PLEASE ADMIT THE BEARER
Marguerite A. LeHand
TO THE WHITE HOUSE GROUNDS
SUPERVISING AGENT
U. S. SECRET SERVICE

*Missy's White House I.D. card.*

Missy's third-floor suite of rooms—sitting room, bedroom, and bath overlooking Pennsylvania Avenue—was near the sewing room used by an observant and gossipy maid, Lillian Rogers Parks. She remembered in her tell-all book *The Roosevelts: A Family in Turmoil* that all the White House domestic staff loved Missy "because she was so much fun and so kind," and declared she "could be the most glamorous woman in the room with her chandelier earrings swaying and her blue eyes flashing. . . . Once the elevator guard at the White House commented, as Missy flipped by, 'I'd rather see her walk than anything.'" Much as she liked her, Parks ascribed to the belief that Missy was the president's in-house mistress. "After you accepted the situation," she said, "there was no shock in seeing Missy come to FDR's suite at night in her nightgown and robe or sitting on his lap in the Oval study." Curiously, Elliott Roosevelt, who had been the only one of the siblings to insist Missy was his father's lover in his pre presidential years, took the position that in the White House their relationship underwent a "marked change" that removed the sexual intimacy. Still, he opined, "She lost little of her value to him as confidante, companion and counselor, which was enough for her at age thirty-six."

Elliott became the first of the Roosevelt children to obtain a divorce. (In total the five children were married nineteen times and divorced fifteen, with Elliott and Franklin Jr. each tying the knot five times. James married the first of his four wives, charming and vivacious Betsey Cushing, in 1930.) Anna had separated from her first husband, and in September 1933 brought her children, Curtis and Anna Eleanor, into the White House as full-time residents with her. The nursery of three-year-old Buzzie and six-year-old Sistie was also located on the third floor near Missy, as were rooms for John and Franklin Jr. when they were home from school.

The White House gained another full-time resident the same month. Feeling she had lost her objectivity as a reporter because of her intensifying relationship with Eleanor, Lorena Hickok resigned from the Associated Press. In May, FDR had brought his New York relief coordinator Harry Hopkins to Washington—with Missy's enthusiastic support—to create the Federal Emergency Relief Administration. It was the first time the federal government had attempted widespread assistance to the unemployed, and Hopkins said the effort to organize FERA was "almost as if the Aztecs had been asked suddenly to build an aeroplane." To assess needs, Hopkins sent field investigators across the country, and Eleanor secured the position of chief investigator for her friend. Hick gave up her New York apartment and between fact-finding trips moved into Eleanor's study on the second floor, down the hall from Louis Howe and FDR.

Demanding as her job was, Missy was much better off than any number of white-collar women who had been laid off as the economy tanked. Hick learned of their plight from New

York social worker Mary Simkhovitch, quoting her in a report to Hopkins: "Single women? Why, they're just discards. I'll tell you how they live! Huddled together in small apartments, three or four of them living on the earnings of one, who may have a job." Missy's hours were long and the food at the White House was nothing to write home about, but she had job security, a ringside seat at a fascinating time in American history, and the most famous roof in the country directly over her head when she fell into her bed at night, so tired she could barely keep her eyes open to read one of the biographies she loved.

Congress passed the last four of the original New Deal bills on June 16, 1933, and the next day the extended Roosevelt "family" left for the Roosevelt vacation home in Campobello. Missy and Grace were part of the entourage, along with Louis Howe, Steve Early, and Raymond Moley, among others. A rare glimpse of their exultant mood is displayed in footage from Missy's home movie camera, discovered by her great-niece Barbara Jacques in 2013. In it, the two secretaries clown around a cabin cruiser, Missy cuddling in the bow with the pipe-puffing Moley as they follow the wake of a motorboat driven by the president. The film also shows a leisurely picnic at Val-Kill Cottage in Hyde Park; the grandchildren riding in a pony cart, and their mother, Anna, capering about the porch at Springwood, pretending to be a monkey with a tail made of swimming pool floaters.

Upon their return, Missy endured her first steamy summer in Washington; the humid weather was a constant complaint in letters to friends and family, though her bedroom was one of the few with an air conditioner. Then the August 12 issue of *Newsweek* thrust her into the spotlight with an admiring profile, "MISSY: Marguerite Le Hand Is President's Super-Secretary."

"She calls the President 'F.D.' She comes to his bedroom, while he is still fussing with eggs and bacon, to report on the state of his correspondence," the article revealed. "She will interrupt the most statesmanlike conference to announce that the time to take cough medicine has arrived, or that the President had better don his coat because of the draft. At the end of the day she declares: 'It's about time for you to stop work.' And the new 'American Dictator' usually does as he's told, though he may call for Missy and her stenographer's pad at midnight."

The profile extolled Missy's ability to "read" her boss: "She knows when he is bored before he realizes it himself; she can see his streak of Dutch stubbornness emerging during an argument; she can tell when he is really listening to an interlocutor and when he is merely being polite—which no one else can—and she sometimes senses when he is beginning to disapprove of something that he still thinks he likes." The caption under her picture said, "Miss LeHand, the President's Boss."

There it was. Missy was out of the shadows.

The most popular "chick lit" writer of the 1930s was Faith Baldwin, who published as many as four books a year and numerous magazine serials featuring working women, many of them private secretaries such as Missy. She had popularized the term "office wife," the title of one of her best-known novels, to describe a secretary as essential to her male boss at work as his legal wife is at home—minus a physical relationship. Baldwin's foreword in *The Office Wife*, published in 1929, foreshadowed the *Newsweek* article: "The position of private secretary to a man of breadth, significance and power in his particular line of business is almost a twenty-four hour job. . . . He demands of the woman in his private office not only alertness, efficiency and the clairvoyant quality of being able to carry out even the orders he does not give, but also a certain amount of charm, of personal attraction. He shares with her an intimate knowledge of himself that not even his closest friend may possess." Missy was the embodiment of a Faith Baldwin heroine—pretty, smart, principled, from a struggling family but able to blend in with the upper class. The only attribute she lacked was a dashing and wealthy suitor. In the fall of 1933 that void would be filled in the person of William Christian Bullitt.

CHAPTER ELEVEN

# *The Ambassador to Russia*

Bill Bullitt could easily have stepped out of a Faith Baldwin romance novel in the role of the "very attractive man." "A man of mystery and paradox," according to his biographers, he had a quick, engaging smile, long-lashed blue eyes, and dressed and moved with natural elegance. He danced beautifully, spoke fluent French and German, had marvelous taste in jewelry and flowers, and penned charming notes in a bold hand. He was wealthy—though not fabulously so—the middle son of a socially prominent Philadelphia family, a brilliant graduate of Yale, a distinguished journalist and war correspondent, and, while still in his twenties, served as a diplomat in President Wilson's delegation to negotiate the peace after World War I.

But the true stripes of many of the suitors who pursued Baldwin's heroines were a scarlet fingernail scratch below the surface, and so it was with William Christian Bullitt. Many people suspected he used Missy for access to FDR, and his detractors over the years said "Christian" was a "singularly ironic middle name." Actually it was a family name, for his antecedents included Fletcher Christian, who led the mutiny on the *Bounty*. In that sense, it was an appropriate moniker for a man who constantly rebelled against his patrician background while simultaneously working every possible social connection to make his mark in the world.

The struggle was evident as early as his boyhood, when at

age eight he brought a female street urchin home, where his horrified mother caught them playing doctor. In prep school he crossed swords with a German teacher who accused him of cheating; it cost the teacher his job. Bullitt never hesitated to stand up for himself and his beliefs. He resigned from the 1919 peace delegation deeply disillusioned, convinced the Treaty of Versailles paved the way for future world conflict, and testified to that effect before Congress. This outspoken criticism of Woodrow Wilson and the treaty did not sit well in the hallowed halls of the U.S. State Department. (Years later he collaborated with the celebrated psychiatrist Sigmund Freud on a controversial book psychoanalyzing Wilson.)

*Bill Bullitt was courting Missy's affection at Warm Springs when this photo was taken in 1933.*

Bullitt's first marriage, to a woman of his social class, lasted only slightly longer than his diplomatic career. In 1923, he fell in love with radical journalist Louise Bryant, the beautiful widow of the American communist John Reed, who had chronicled the Bolshevik Revolution in Russia. Louise accompanied him to Istanbul, where they lived in a villa overlooking the Bosporus Strait while he wrote an autobiographical novel. They were married a few months before she gave birth to their daughter, Anne, in 1924.

His novel *It's Not Done,* which satirized Bullitt's family and their Philadelphia social set, was published in 1926. (As an example of his barbs, the last words on the dying matriarch's lips were "Bored . . . bored . . . bored . . .") The novel sold 150,000 copies, compared to 20,000 in first-year sales of F. Scott Fitzgerald's 1925 masterpiece, *The Great Gatsby*. Bullitt's brother Orville tried unsuccessfully to buy up every copy in Philadelphia to spare his family embarrassment. Although Bullitt dedicated his novel to "Louise Bryant, my wife," their marriage was over by 1930. He won full custody of Anne, and Louise died six years later of a brain hemorrhage after years of illness and heavy drinking.

By the time Missy met Bullitt in 1932, he was forty-one, almost completely bald, and furiously working his connections to regain a toehold in the U.S. diplomatic corps. He arranged a meeting with FDR through a mutual friend, New York attorney Louis Wehle, and undertook two unofficial diplomatic trips for the president-in-waiting at his own expense. The trips to Europe in the fall and winter were not altogether successful. In Germany during the first trip, Bullitt misjudged Adolf Hitler, writing to FDR, "Hitler is finished . . . the [German] Government is no longer afraid of the growth of the Nazi movement." He had barely arrived in Europe on his second mission when Hitler was named chancellor.

Bullitt called Missy shortly before sailing on January 14, 1933, "to ask her please to be sure that no word about my present trip escapes to the public." Missy had received several of his coded messages in Warm Springs when the news broke that Bullitt was serving as FDR's "secret agent" in Europe, a violation of the Logan Act. (The act sanctioned such freelance diplomacy with a fine of up to $5,000 and three years in prison.) Republican senator Arthur Robinson of Indiana raised a fuss on the Senate floor, and though Roosevelt denied that Bullitt was his envoy and Bullitt refused to comment, he cut the trip short. Arriving in New York in mid-February "with his hat turned down over his eyes and face mostly concealed under a turned-up fur collar," he hid out at Louis Wehle's apartment, terrified he would be arrested.

In light of the financial crisis engulfing the country by then, Bullitt's cloak-and-dagger adventures were soon forgotten, though when he arrived in Washington seeking an appointment at the State Department, he got some ribbing from Senator Huey Long at a cocktail party. "Damn near sent you to jail for twenty years, hey, boy?" the Louisiana demagogue jeered. Bullitt ingratiated himself with Raymond Moley, who lived at the same hotel and was then FDR's closest policy advisor. By late April he had visited the White House half a dozen times and been appointed special assistant to Secretary of State Cordell Hull. By early November, he was almost a daily visitor to FDR's offices, and he and Missy had become an item.

"Your Ladyship," he wrote in late September, "Herewith the pearls, which turned up on the floor of the car." The note hardly implies a passionate tussle in the backseat, as it was typed by Bullitt's secretary, but the familiar tone indicates their relationship was not strictly professional. His visits to the White House escalated through the fall, culminating with the announcement on November 17 that the United States was establishing diplomatic relations with the Soviet Union, and Bullitt would be the first U.S. ambassador there since the czarist government fell in 1917.

"Well, Russia is recognized. Bullitt goes as ambassador. I wonder if that is why F.D.R. has been content to let Missy play with him?" Eleanor wrote rather snarkily to her friend Lorena Hickok. "She'll have another embassy to visit next summer anyway!"

Bullitt was a natural choice for the position. As part of the Wilson peace delegation in 1919, he had been dispatched with press aide Lincoln Steffens to meet with Lenin and explore the possibility of America's recognition of the Soviet Union. He had met the wily Soviet leader and Maxim Litvinov—who was now people's commissar for foreign affairs—and been dazzled by the promise of the new country. There is some debate about whether Bullitt or Steffens made the famous—and later much reviled—statement "I have been over to the future and it works," but Bullitt fully believed it at the time. He was bitterly disappointed that Wilson declined his recommendation that relations be formalized. His subsequent marriage to Louise Bryant was further evidence of his romantic obsession with the Russian communists.

Bullitt departed by ship to present his credentials in Moscow on December 6, 1933, after a brief visit with FDR at Warm Springs. In his farewell letter to Missy he reminded her that she was expected to visit the following summer when "I . . . shall hope to have some sort of embassy in which to entertain you." He was greeted with open arms by the Soviet leaders, who feted him at a lavish Kremlin banquet, punctuated with dozens of vodka toasts and ending with a kiss on the mouth from Lenin's successor, Joseph Stalin. "I swallowed my astonishment, and, when he turned up his face for a return kiss, I delivered it," he reported to the president.

Missy went home to Somerville where she spent Christmas with her family. A newspaper reporter came calling and wrote of a house festively decorated and Missy relaxing in "blue velvet lounging pajamas." She posed with a phone, reenacting a telephone call from the White House. "But she admitted that the most important of the gifts was not among the boxes. It was a check from the President and she mentioned it excitedly, even though she didn't state the amount. 'I am going to use it for a trip to Europe next summer,' she gurgled."

Her correspondence with Bullitt began in mid-January 1934 and continued unabated for almost seven years, mostly through letters slipped into the diplomatic pouch to his embassies in

Moscow and, later, Paris. In her first quick note, she thanked "Dearest Bill" for the foie gras he had sent. "You really are an angel and I do miss you so much, but you leave lovely pleasant memories—they help a lot." Three days later she wrote even more explicitly of her feelings for him. It was a Saturday afternoon, she was just back from lunch with friends, and "I am longing to take a taxi to 2414!" This may have been the street number of his Washington hotel or a place they had spent time together. "I hope you will find an Embassy ready for you which will have at least the essentials of comfort—I hope, too, that this note will be there, just to say I am thinking of you, and that a week filled with happiness is still fresh and alive in my memory. . . . My love to you—much more of it than I like to confess."

Bullitt was back in the United States by the end of January, and he spent enough time squiring Missy around Washington to cause speculation in the press that they were engaged to be married, but he returned to Moscow to get down to business in earnest in March. At mid-month Missy took him to task for failing to write. "I am, my dear Mr. Ambassador, with great respect (spinach!) and with horrid thoughts—not going to write another line to you until I hear from you. That may be taken as a threat or a promise," she closed, signing the letter simply "M." ("Spinach" was one of the president's favorite "swear" words.) A short note soon arrived, and Missy's reply was a long, whimsical letter in which she referred to the part of herself that longed for Bullitt as "Marguerite." The following passage is a telling one about how she was trying to deal with the uncertainty and loneliness of their long-distance relationship:

> Marguerite has been behaving very badly—every quiet moment finds her concerned with disquieting thoughts—this has been especially true after she was put away for the night. After reading a few words in her book she would suddenly find herself—of all strange places—in Moscow! Playing—not with an Ambassador, but with a very nice man called "Bill" and with

> a little white dog called "Piepie" (spelling?) This would have been very well if the return to Washington had not left her so far down in the dumps. This same young lady had been so confident of her ability to control her emotions, so sure they could be regulated like her watch, that I finally became thoroughly disgusted and set myself down to reason with her. You know all the things one should say—"You should never be sorry for happy times just because they leave you feeling very lonely—the only happy person is the one who loves nobody, etc. etc. etc." When I finished I found we were in complete agreement. Marguerite agreed that she was an idiot, and from that moment on she would discipline her mind. She switched off the light, turned comfortably over, closed her eyes—and trotted right back to find Mr. Stalin!! Now what can one do with her??

Bullitt apparently made her promise to destroy his letters, as there are very few in his papers at Yale University or among Missy's other papers. However, her responses to him indicate he wrote her fairly regularly, and she devoured the long official dispatches that he sent to FDR. Often she mentioned the president's responses to the witty reports to the man Bullitt and his personal secretary, Carmel Offie, called "the Great White Father." Her 1934 letters filled him in on mutual friends such as Bullitt's major ally at the State Department, R. Walton Moore, Washington gossip, her social engagements, and her ongoing battles with colds and coughs. She also shared the surprising news that she was "on the water wagon." Perhaps Bullitt had chided her for drinking and shared the havoc his ex-wife, Louise's, alcoholism had wreaked on her life and their marriage. She didn't drink for three months.

In an April letter following "five miserable days in bed" she again confessed her loneliness. "I am sure that Moscow cannot be as lonely as Washington even though this place has lots of people I know," she wrote, and immediately apologized, "The quiet of my room, the warm bath, the sofa are making me feel more sentimental—I must stop. Goodnight—bless you, my dear."

Had Missy known what Bullitt's life was like at Spaso House, the temporary embassy in Moscow, she might have ended their correspondence and relationship with that letter. It was very much a fraternity—Bullitt's staff of forty was all-male—with George F. Kennan and Charles Bohlen among his chief lieutenants, and it had some aspects of a fraternity house. While contact with ordinary Russian citizens was carefully regulated, the Soviet authorities handpicked lovely members of the Moscow Ballet to mix with the Americans. Bohlen recalled, "There were usually two or three ballerinas running around the Embassy," and the resulting cultural exchange was much as expected. Bullitt, Bohlen, and another staff member shared the favors of one of the dancers, who regularly slept in a bedroom at Spaso House. She was described cavalierly as "an acquisition of the Embassy."

Blissfully unaware of Bullitt's exciting new life in an embassy equipped with hot and cold running ballerinas, Missy wrote in early June, "I do wish you would tell me the things you are doing—I hate having to read everything in the newspapers." Her personal experiment with Prohibition had ended, she confessed. "I am just back from luncheon—fell off the wagon with a terrific jolt—and am just silly enough to write to you . . . Marguerite is—well—I just hope she will not take to alcohol seriously, because the responsibility would be all yours!" She told of the past week traveling with the president to New York to see the review of the fleet, "which was thrilling beyond words," and then spending three days with her family in Boston, "which was boring beyond words! However, I always enjoy seeing my nieces." She shared her plans to sail in June with Grace Tully on the luxury liner SS *Manhattan* for a long vacation in Europe. They planned to visit France and Italy, but she would not be able to reach Moscow. (Antoinette Bachelder, a member of her staff, sent a telegram to the ship: "Do bring back a count or somepin.")

Missy told the press it was her first vacation in four years, made possible because FDR was taking a long cruise to Hawaii and didn't cotton to having women along. (Eleanor spent three weeks in California and Nevada with Lorena Hickok, rejoining her husband when he disembarked in Oregon.) A newspaper clipping in the scrapbook of Missy's sister, Anna, gives the only detail of the trip: "On her arrival in Paris she was met with the six-months-old story that she was going to be married to Ambassador Bullitt and was on her way to join her fiancé in Moscow. The yarn met with a prompt denial by Miss LeHand, as it did when it was first published."

*A nattily dressed Missy emerged from her Paris hotel in the summer of 1934, when she was rumored to be meeting Bullitt to marry him.*

FDR teased his secretary in a laughing letter to her and Grace from the USS *Houston*. "By the way Mac [Marvin McIntyre] thinks from Marguerite's photo she is yearning for him but this big news story about Bill Bullitt upsets him a lot especially because it says C. Vanderbilt, Jr. is to be best man—However, don't worry!" (Despite his huge family wealth, Neil Vanderbilt was a working journalist and may have been the source of the news item. Missy was on a first-name basis with Neil, and wrote Bullitt after she got back home, "I am prepared to shoot him on sight!") FDR closed, "Don't go to Germany and stay away from Riots & Revolutions. The U.S.A. needs you & so do I. Much love from your devoted Father."

Even though she avoided European hotspots, in July Missy developed a serious but unspecified health problem that cut the trip short, and she spent the rest of the summer in the care of Sam and Dorothy Rosenman at their vacation home at Blue Mountain Lake, New York. Eleanor wrote a consoling note in August from Val-Kill Cottage. "I am glad you are better & do hope it won't be too hot these next few weeks before you come up here. I would have come home of course had I known you were ill or wanted me but going to the Rosenmans was a grand thing to do & I'm glad you all had such a happy time." By then FDR had returned from his cruise—"a perfect trip," his wife said. "I had a good trip too & I'm only sorry you . . . children didn't pull it off so well. Another time you must let me help plan & perhaps we can do better." The letter, which offered "a hug and a kiss for you," epitomizes Eleanor's mothering instincts when it came to Missy, and also contains a huge dose of irony. On her trip west with Lorena, Eleanor was hounded by the press, chased at high speed by a carload of reporters, and stared at and pestered by ordinary Americans wherever she went. Hick responded several times with bad humor and worse language, much to Eleanor's embarrassment.

Bullitt weighed in on Missy's bummer of a summer at the end of a letter that primarily concerned embassy affairs. "I was really sorry to hear that you had had such an unsatisfactory trip and even more so to hear that you had been ill. Take care of yourself." Considering his rather perfunctory tone, it's hard to believe in the existence of an engagement at this time between

Missy and her ambassador boyfriend. Fifty years later, Dorothy Rosenman told FDR biographer Ted Morgan that Missy had traveled to Moscow and discovered Bullitt was involved with a ballet dancer and broke off the engagement. Mrs. Rosenman should have been a credible source, having cared for the ailing Missy in her home after her return from Europe, but the Bullitt papers containing Missy's letters, which were donated to Yale University in 2008, set the engagement story to rest. Missy's reply to Bullitt's September 1, 1934, letter makes it clear she did not see him that summer: "From all I can gather Grace (Tully) and I are the only two white people who did not visit Russia this summer. Everyone returns with glowing stories of you," she wrote, using a mildly racist reference that was fairly common at the time. (Among his visitors was eccentric Washington heiress Evalyn Walsh McLean, owner of the sixty-seven-plus-carat Hope Diamond, who had threatened to flaunt her spectacular blue bauble in the streets of Moscow as a symbol of the superiority of capitalism. Bullitt talked her out of it.) Although Bullitt remained ambassador to Russia until early 1936 and was ambassador to France from 1936 to 1940, Missy never visited him at either embassy. There is no indication in her letters that she believed their relationship would lead to marriage.

Bullitt was important to Missy, but she doesn't seem to have wanted a commitment from him, and even doubted his exclusivity. Their love affair, conducted mostly by letter and phone, was the secret to hold close in her bedroom at night, the secret that made her smile to herself as she worked at her desk outside FDR's office, the secret that set her pulse racing when the diplomatic pouch arrived or the phone rang with an international call. Even FDR could not penetrate the place she kept that secret in her laboring, damaged heart.

## CHAPTER TWELVE

# *Woman of Influence*

The West Wing where Missy returned to work after her 1934 summer vacation was a construction zone, and would remain so through the fall as the executive office was renovated and expanded. Missy set up a temporary office in the Red Room at the White House with Grace and Paula Tully, complaining in a letter to Bill Bullitt in Moscow, "The noise is terrific, goes on 24 hours a day, and they tell us it will be worse later!" The $325,000 project—$5.6 million in current dollars—added office space by building a basement and a penthouse for 120 executive staff members.

When all the dust cleared, Missy again had the most enviable office in the West Wing, the only one that opened directly into the enlarged Oval Office—and the only one with walls painted pink rather than pistachio green. Her windows gave her a lovely view of the White House Rose Garden, a source of much joy: she interrupted the president at lunch one day to tell him "that there are two robins sitting in my garden." Her office had a separate outside entrance with French doors, providing a surreptitious way for visitors to reach the president's office—as long as Missy, the ultimate gatekeeper, would admit them. Her small desk held one telephone—"I can only use one telephone at a time," she explained to journalist Doris Fleeson—a lamp, ashtray, files, and other clutter, and a small bronze bust of FDR by the sculptor Jo Davidson. If her glasses were not on her nose, they were somewhere nearby. She invariably removed them when she posed for photographs. Members of the cabinet and Congress and heads of the New Deal's alphabet agencies—AAA, CCC, CWA, FERA, and on down the line—had gotten wise to the advantage of befriending "Miss LeHand." Powerful men—but seldom women, as the president's wife was their most passionate advocate—dropped by her desk, called her on the phone, or sent her notes and memos and the occasional small gift. Could she find them just a moment on the president's schedule? Would she mind looking over this document and possibly finding a time to share it with the president? What had she heard the president say about this vital issue or that pending job appointment? Tactful and charming, Missy sized up her "suitors" behind her lovely smile. The bottom line was always the same: Was this person out to help the president further the New Deal agenda, or did he have one of his own?

The *Time* magazine cover story on December 17, 1934, was devoted to "The White House Secretariat" and their new "palace." Four faces shared the cover: Louis Howe, Steve Early, Marvin McIntyre, and Marguerite LeHand, further validating her importance in the Roosevelt administration. *Time* covers featured women only two other weeks that year, one devoted to fashion designer Elsa Schiaparelli, the other to a group of children's activists, including Eleanor Roosevelt. Missy was the only one sharing a cover on an equal basis with men.

The male secretaries had come to FDR from a background in journalism. Early, a handsome, short-tempered native of Virginia and descendant of the legendary Confederate General Jubal Early, was widely considered a first-rate press secretary. Steve staged two press conferences every week through most of FDR's presidency, managed press questions, and carefully groomed his boss's image. It was he who made sure that the American public never saw a picture or newsreel of FDR in a wheelchair. Steve and Missy had a close, joshing relationship that included making silly bets and going out for occasional drinks and dinner. He once presented her with a photo of himself seated between Howe and FDR's jovial military aide, Colonel Edwin M. "Pa" Watson, with the inscription "To Missy from the rose between 2 thorns."

*Press Secretary Steve Early called himself "the rose between 2 thorns" in this photo with Louis Howe and Edwin "Pa" Watson.*

If Early had an especially sensitive matter to broach with the president, he often ran it by Missy. In the fall of 1934, he wrote a "confidential memo" to her about the president's Sunday recreational activities, including fishing and attending a raucous press baseball game in Hyde Park. "There are many, perhaps too many, people through the country who still take Sunday observance seriously—who take their religion seriously," he wrote. "Such publicity as the Sunday stories I mention is harmful. It not only appears in the daily press but the religious press follows it up editorially and puts exaggerated religious implications regarding the President's conduct on Sundays. . . . This is just between us unless, of course, you want to talk to the President about it." There's no record if she did, but the president continued to fish on Sundays.

Like Missy, Howe, and Early, appointments secretary McIntyre was an original member of the 1920 Cuff Links Gang. Like Missy, he struggled with his health, becoming as thin as a whisper and periodically checking into a hospital for treatment of tuberculosis. The son of a Kentucky minister, he was described by a contemporary writer as the most "average" of men, a slap-'em-on-the-back sort of guy well suited to being the "official greeter" to the people cooling their heels in FDR's outer office. As the scheduler of FDR's office appointments, Mac waged a losing battle against the clock, for the garrulous president invariably overran the time slots. Once Missy began slipping people through the back door, Mac's job grew even harder. She sometimes criticized him, telling Interior Secretary Harold Ickes—who rightly suspected that Mac disliked him—that he was rather too fond of rich people. "She said that he would go out to parties and come back and tell her whom he had been with and would then relate how many millions the person was worth," Ickes confided in his "secret" diary, which he kept throughout his dozen years at Interior and which was published after his death in 1952. Yet the two were fast friends, and Missy worried over Mac's health.

She was less sympathetic toward Louis. By the time of the secretariat *Time* magazine cover, he was clearly a dying man. He maintained an office in the West Wing but was seldom well enough to use it, instead spending most of his time in his bedroom, sometimes under an oxygen tent, sometimes on hands and knees, the only position that enabled him to catch his breath. By April 1935 he was thought to be so close to death that the president postponed his vacation to be at his bedside, and Howe's wife and children came to stay at the White House. Missy complained to Bullitt that Grace Howe is "no help at all, and the President and Mrs. R more bound to Louis' bedside than ever—terrible person!" After several days in a coma, Howe came to and growled, "Why in hell doesn't somebody get me a cigarette?" but his effectiveness as an advisor was all but gone.

When the White House again became a construction zone in the summer of 1935—this time the kitchen was renovated, leaving its residents with "neither hot water, cold water, lights or food," according to Missy—Louis was moved to the nearby naval hospital where he spent the rest of his life. Provided a telephone in his room, he sometimes made meddlesome calls to cabinet members, and FDR spread the word to check in with him before acting on a Howe directive.

Louis and Missy had always gotten along, though there was friction, as an inscription on a portrait he gave to her implies. The romantic, soft-focus photo of Howe with a cigarette in his fingers and smoke curling beside his ear is signed, "For 'Missy' who has fought so many battles—For me—with me—and against me—for Lo!—these many years (let's not tell how many) from Louis McHenry Howe." His long illness wore on Missy to the point that a few weeks before his death in March 1936, she wrote Bullitt that she felt "resentful" he was still hanging on as he had "had a fine share of life. However, I guess there is nothing I can do about it."

Louis's genius in political strategy, Steve's inspired press management, and Mac's genial handling of appointments all served Roosevelt well. But Missy was the Swiss Army knife of the White House. A formidable, multitalented multitasker, Missy might on any given day be directing the work of fifty staffers, writing a check to Franklin Jr.'s doctor for treatment of hemorrhoids, telling the president the wording in a speech "just doesn't sound like you," soothing an irate bureaucrat who couldn't get an appointment, and then racing over to the White House to "pour tea for a crowd of archaeologists." In a letter she dashed off to her niece Babe, Missy lamented, "I am having a devilish time trying to finish this—the telephone—callers & <u>that man</u>—the P!!"

Her day began about 9:25 each morning when, after having coffee and orange juice in her suite and scanning several newspapers, she briefly met the male secretaries in the president's bedroom. FDR would still be in bed, wearing an old blue sweater or a navy cape to keep his shoulders warm as he finished his breakfast and read the *Congressional Record*. "In this way it is possible for me to keep informed of the various things that are discussed at this morning conference about which I might not otherwise know," she wrote in the draft of a magazine article for *The Saturday Evening Post* that she never completed. They would go over the day's appointment schedule and any other pressing matters, and then disperse to their individual offices. Missy generally ate lunch at her desk each day, usually crackers and milk or a cup of broth to keep her weight at 130 pounds, and then joined the others for the Children's Hour. When the work day ended, Steve and Mac went home to their wives but Missy's duties could continue late into the evening, as she attended a White House state dinner, arranged a quiet night of poker to help the president relax, or simply sat with FDR in his study as he worked on his stamp collection or listened to music. FDR was said to do his "best intellectual work" between nine and midnight, as the information he had taken in during the workday percolated through his brain. He liked to have someone with him then to write down a thought or idea. At least her third-floor suite became a little quieter in mid-1935, when the rambunctious grandchildren, Sistie and Buzzie Dall, moved out of their nearby nursery. Their mother, Anna, married John Boettiger, the journalist she had met on the campaign train in 1932, and the family moved to New York.

Missy's weekends were not her own, either, as she invariably accompanied FDR on trips home to Hyde Park or on day or weekend cruises on the presidential yacht the *Sequoia* and its successor the *Potomac*. During these watery journeys she was often working on letters, weighing in on policy discussions, or serving as the cruise hostess, as Eleanor did not usually go on overnight trips, but Missy enjoyed them immensely. She repeatedly mentioned how relaxing they were in letters to Bullitt. Sometimes her nieces, Aunt Nellie, or friends joined her. As

FDR's semiannual fishing cruises were strictly stag affairs, the trips on the yacht were reminders of their months of fishing in the Florida Keys. "We are just back from two lovely days on the *Sequoia*—much fishing but no fish!!" she wrote Bullitt.

Her 1935 letters to Bullitt included many political observations among the tidbits about Washington society and declarations of her love, reminding him of her value as his pipeline to the Oval Office. By the spring of 1935, FDR's reelection bid was very much on her mind. "I feel very strongly that it should not be won by a small margin of votes—in order to carry on what has been started there should be a really authoritative majority," she wrote. She also weighed in on the U.S. Supreme Court decision that had nullified the National Industrial Recovery Act. It had spawned the most controversial of the alphabet agencies, the National Recovery Administration, which had negotiated wage-price "codes" in hundreds of industries. Adhering companies—including Eleanor's Val-Kill Industries—proclaimed their compliance with the Blue Eagle emblem and the slogan "We Do Our Part." But instead of bringing prices down and wages up, the opposite occurred, and businesses rankled under the growing power the NRA gave to trade unions. On May 27, 1935, the court declared the codes section of the NRA unconstitutional. "Wasn't the Supreme Court decision terrific?" she asked Bullitt. (Missy routinely used the word "terrific" to mean "terrible," as in "The heat has been terrific.") "The conservatives in both parties feel, apparently, that the President no longer can 'seduce' the Congress and the Court, and they have become extremely vocal. Price-cutting, reduction of wages and lengthening of hours of labor are started again, and strikes are threatening everywhere with the government powerless to help. Should we send for Stalin?!!!"

Despite the NRA setback, as the Roosevelt presidency hit the middle of its first term it had much of which to be proud. The summer of 1935 saw the passage of a raft of "Second New Deal" legislation, including the Social Security Act and the

National Labor Relations Act. The banking system had been saved: only nine banks failed in 1934, compared to more than four thousand in 1933. Hundreds of thousands of young men had gone into the forests to work for the Civilian Conservation Corps. One of FDR's favorite programs, it led to the planting of two billion trees and improvements at national parks, including Gettysburg, where the young men rebuilt the stone walls of the battlefield. Unemployment had dropped from almost 25 percent to just over 20 percent. (Missy's connections improved the statistic among the LeHands. Her brother Dan got a job in Boston with the Reconstruction Finance Corporation, a federal agency that made loans to state and local governments; Bernard was hired by Joseph P. Kennedy's alcohol importing firm; and her niece Barbara became James Roosevelt's secretary at the Boston insurance company where he was a partner.)

*Joseph P. Kennedy got the appointment he craved, ambassador to the Court of St. James's, but botched the job.*

The two men responsible for most of the employment programs were Harry Hopkins and Harold Ickes. They were both totally dedicated to the New Deal, FDR, and work for pay rather than straight relief payments, yet their approaches were diametrically opposed and they heartily disliked each other. Ickes took pride in his reputation as an irascible curmudgeon and his nickname "Honest Harold," and he strived for accountability as head of the Public Works Administration. Started in June 1933, it funded major projects such as bridges, dams, hospitals, schools, and aircraft carriers, using private sector contractors. The Grand Coulee Dam and New York's Triborough Bridge were PWA projects and highly visible reminders of the success of the New Deal.

*Harry Hopkins filled a number of roles in FDR's government, despite ill health.*

Hopkins's Works Progress Administration, or WPA, begun in 1935 with an appropriation of $4.8 billion—$82 billion in current money—primarily funneled money to states to put unskilled men and women into public works projects in order to get them off the relief rolls. Workers constructed or improved thousands of public schools, airports, and playgrounds, and built more than half a million miles of roads. WPA also had a division for artists and writers. To critics, Hopkins replied, "Hell! They've got to eat just like other people." In Missy's hometown of Somerville, a mural by WPA artist Ross Moffett depicting a Revolutionary War skirmish was painted on the post office wall in Union Square and remains there today.

There was considerable disagreement about which projects should be PWA and which should be WPA, thrashed out at contentious Allotment Advisory Committee meetings at the White House. Headed into the first one in May 1935, Missy was braced for trouble. "The Allotment Board of the new Work-Relief meets for the first time this afternoon—that should be fun!" she wrote Bullitt. Afterward, Ickes groused that Hopkins was presenting "thousands of inconsequential make-believe programs in all parts of the country" for WPA while he was focusing on "useful and socially desirable public works" for PWA. Editorial cartoons caricatured WPA workers as lazy, and people joked that its letters were an acronym for "We Poke Along" or "Whistle, Piss and Argue." Careful Ickes doled out aid with a teaspoon, passionate Hopkins with a fire hose. Hopkins made no apologies, replying to an observation that a more careful approach would work in the long run by saying "People don't eat in the long run."

Ickes began using Missy as a sounding board and source of inside information late in 1934, yet her relationship with Hopkins—whom she had known, liked, and respected since Albany—continued to be a strong one. The fact that two men who disliked each other both trusted and liked Missy speaks volumes for her diplomacy and discretion. Ickes funneled personal letters for FDR through Missy and pulled her aside for private words. He was delighted when Missy invited him to the White House in December 1934 after a cocktail party she and Grace Tully gave at the Willard Hotel for Grace's sister, Paula, who was engaged to be married. The revelers went to FDR's private study, where he was finishing up some work with Raymond Moley. "Two bottles of champagne were brought up and we had a jolly time until close to midnight," Ickes happily confided to his diary. "The President was at his best, laughing and joking, telling stories and relating incidents."

As Missy gained confidence, she became more adept at creating social occasions for people she favored to spend time with the president away from Louis Howe's jealous eye. In this way, she introduced FDR to Thomas G. Corcoran, who would become one of the most useful implements in his presidential toolbox.

*Interior Secretary Harold Ickes and FDR's chief lobbyist Tommy Corcoran leave the White House after a conference with the president in 1935.*

## ❁ CHAPTER THIRTEEN

# *Mixing Work and Play*

Tommy Corcoran had been a student of Harvard University Law School professor Felix Frankfurter, one of a group of Frankfurter alums known around the capital as the "Happy Hot Dogs." Frankfurter, a frequent Oval Office visitor whom Missy called "one of my pets," sent her a note in the fall of 1934 commending Corcoran as "a very dear friend" and "a person of entire dependability." Missy quickly sized Corcoran up as a man who could do the administration much good. With his deeply dimpled cheeks, curly hair, ebullient personality, and musical talent, the Irish American Catholic lawyer would not have been out of place in any bar in Dublin, though he seldom drank. Missy brought him to the White House one night to sing and play the accordion after dinner when Eleanor was away. FDR, who loved such informal musical evenings, was charmed, and bestowed upon him the nickname "Tommy the Cork." He was in like Flynn.

Corcoran, who worked for the Reconstruction Finance Corporation, began arriving at the White House almost daily for a visit with Missy. "In that way I avoided crossing paths with any of Roosevelt's old guard and kept the jealousies down to a manageable level," he said. Wrote Corcoran's biographer David McKean, "Corcoran would tell LeHand anything he felt the president should know, and she in turn would inform the president. If Roosevelt wanted some action taken on an issue, then, as he described it, 'she showed me in.' Indeed, Corcoran's close friendship with LeHand was central to his rising influence."

Corcoran also talent-scouted other young Catholic and Jewish lawyers to join the WASPs dominating the government's ranks of legal eagles. With his Jewish colleague and housemate Ben Cohen, Corcoran drafted some of the most crucial New Deal legislation, and FDR used him as a lobbyist for the White House—a first in Washington. More darkly, he was described as FDR's "hatchet man" by Supreme Court Justice William O. Douglas. He may have been alluding to Corcoran's role as a "fixer" for the legal problems of the Roosevelt children, keeping the lid on their financial and domestic scandals. "Some people thought Corcoran capable of murder, literally," in his zealous devotion to FDR, wrote historian Frank Costigliola.

Eleanor did not share her husband's enthusiasm for Tommy. Corcoran's religion may have been part of the reason, for Roman Catholicism was Eleanor's one bigotry blind spot. Her close friend and biographer Joseph Lash said he was "struck by her hostility" to the Catholic Church, which her cousin, the political columnist Joseph Alsop, said was a remnant of "the anti-Catholic nonsense she heard during childhood." In her memoirs, Eleanor said Corcoran "exploited Missy's friendship." Nevertheless, Missy, Tommy, Grace, and other Catholics provided valuable service in mitigating the destructive influence of the radical "radio priest" Father Charles Coughlin. His national program had tens of millions of listeners, and he vociferously turned on the New Deal in 1936.

Besides his professional ability, Tommy was just plain fun to have around. A prime example of the relaxing sort of evening Missy engineered took place at Joseph Kennedy's rented estate in Maryland in the summer of 1935. Kennedy was then chairman of the Securities and Exchange Commission, created to regulate the stock market. His appointment was controversial, because his own stock manipulations had helped make him an even wealthier man as others were wiped out by the crash. FDR's response, "Set a thief to catch a thief," turned out to be inspired. Kennedy did an excellent job as the first czar of stock market regulation. Missy described his Marwood estate in a letter to Bill Bullitt as "like the palace at Versailles—it must be seen to be appreciated! . . . One of the bathrooms is more fantastic than anything Hollywood could produce." While movies were shown at the White House in the hall outside the president's study and bedroom, Kennedy's house boasted a dedicated movie theater, as well as twelve bedrooms. Missy's relationship with Kennedy was complicated. Even as she enjoyed his friendship, her private comments to Bullitt were often snarky: "Joe is terribly worried for fear the government will take all his money & the poor little Kennedys will be left to starve!"

On the last evening in June 1935, two White House cars arrived at Marwood, disgorging six Secret Service agents, the president, and a contingent of Irish American Catholics: Missy, Grace Tully, Tommy Corcoran, and SEC general counsel John Burns. They had called inviting themselves to dinner that afternoon, and Joe had quickly consented, though he was in a fix. Arthur Krock, the *New York Times* Washington correspondent, was there as his guest, and Krock was on the outs with the White House. Krock hid in his second-floor bedroom, but he made notes on what he overheard.

After the guests enjoyed dinner and a movie, liberally washed down with mint juleps, Corcoran pulled out his accordion and the singing began. They invented a GOP campaign song to the tune of "The Old Gray Mare She Ain't What She Used to Be," and then FDR began telling some of his favorite stories, many involving boats. "The President gave this as 'bhutt,'" Krock wrote. "From that time on, whenever he said 'boat' or 'float' or any similar word, Miss LeHand would chime in with 'bhutt' or 'fluhtt.' This must have happened twenty times. . . . The singing and talk went on until well past midnight. About that time I fell asleep, pondering what paradoxes of the men who occupy the highest office in the land." Eleanor and Lorena Hickok had left on a motoring vacation earlier in the day and weren't disturbed by FDR's and Missy's return home after 1 a.m. Marwood probably would not have been much fun for them.

Eleanor did have a lot of fun at other times, as Missy's home movie camera recorded her at Val-Kill ice-skating with Nancy Cook and Marion Dickerman, and at large picnics cooking hot dogs on a stick, carrying an egg on a spoon in a relay race, and even playing an adult version of ring-around-the-rosy. Because the winter Gridiron Dinner was a stag affair for the male press, Eleanor created a simultaneous Gridiron Widows affair at the White House, where women came in costume. Labor Secretary Frances Perkins wore cap and gown as a Brain Truster and five women arrived as Canada's most famous citizens, the Dionne Quintuplets, the first quints in the world known to have survived infancy. Louis Howe so disguised Eleanor as an old apple woman that no one recognized her.

Interior Secretary Harold Ickes initially had a positive opinion of the first lady, describing her at a picnic held a few weeks after the inauguration as "a very charming woman, natural, simple and friendly." By the fall of 1935, however, his department had been on the receiving end of so much of her "interference" that he complained in his diary, "Soon I will expect Sistie and Buzzie to be issuing orders to members of my staff. Fortunately they can't write yet."

Missy's role as a stand-in hostess was crucial to Eleanor's activism. She traveled widely, plunging down a coal mine shaft in Ohio and visiting the slums of Puerto Rico, where she saw firsthand the plight of the most downtrodden Americans, especially unemployed young people, African Americans, women, and children. Idealistic always, she lobbied Franklin to be more liberal. He listened, but he better understood the limits of how far he could push Congress. By early 1935, Ickes was echoing many people around the country when he wrote in his diary, "After all, the people did not elect her President, and I don't think the country likes the thought of the wife of the President engaging prominently in public affairs to the extent that she does." Yet when

Ickes's wife, Anna, was killed in an automobile accident that August, Eleanor Roosevelt and Harry Hopkins were among the administration representatives at the Chicago funeral, while the president and Missy went to Hyde Park for a planned vacation.

Fulton Oursler, Missy's close friend and *Liberty* magazine editor, got a jaw-dropping look at the Roosevelts at dinner during a May 1935 visit he and wife Grace made to the White House. "We arrived in time to see the two children with the emetic nicknames [Sistie and Buzzie Dall] in a gasping deathgrip at the foot of the stairs," he wrote. At the small family dinner table, the president wore a "black velvet smoking jacket cut in tuxedo fashion"—a style Oursler liked so much he had one made for himself—while Eleanor wore a "shrimp pink" evening gown, and Missy one of red chiffon. They were formally dressed for a large reception to follow in the Blue Room. "I wanted to look around and take in everything," he wrote. "But who could go on noticing mundane details when there was a brawl going on at the table—I mean a very unpleasant and bitter scene between President Roosevelt and his First Lady."

The topic on Eleanor's mind that night was jobs for young people, and it was one she had been lobbying her husband about for two years. Oursler described the scene: "Mrs. Roosevelt launched into a long discussion of the impatience of the American youth against the older generation which had bequeathed it only war, then boom and then smash. It was a very familiar tune. Every magazine and newspaper had carried reams of the stuff." FDR told her she had to look at the whole picture; men over forty who couldn't get jobs were in just as much "misery" as the youth. Then he suggested she refer the youth to his beloved Civilian Conservation Corps camps.

"The snort she gave was equine in contempt. . . . 'I'm not criticizing your CCC camps, Frank, but I know there is nothing really being done there. . . . My dear, forestry is a joke," she told him, castigating the program closest to his heart: FDR liked to describe himself as a Hyde Park tree farmer. The conversation went downhill from there, but at the end FDR winked at his wife and promised to "consider the matter." Sure enough, when the WPA went into action a few weeks later, it included a program of education and job training for youth age sixteen to twenty-five, run by Eleanor's friend Aubrey Williams.

Missy sat quietly through the dinner, letting the Roosevelts thrash out their differences in front of their mortified guests. Oursler made a word portrait of her face: "Back through the years I look tonight and see her there, Marguerite LeHand, in flowing red chiffon, blue eyes sparkling, lips parted in that strange secret smile, compound of cunning and innocence forever baffling." This was typical behavior for her, quietly listening, and then sharing her opinion with the president when they were alone. Her outward reserve may have enabled Eleanor to convince herself that Missy had no interest or influence when it came to politics, indeed that some of her behavior caused problems for FDR. In her autobiography, *This I Remember,* published after Missy was dead, she wrote "Missy was young and pretty and loved a good time, and occasionally her social contacts got mixed with her work and made it hard for her and others."

Yet Missy never let on to anyone—including Bullitt—that she had anything but admiration for the first lady. In Christmas letters she wrote to the Roosevelts in the mid-1930s, she appealed to them both as a loving child—one with tremendous insight into what made them tick. "You must know how proud I am every time you get something accomplished, which is *all* the time—just being with you is a joy I can't express," she wrote to Franklin. "I've had a happy year—for all the times I've misbehaved I hope both you and Mrs. Roosevelt will forgive me—that would be my nicest present." To "Dearest ER," Missy wrote along the same lines. "I hope you know how very much I appreciate being with you—not because of the W.H. [White House]—but because I'm with you!" She complimented Eleanor on all she did for others—"I know the 'doing' has been fun for you too. I love you so much—I never can tell you how very much." Eleanor repeatedly vowed her love to Missy in letters, closing them with declarations such as "Much, much love to you my dear" and "I love you always." A studio portrait of Missy, taken in the late 1920s, hung in Eleanor's bedroom at Val-Kill until her death in 1962, along with photos of her husband and other close friends.

*Missy's fun-loving side is evident in this photo taken with Grace Tully and what appears to be a live donkey.*

In the fall of 1935, Missy's actions demonstrated beyond words her feelings for her White House "family." She made out her will, leaving most of her White House furniture to the Roosevelts and the Tully sisters, and instructing that Eleanor, Grace, and Paula should also inherit her jewelry, clothing, and personal effects, but asked that they distribute items as they saw fit to her nieces and friends "as would, in their opinion, be in accordance with my desires." She suggested that the nieces be given specific items of jewelry, furs, movie cameras, her car, and "a small hanging bookshelf made for me by President Roosevelt." She left her home in

Somerville to her brothers and her cottage in Warm Springs to her nieces. "I am deliberately omitting my sister, Anna LeHand Rochon, from this devise inasmuch as she has already enjoyed the use of said real property rent free and tax free for several years," Missy said of the house on Orchard Street. She left Anna $500, stipulating the same amount be given to Grace and her Aunt Nellie. Although Anna would be the person who cared for Missy at home in her last years, she never altered her will. It was witnessed by Raymond Moley, Steve Early, and her assistant Mary Eben.

That fall of 1935 had passed in a whirlwind. Eleanor threw Missy a birthday party at Val-Kill Cottage in September, and she was thrilled to get a telegram from Bullitt: "Maybe Friday thirteenth but happiest greetings all good wishes miss you. Bill." The next week her nieces were married in a double wedding in Boston, with Eleanor and James Roosevelt among the guests, and in October she joined a party of about eighty people on a cross-country train with the Roosevelts. They inspected public works projects, dedicated the Boulder Dam, and in California saw the president, the feuding Hopkins and Ickes, and a few other men off on a fishing trip that would take them through the Panama Canal and back to Washington via the port of Charleston, South Carolina. (Ickes, a recent widower, had a surprisingly good time and came to appreciate Hopkins's "easy manners and keen wit.") Missy stayed with Grace in California, visiting child star Shirley Temple on the set of her movie *The Littlest Rebel,* and wrote breathlessly to Bullitt from San Francisco. "We have had such a gay time I have only been able to drop into bed when I got to my room. . . . I am off for a day in the country—the weather is gorgeous and I am looking forward to it."

Her heart lifted in late November when a telegram came from Bill, telling her he expected to reach Washington on December 12 "and hope you will dine with me on that date." She did. She had just gotten back from two weeks in Warm Springs with the president and his polios.

CHAPTER FOURTEEN

# Polio Redux

"If you ever come to Washington," Missy told a college student from her Somerville neighborhood who had worked for FDR's election, "give me a call at the White House." One summer day while visiting family in the capital, Thomas P. O'Neill took her up on the offer. He described it as "the political thrill of my life."

Missy greeted him at the gate and asked if he would like to meet the president. "I was speechless," her visitor recalled. "Franklin Delano Roosevelt was like God to me. . . . When I saw the president sitting in a wheelchair, I was so shocked that my chin about hit my chest. Like most Americans, I had absolutely no idea that Franklin Roosevelt was disabled." He guarded the extent of FDR's disability as if Missy had revealed a state secret. "Tip" O'Neill led one of the most storied political careers of the twentieth century, culminating with his service as speaker of the U.S. House of Representatives. He was a New Dealer until the day he died.

For FDR and the people around him, his paralysis was a fact of life, evident from the moment he opened his eyes in bed and called for help to get to the bathroom until he was tucked in for the night. He could never forget the extent of his disability, or the struggles of the other polios he knew. Within the White House, they included Antoinette "Toi" Bachelder, a former patient from Warm Springs whom Missy hired for her staff, and the chatty maid Lillian Rogers Parks, who performed her duties while hobbling on a crutch.

Especially during his first two terms, his cottage on the grounds of the Georgia Warm Springs Foundation was the place FDR went to relax and recharge his batteries. On the Foundation grounds, braces and wheelchairs and staggering gaits didn't attract a second glance, the buildings were designed with access in mind, and he felt at home there with his fellow survivors and the Georgians who had taken him into their hearts.

Missy was FDR's consort at the Little White House. When Eleanor went to Warm Springs as first lady, it was usually for ceremonial occasions, and she didn't stay long. She was even absent on a spring morning when a handsome brick schoolhouse for the community's African American children—named for her—was dedicated. The plight of these children is painfully evident in one of Missy's home movies, which shows three wretchedly dressed little boys. A white man throws a coin to them and the three tussle in the dirt until one pops up, the grinning winner. Watching the film from a distance of eighty years is painful; it's easy to imagine how sickening Eleanor, with her strong social justice convictions, would have found such scenes. At any event, she had willingly abdicated her place to Missy long before, not only because she disliked Deep South attitudes, but because she felt the Warm Springs visits were her husband's "time with Missy."

Many members of the White House staff traveled to Warm Springs, but only Missy had her own bedroom in the Little White House, with a private bath and screened porch, furnished in maple Val-Kill furniture. Her twin bed was similar to the one in the president's bedroom on the other side of the house, but with a pink flowered chenille bedspread that matched the rose-colored drapes at the window and a chintz-covered slipper chair.

For Missy, life at Warm Springs was a constant whirl of activity that ranged from hosting luncheons to welcoming politically and socially important guests, from attending somewhat raucous parties to making serious efforts on behalf of polio victims. Poliomyelitis remained a feared public health threat and a terrible burden to those it crippled. The Depression, which had made it hard for even many able-bodied people to find work, was especially hard on the disabled. "We had a nice little piece of money once, ready to build and furnish [a home] and pay cash," one man wrote to FDR. "Then my boy took sick with infantile and we spent the whole thing, but I never begrudged one penny."

*Missy was the queen of the Little White House and presided over many a picnic at Warm Springs.*

Warm Springs had always accepted charity cases, but the Depression increased the number while drying up donations to support them. When FDR was elected New York governor, he handed over the financial reins of the Foundation to Doc O'Connor, who recruited a successful insurance salesman named Keith Morgan as his fundraiser and charged him with sharing the Warm Springs story with wealthy philanthropists. At first it worked. In 1929, donations to Warm Springs totaled $369,000, but by 1932 they had fallen to just $30,000. A new approach was needed if Warm Springs was to survive.

Morgan turned to a man named Carl Byoir, a wizard in the new field of public relations, and he came up with a groundbreaking idea: instead of courting the dwindling rich, who distrusted

Roosevelt if they didn't outright hate him, the Foundation should appeal to the much larger base of people who had elected him president. If enough "forgotten men" (and women) stepped up to the plate, it would make up for the wealthy folks who were triple-knotting their purse strings. And what better way to do it than to invite them to a party? Byoir suggested to the president that a nationwide birthday party be thrown for FDR in January 1934, with proceeds donated to Warm Springs. "If my birthday will be of any help, take it," the president said.

Byoir's innovation "turned traditional philanthropy on its head," wrote polio historian David Oshinsky. "Large gifts were hard to come by in the 1930s; the secret lay in small donations. Who wouldn't contribute *something* to see a crippled child walk again?" Who indeed? With just two months to prepare, Byoir launched the President's Birthday Balls with the slogan "We Dance So That Others Might Walk." Some six thousand balls and parties were held on January 30, FDR's fifty-second birthday. The Birthday Balls reflected their locales and patrons, ranging from a high-society shindig at the Waldorf-Astoria in New York to a tribal dance on the Blackfoot Reservation in Browning, Montana. At Warm Springs, the patients held a square dance in their wheelchairs.

Byoir didn't depend on goodwill alone to line up volunteers. Post offices nationwide were headed by presidential appointees, and all of them were tapped as honorary chairs. In Potsdam, New York, Missy's Aunt Nellie was a patroness of two birthday fundraisers, chaired by her close friend Ruth Perrin, who was Potsdam's postmistress. One was a card party held at a social club, the other a dance with orchestra at a local gym that was decorated, said a local newspaper, with "festoons of colored lights" and a large picture of FDR. A national radio hookup delivered the president's 11:30 p.m. address live. "I wish I could divide myself by six thousand and attend in person each and every one of these birthday parties," he said, thanking the contributors for "the happiest birthday I ever have known." The

Potsdam events raised $150, a trickle pouring into a torrent of money. All told, the Birthday Balls netted more than a million dollars ($17 million in current dollars), which was ten times what O'Connor had expected.

FDR celebrated that night with family, staff, and his Cuff Links Gang at a "Hail, Caesar" party dreamed up by Louis Howe. The men dressed as centurions and toga-clad senators, the women as Vestal Virgins, and FDR wore a crown of laurel leaves, looking every inch a Roman ruler. A photograph shows a virginal Missy seated at his feet, beside a three-tiered cake big around as a truck tire, arms clasped around her knees and a look of unalloyed delight on her face as she gazed at her "Caesar."

*FDR's infamous 1934 "Hail Caesar" birthday party was held the same night as the first Birthday Ball. Missy is sitting at lower left.*

At 11:30 p.m., the "gentlemen" retired to the study and Eleanor Roosevelt journeyed out to two hotels to attend their balls. Missy was part of her retinue, squired by Bill Bullitt, who was home for a brief visit after presenting his credentials as ambassador in Moscow.

The popular and profitable balls did more than replenish the coffers at Warm Springs. In 1935, more than two thirds of the money raised at the second Birthday Balls stayed in the communities to assist and treat local victims of the disease, and the rest was earmarked for research. Even so, critics and political enemies began charging that the president was using the proceeds of the balls to line his own pockets, and the revenue began to decline. To de-politicize the cause, FDR announced in 1938 the formation of the National Foundation for Infantile Paralysis, headed by O'Connor as its unpaid executive director, its mission to research a cure for polio and care for its victims. The NFIP became one of the most successful charities in history, breaking new ground in fundraising techniques and eventually working itself out of a job. Between 1938 and 1955, the NFIP spent $233 million on patient care and funded the research that resulted in the polio vaccine.

As FDR's private secretary, Missy handled and appropriately referred all business related to the Warm Springs Foundation, the NFIP, and his Meriwether County farm property that came across her desk. (An example of the latter was a badly spelled letter from a farmer's wife who complained that Roosevelt's cows had eaten some of her velvet beans, and she was still awaiting compensation: "I am sorrow that I halft to write you about it.") One of her most puzzling foundation-related experiences came when a young girl from North Carolina arrived with her mother, claiming to have won a week's stay at the White House for winning an NFIP poetry contest. It turned out she had faked a letter of invitation from Missy and even fooled the local newspaper into writing a story about it.

Missy enjoyed a close and friendly working relationship with O'Connor, who had made his fortune in his Wall Street law business. Though initially uninterested in charity, he became as enthusiastic about the NFIP's work as Roosevelt was. "Like Andrew Jackson at the Battle of New Orleans, I found myself up to my rump in blood and liked it," he said. A later addition to the Cuff Links Gang, Doc often traveled with FDR, stood close by on election nights, and was among the favored few included on the president's stag fishing trips. He was an Irish American Catholic like Missy, and he had his own nickname for her: Peg.

A major fundraising breakthrough occurred when entertainer Eddie Cantor offered to use his popular radio program to launch a "March of Dimes" to the White House, a spin on the *March of Time* radio show and newsreels that preceded the main feature at movie houses. Two days after the program aired in 1938, the number of letters arriving each day in the White House mail room rose from the usual five thousand to fifteen thousand. On the fourth day, 150,000 letters arrived. And they contained money. Delighted, FDR sent a note to the mail room that said, "I hope you are having a good dime." (His connection with the dime is the reason the profile of Mercury was replaced by the profile of FDR after his death.)

*Missy posed for a picture in the mail room as dimes poured into the White House after the first March of Dimes broadcast in 1938.*

Missy posed for publicity photos that ran in newspapers all over the country, sitting at a desk covered with envelopes, laughing at two men with huge mail bags slung over their shoulders, holding up a shiny silver dime for the camera, but the work of counting the dimes was too much for the White House staff. The coins eventually were shipped off to the Treasury Department. The final tally: $268,000 in dimes, plus thousands in larger bills and checks. It took four months to clear the ocean of silver out of the White House.

During every visit to Warm Springs, Missy could see the results of the American public's donations to the polio fight. A three-story orthopedic surgical hospital opened in 1939 as well as an occupational therapy building. Patient enrollment surged from 267 patients in 1934 to more than 400 in 1941. The resulting employment creating an economic boom in Meriwether County. Missy could also observe the New Deal in action at Civilian Conservation Corps Camp No. 1429 adjoining the Foundation campus and the Pine Mountain Valley Project, a subsistence homestead community that moved people living on welfare to model farms. (It was a sister project of Arthurdale in West Virginia, one of Eleanor Roosevelt's most beloved New Deal causes.) These sights brought her White House labors to life, vividly reminding her that her long days of work were having a positive impact on people's lives.

After his 1932 election, FDR made fourteen visits to Warm Springs with Missy, and he dedicated something—from a chapel to a flagpole—on almost every trip. But the visits were also a time to escape the pressures of Washington, drive Missy around in his car with only a discreet Secret Service detail—or none, if he could evade it—talk to Otis Moore, the manager of his farm, eat the crispy Southern fried chicken of Little White House cook Daisy Bonner, and work on his stamp albums. And of course, even though he had long given up hope of walking again, he enjoyed daily swims in the buoyant waters of the Warm Springs pools and games of water football with the younger patients. Missy's home movies capture pool scenes such as Postmaster General James Farley looking like a gigantic beach ball, picnics with guests swigging from tiny bottles of Coca-Cola, and that rarest of images: FDR sitting in his wheelchair, a towel draped over his spindly legs.

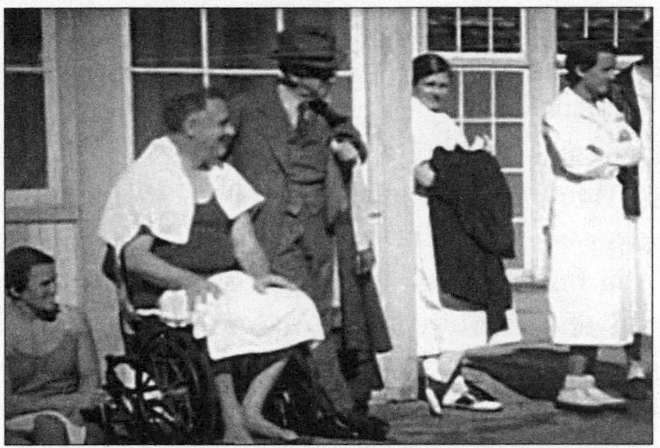

*Missy's home movie captured FDR in his wheelchair poolside in Warm Springs.*

Missy began devising social events for his vacations long before they left Washington, writing letters to invite friends and Foundation staff to lunch, dinner, or cocktails and planning elaborate picnics at Dowdell's Knob, with its spectacular panorama of Pine Mountain Valley. Missy, her silvery hair held back in a broad cloth band and smoking Lucky Strikes in an ivory cigarette holder like the one her boss used, moved easily among the guests. Surrounded by close friends and fellow polios on the knob, FDR wore his braces outside his pants and lounged on a bench seat removed from his car.

Crisp fall days spent by the fire in the Little White House or sitting on the ship's fantail-shaped back porch in the warm spring sunshine were the best times for Foundation officials to update the president on polio matters. Missy was always close by, a steno pad on her knee, taking down notes and chiming in with her own thoughts.

Sometimes FDR rounded up his own company. One day the Marine sentry behind the Little White House apprehended some Boy Scouts who had gotten lost while trying to earn their orienteering badge. The president invited them up for lemonade and cookies and a chat on his back porch. When the boys arrived home, their parents did not believe their tale of a late afternoon snack with the president—until FDR's departure from the train depot a few days later. Recognizing the boys, he called to them, "Maybe we can have ice cream next time!"

About twenty families, many of them very well-to-do people with a polio sufferer in the family such as the Lynn Piersons of Detroit and the Stuart Chevaliers of California, owned vacation homes near the Little White House. They were the sites of social gatherings, as was the home of Dr. C. E. Irwin, the Foundation medical director. At Irwin's home, FDR insisted on mixing the potent martinis. He was a shameless pusher, urging guests "How about another little sippy?"

Missy presided over the Little White House dinner table where local favorites such as collards, cornbread, and Country Captain—a spicy dish said to have forty-five ingredients besides the chicken—were served. Daisy Bonner concocted the delectable meals in a galley kitchen where the most modern appliance was the stove. There was no refrigerator; an icebox sat on the back porch. Sometimes the guests enjoyed fancier fare. When Joseph Kennedy curried favor with the president by shipping Maine lobsters to the Little White House, FDR had Missy send a jocular telegram: "THIS IS FIRST TIME LIVE LOBSTERS EVER FLEW TO PINE MOUNTAIN WE ARE INFORMING SMITHSONIAN."

Life at the Little White House was punctuated with FDR's corny jokes and pranks. On a freezing November day, he bundled Missy and Eleanor into his open car along with his long-suffering appointments secretary and drove to a site marked with a new sign: "The Marvin H. McIntyre Memorial Possum Reserve." It was a birthday gift that came complete with a deed—not quite a legal one but in the president's own hand. Eleanor reported that the president appeared to have gotten lost and had to consult his map, a sight that made Missy laugh with poke-out-her-tongue glee.

Naturally, the number of out-of-town visitors flocking to the tiny Georgia town increased exponentially after the 1932 election. "We have had three lovely days for sunbaths," Missy wrote her assistant Paula Tully in November 1933. "The whole world is gradually descending upon us but as long as we can stay in our corner—we will." Heads of state, ambassadors, cabinet members, advisors, reporters, favor seekers, and celebrities came, some for scheduled visits, others hoping to get a scoop or a few minutes of the president's time when he was less insulated by staff.

*FDR consults his map while taking his appointments secretary Marvin McIntyre and Missy on a ride at Warm Springs. Eleanor is also in the backseat.*

Even for a harried visiting head of state, Warm Springs held appeal. Canadian prime minister William Lyon Mackenzie King stayed at a guest cottage on the grounds one April. He joined the president for meals, posing for pictures with Canadian polio patients, and motoring around Pine Mountain with Roosevelt at the wheel. Even as the head of one of the most naturally beautiful countries in the world, Mackenzie King was struck by Warm Springs at Easter, with its flowering dogwood trees starring the hills and bright violets peeping out from under the pine trees. Missy presided over several meals the days he visited, and the prime minister retired for the night thoroughly exhausted, writing in his diary, "Felt I had had as enjoyable day as any in a very long time."

Aide Harry Hopkins recounted a typical day spent in the Little White House's combination dining and living room, where the maritime prints, ship models, and portrait of John Paul Jones had been joined by a hand-hooked rug on the living room floor featuring an NRA blue eagle. He described lunch with just Missy and the president as "the pleasantest because he is under no restraint and personal and public business is discussed with the utmost frankness." The day meandered along.

> The ceremonial cocktail with the President doing the honors—gin and grapefruit juice is his current favorite—and a vile drink it is! He makes a first rate "old fashioned" and a fair martini—which he should stick to—but his low and uncultivated taste in liquors leads him woefully astray. Missy and I will not be bullied into drinking his concoction which leads him to take three instead of his usual quota of two. . . . Dinner therefore is gay—as it should be—and the President reminisces long over the personal experiences of his life—he tells incidents well—tho he has a bad habit of repeating them every year or so. I fancy Missy has heard them all many times but she never flickers an eyebrow.

Roosevelt was a master of the embellishment, of course, which as all good storytellers know is different from lying: you lie to save your skin, but you embellish to entertain your friends.

This uneventful day was not the norm for a Warm Springs gathering. "Man, when FDR showed up, the party began," said Hal S. "Toby" Raper, whose physician father and physical therapist mother met as staff, married, and lived on the Warm Springs campus. One of FDR's and Missy's favorite local celebrities was Cason Callaway, a textile mill owner from LaGrange who had led the drive to build Georgia Hall, the main building on the Foundation campus. He and his wife, Virginia, owned Blue Springs, a beautiful retreat near a lake about fifteen miles from the Little White House. Missy was among the guests at a lively drinks, dinner, and dancing party there one night, the ladies taking turns sitting out dances with the paralyzed president. As the evening wore on and the level of hilarity rose, the guests repeatedly slid down the canvas fire escapes the Secret Service had rigged from the second-story windows, while the president egged them on from his chair.

The most important annual occasion for FDR—and the one he missed only twice during his presidency before America entered World War II—was the Founder's Day dinner held close to Thanksgiving in the Foundation dining room. It was a formal affair, with the patients gathered in their Sunday best, white linen on the tables, and the president wielding the carving knife on the turkey, a smiling Eleanor at one elbow (usually dropping in for just a day or two) and a polio patient at the other. The latter seat was a coveted one, determined by lottery. One year the winner was Ann Smithers, a seven-year-old Kentucky girl. "Ann was more excited over a pair of new shoes she had been promised than the fact she was to sit beside the president," reported the *Warm Springs Mirror*. With the plum seats taken, Missy was exiled to a distant spot in the dining room, but she was used to sitting "below the salt." The patients rehearsed for weeks to present post-dinner entertainments, such as a performance by the Polio-politan Opera Company and the singing of the "Warm Springs Blues":

> Oh, what's become of Hinky Dinky Palez Vous,
> Who danced the Rhumber and the Carioca, too?
> He isn't wearing army clothes
> For he's joined the Polios.
> Hinky Dinky Warm Springs Blues.

Although Eleanor smiled for the cameras at the Founder's Day dinner, she did not fit in with the prevailing party atmosphere. Writing from Warm Springs to daughter Anna, she confessed, "I always feel like a spoilsport & policeman here & at times elsewhere because I lost my temper last night." Her friend Nancy Cook was with her, and Eleanor felt FDR had deliberately gotten Nancy drunk by making her cocktails too strong. "I'm an idiotic puritan & I wish I had the right kind of sense of humor & could enjoy certain things," she lamented.

Missy, of course, had no problem letting her hair down. And at the end of every day, when all the guests had gone home, and the president had gotten his rubdown and was ready for bed, the only inhabitants of the Little White House were often Missy and F.D. The sun went down, the crickets chirped, and in the morning the whole circus started anew.

❁ CHAPTER FIFTEEN

# *Hubris and Hell*

Louis Howe was barely five feet tall and Franklin Roosevelt was six-foot-two in the early days of their political partnership. Polio knocked the Boss down to eye level, but they still didn't see eye-to-eye on many things. Even in the White House, Louis wasn't afraid to tell Franklin he was wrong and, on occasion, to just plain "go to hell." He was one of the few who dared.

When Louis died in his sleep on April 18, 1936, FDR pulled out all the stops, giving the little man a state funeral at the White House. Missy joined the presidential entourage that traveled to Fall River, Massachusetts, for the interment, though she had complained to Brain Truster Raymond Moley—who intentionally skipped the funeral—that Louis had mostly been a nuisance and mischief maker for some time. Even so, his death left only three close advisors unafraid to speak frankly to FDR: Moley, Missy, and Eleanor. Moley would soon be gone. Though he had not held an official post in the administration since the summer of 1933, he had been an advisor and speechwriter, entering FDR's office via Missy's to avoid notice by the press. However, he had grown more conservative since the early days, writing articles critical of the administration for the newsmagazine he had cofounded, *Today*.

It was a spring of transition. Missy's love Bill Bullitt was thoroughly disgusted with the Soviet Union, where Stalin was sending hundreds of thousands of people into exile in Siberia.

Ambassador to France Jesse I. Strauss was dying, and FDR had dangled the possibility of that embassy before Bullitt. He wanted it badly. In May Missy wrote to reassure him, blaming the delay on the "stodgy poky [State] Department." She also shared the thrilling news that she had won nearly $600 betting on Bold Venture, the winning horse in the Kentucky Derby, and was "feeling very rich." (Her win was worth more than $10,000 in current dollars.) Bullitt returned to Washington in June with few fond memories of Russia, although a tiny enameled Easter egg with the letters XB—Slavic for "Christ is Risen"—dangles from one of Missy's charm bracelets, almost certainly a souvenir from him.

While waiting for his appointment, Bullitt joined Roosevelt's reelection campaign in which he was facing Kansas governor Alfred M. Landon. Sam Rosenman, who had remained on the judicial bench in New York, came to the White House in late June to work on the nomination acceptance speech to be given in Philadelphia. One night FDR invited Moley, Rosenman, Tommy Corcoran, Missy, and a talented "phrase-maker" named Stanley High to a working dinner. For Rosenman, it was a most memorable occasion because "for the first and only time in my life, I saw the President forget himself as a gentleman." At the table, FDR began "twitting" Moley about his "new, rich friends" and his pro-business articles in *Today*. "Moley responded with what I thought was justifiable heat," Rosenman recalled. "The President grew angry, and the exchanges between them became very bitter. We all felt embarrassed; Missy did her best to change the subject but failed." Although Moley subsequently insisted that this argument was no worse than others with FDR, it signaled the end of their working relationship.

Nevertheless, they managed to come up with a fine speech, and the final night of the convention was a triumph, with over 100,000 people jamming the University of Pennsylvania stadium. The most memorable sentence, "This generation of Americans has a rendezvous with destiny," was Corcoran's contribution. FDR and Moley talked afterward, the old Brain Truster concluding that "Roosevelt would ultimately sweep his administration into the extreme positions that would expose it to the devastating counterattack of reaction. But that was his choice and his risk. . . . Now I was in a position to leave his service permanently and happily."

That left two "no men": FDR's wife, Eleanor, and his "office wife," Missy, both secure enough in their positions and convictions that they could frankly tell him things he did not want to hear. As usual, Eleanor spoke openly and caustically, Missy privately and diplomatically.

The presidential campaigns of the 1930s were nothing like the lengthy slogs of today. After the convention, FDR followed his usual summer practice of long vacations and relaxing weekends on the USS *Potomac*. Missy sounded out Harold Ickes about hosting the president for dinner at his country home, and FDR's jovial state of mind after the "coronation" was obvious when he arrived there with a small party that included Missy, Grace Tully, and Tommy Corcoran. They dined al fresco, FDR seated in Ickes's favorite chair. Ickes lovingly described the menu and drinks in his diary, right down to "my own special ice cream, black raspberry, with cookies and coffee to finish with." He observed, "The President certainly carries his liquor well. He must have had five highballs after dinner. He drank gin and ginger ale but he never showed the slightest effect." The group "stayed until half past twelve and then only after Miss LeHand prodded him two or three times and insisted that he must go home and go to bed."

The respite lasted until August, when the speechwriting got under way in earnest. Rosenman admired Missy's frank and spirited response during one of these sessions at the White House. They were listening to Treasury Secretary Henry Morgenthau droning out a speech he had written for a bankers' convention that he thought could be adapted for the president to deliver at a baseball stadium. Sam wrote, "The President realized right away that it would never do; however, he apparently was steeled to hear it to the end; Missy was not quite so polite. At the end of the second page, she stood up and with great firmness announced: 'By this time all of the bleachers are empty and folks are beginning to walk out of the grandstand.' As she sauntered out of the room, we all burst out laughing, including the Secretary of the Treasury himself. Further reading of the draft was discontinued."

Bullitt made a valuable contribution to the only campaign speech that dealt with foreign affairs. The militarism of the Japanese, Benito Mussolini in Italy, and Hitler in Germany was being viewed with much concern in the United States, although most Americans were resolutely isolationist. In the speech given in mid-August, FDR graphically described the human cost of conflict: "I have seen war. I have seen war on land and sea. I have seen blood running from the wounded. I have seen men coughing out their gassed lungs. I have seen the dead in the mud. I have seen cities destroyed. I have seen 200 limping, exhausted men come out of line—the survivors of a regiment of 1,000 that went forward 48 hours before. I have seen children starving. I have seen the agony of mothers and wives. *I hate war*." Neither he nor Bullitt had served in the military, but wrote and spoke of what they had seen as civilians visiting Europe during World War I. The phrase "I hate war" had been uttered to Bullitt by a tearful President Woodrow Wilson in 1917.

In late August, FDR gave Missy the go-ahead to "Tell Bill Bullitt he is going to Paris." The appointment was received with mixed feelings at the State Department, and Eleanor uttered a rare expletive. "Damnit!" she told Democratic Party chairman Jim Farley, who wanted the post, "That's just like Franklin."

Bullitt stayed in Washington until the end of September, attending Missy's White House birthday party on the 13th and presenting her with a puppy. (This may be the pooch named Aaron that Missy mentioned in a letter to the vacationing FDR in December, saying "he is housebroken at last, and is the sweetest puppy ever. He went to your door and cried but you were not there!") Missy had little time to pine for Bullitt, as she joined the campaign trains that carried FDR as far west as Wyoming and all over the Midwest and Northeast, laboring with the speechwriters and stenographers over draft after draft. Rosenman described the experience:

> The excitement and exhilaration are too absorbing to you to notice that you are not getting enough sleep, or that you never get your food at the right time, or that you do not get a chance to take a bath. . . . It is impossible to describe . . . the thrill of crowds of cheering people station after station, city after city, the applause of 10,000 enthusiastic rooters inside an auditorium or the shouts of 100,000 people in a ball park, the mounted police holding back the crowds as the cars parade through the streets, the excitement and rush of getting out one speech and starting almost immediately on the next, the few precious minutes of kidding and laughing as you gulp your food—and, in 1936, the look of hope and confidence on the faces of people who four years before were despondent and desperate.

Besides his opponent, FDR was attacked by his former ally Al Smith, newspaper baron William Randolph Hearst, and Father Charles Coughlin, the radio priest. All three accused him of being a communist sympathizer. Smith switched parties to endorse Landon, who he said could "suppress class warfare and revolution" in this country. Coughlin labeled FDR "the dumbest man ever to occupy the White House" and "anti-God." He began to reveal his anti-Semite stripes by carping about the president's Jewish advisors. Writing to Bullitt, Missy said, "I do feel very deeply about the fact that W.R.H. [Hearst] and Father Coughlin have such terrific obstructive power . . . and while I am always cynical about the intelligence of my fellow Americans I think I must always have hope. For the people who have convictions I have the greatest respect; for the sheep——." Missy and Ed Flynn, the Irish American Catholic party boss from the Bronx, told Ickes they were thinking of leaving the Church because of

Coughlin. "I do not think that either of them meant it seriously," Ickes wrote in his diary, "but it shows how deep the feeling is running, even among Catholics, over Coughlin's political activities."

FDR met his right-wing critics head-on in the final major speech of the campaign, given at Madison Square Garden on Halloween night. He identified the bogeymen of the Depression as practitioners of "business and financial monopoly, speculation, reckless banking, class antagonism, sectionalism, war profiteering" and declared, "I welcome their hatred." The prolonged ovations and clanging cowbells had to be thrilling to Missy, yet she wasn't convinced it was enough. Some polls had predicted a decisive victory for Landon, and Missy had almost cried when she left the White House for New York, believing she was about to lose her "home." Not to worry, consoled Jim Farley, correctly predicting FDR would carry every state except Vermont and Maine. When the votes were tallied November 4, FDR had won almost 61 percent of the popular vote and 523 electoral votes to Landon's eight, a record-setting landslide. As was his practice, FDR sat with Missy in the dining room of his mother's Hyde Park home, keeping a hand tally of the results. At 11 p.m., he signed his name with a flourish and gave the paper to Missy as a souvenir. Bullitt, back in Paris, sent her a proud telegram. "What do you think of my country today? Please give the President an enormous embrace for me and please give another to the American people."

FDR and company returned to Washington on November 6, where the Usher's Log at the White House bore a typed insert that began, "Fresh from the most complete public reassurance ever granted a President of the United States, Franklin Delano Roosevelt came home today like the conquering hero that he is." He breakfasted with Missy and his son James, who would shortly—and controversially—join the White House secretariat. Hubris, that heady feeling of exaggerated confidence so fatal to politicians, was a silent, gloating guest at the breakfast table.

"Wasn't the election swell?" Missy crowed in a note to her niece Babe Collins a few days later. "I did wish you could all have been with me that night although I was not conscious. I have two burns on my chin, and the only way I could have got them was to have rested the lighted end of my cigarette there." Her exhaustion had to be profound. There was no trip to Warm Springs that November, but Missy took Babe's sister, Barbara, who had recently separated from her husband, for "ten days of sleep and sunshine" at Joseph Kennedy's estate in Palm Beach, joined by James Roosevelt's wife, Betsey. She was able to relax because the president was off on another all-male cruise, this time to South America aboard the USS *Indianapolis*. The trip was marred by the unexpected loss of another staffer, the lovable bodyguard Gus Gennerich, who was only forty-nine when he died of a heart attack in Buenos Aires. FDR wrote Missy an unusually emotional letter about Gus, beginning "We are all feeling very low—since the tragedy of poor Gus' wholly unexpected death," and concluding, "Lots of love—I miss you much." "You know how upset we all are about Gus," Missy wrote from Palm Beach. "I hope it has not spoiled your trip." Gus, like Louis Howe, was accorded a White House funeral.

Missy did some Christmas shopping in New York, where Marion Davies, the actress and mistress of the chastened publisher William Randolph Hearst, invited her to have lunch at the Ritz, and spent a few days at the luxurious Greenbrier Hotel in West Virginia. Although Bullitt spent the holidays with his daughter in Florida, apparently he and Missy had some time together, for there is a definite afterglow in a short note she sent to him in Paris in early January: "You are an angel to be so sweet and I love you!" That year her correspondence with him continued to be affectionate, and they reconnected during long visits Bullitt made to Washington in March and October. The telephone connection from Paris was an improvement over Moscow, though Missy found the calls a poor substitute, as did Bullitt. "Dearest Lady," he wrote, "That last talk was tantalizing with Pres. Roosevelt and several others in the room; it was impossible to say anything." In some letters she would wistfully pretend herself to be with him, writing, "May I dine quietly with you tonight?"

There were few quiet dinners in Paris, where Bullitt was reveling in his role as ambassador at the largest and most glittering U.S. embassy in the world. He became famous for not only his diplomacy but the social scene he created as the "Champagne ambassador," including twice-weekly teas during tourist season, dinners almost every night, and elegant balls that lasted until 6 a.m. He once sent a caviar order to Moscow "that broke all records in the Moscow market," according to foreign correspondent Eric Sevareid. (Bullitt paid most of the entertainment expenses from his own pocket.) In addition to his embassy residence, Bullitt leased a château in Chantilly stocked with eighteen thousand bottles of wine. As in Moscow, rumors of female conquest swirled around him. According to a biographer of *Washington Herald* publisher Eleanor "Cissy" Patterson, he tried to convince her to marry him while she was visiting his embassy. Missy got wind of these things, and occasionally asked about the rumors. "Incidentally," she wrote, "Marguerite would like to know if she should stop thinking about you, and just save her pennies to buy a station wagon for your wedding present. Then the question would pop up as to a name for the beastly thing, and the only ones I can think of at the moment are not the kind that could be printed, so-o-o-o- put your mind to work. Seriously, tell me if it is true—I don't want it to be."

The White House social calendar was crammed that winter as the second term began. "This has been an absolutely mad month and a half," Missy wrote Bullitt in February, apologizing for forgetting his January 25 birthday. The inauguration, held for the first time on January 20 rather than in March, had been executed with the usual pomp and circumstance amid torrential downpours. Missy's family again came to town to enjoy the festivities. A few days before FDR's January 30 birthday, Missy ordered a Sky Pilot World Time Clock, described as "the first really new clock in over 500 years," as a gift. Eleanor had decided to make the Cuff Links Gang party a low-key affair, sending a note to Steve Early that she planned a simple dinner and poker party afterward "for the gentleman" as "None of us have the heart to get up the kind of party we used to have, when Louis was the moving spirit." She didn't count on the moving spirit of Steve and Harry Hopkins, who wrote a radio script spoofing the White House staff's reaction to devastating flooding in the Midwest that had killed hundreds of people. Steve and Harry voiced all the parts, which consisted of interviews broadcast by "station FDR." All were portrayed as goofing off during the crisis: Harry asleep in the Cabinet Room, Marvin McIntyre at a four-hour lunch, Steve playing golf.

Missy, the only woman in the story line, was described thus by Steve: "Miss LeHand is dressed in a smart morning outfit. She is wearing a corsage of petunias on her right hip—a trick she picked up in Palm Beach. She is reading—yes, folks, it's *Gone With the Wind*, for the third time. One fist is concealed in a box of Bon Bons. . . . She has just placed an osculation on the ready lips of Joe Kennedy. Here she is folks."

Harry voiced Missy: "I do want the public to know we are doing everything we can to get the Missouri River diverted into the Ohio. If we can only get water into the Ohio, I can go on with my book. And then I have Joe on my hands. He was on the President's hands for almost two years, but he is now resigned to me. I think the flood is very exciting, but I object to having Harry Hopkins sleeping in the Cabinet room, it upsets me." The last word in the skit went to White House physician Ross McIntire, who declared "the reason the President keeps his health is that he is able to laugh." FDR didn't go to bed until almost 4 a.m., and no word of the callous nature of the birthday skit reached the press.

The staff probably looked back on that night with fondness, for the rest of 1937 wasn't much fun for anyone. Feeling empowered by his landslide win, FDR launched a bruising and politically costly assault on the Supreme Court; the economy plunged into the "Roosevelt recession," when an ill-timed budget balancing program caused the stock market to crash and the unemployment rate to shoot back up; and James Roosevelt proved a poor replacement for Howe as well as a lightning rod for charges—some justified—that he used his influence to line his pockets. William Douglas, by then chairman of the Securities and Exchange Commission, offered his resignation to FDR over what he considered a clear case of influence peddling by his son. He recalled that the president "put his head on his arm and cried like a child for several minutes," finally sighing, "Jimmy! What a problem he is! Thanks for telling me. Now get back to your desk. Of course you're not resigning."

It was also a year of tremendous labor unrest and sit-down strikes, in which employees occupied the work premises so strikebreakers could not replace them. FDR personally intervened in a strike at General Motors, where the United Auto Workers won a huge victory and began a stranglehold on the American auto industry. At the Hershey Chocolate Company, however, a minority of pro-union strikers were driven from the Pennsylvania plant by anti-union employees and pitchfork-wielding dairy farmers desperate to sell the milk that went into candy bars.

Personal woes mounted. Missy spent three weeks in the hospital with a blood clot in her leg. Harold Ickes had a heart attack. Harry's wife died of breast cancer, leaving their six-year-old daughter, Diana, in his distracted care, and he entered the Mayo Clinic where he underwent surgery for stomach cancer. It didn't kill him, but he suffered debilitating digestive problems until his death in 1946.

FDR's so-called court-packing scheme was the biggest miscalculation of his political career. Following quiet meetings with his staff and advisors, he assembled the cabinet in early February to present a bill, written by Attorney General Cummings, that would enable him to appoint a new member of the court for every member over age seventy—currently six appointees. The obvious targets were conservative members of the court who had gutted New Deal legislation. The bill caused an uproar, followed by months of legislative battling and brinkmanship. Writing to Bullitt in the summer of 1937, Missy said, "I have never seen the President in better form . . . he loves a battle!" But it was one he would lose.

By then Missy was back at work after fighting the blood clot in her leg during "three endless weeks" at Doctors Hospital in New York. Her main concern was that the press would discover she was a patient before she could get word to FDR. She registered under an assumed name. Grace and Mary Eben came from Washington to stay with her, and the Sam Rosenmans, the Basil O'Connors, and other New York friends rallied around. "I have a lovely room that looks out over the East River and the Triborough Bridge," she wrote FDR, assuring him she would be back at the White House in a few days. They dined alone in his room four nights running after she returned. This may have been the time when he sent her a little note that she put in her scrapbook: "MAL Can I dine with you or will you dine with me? 7:30 FDR." This joined others of her favorite "chits," as the little notes on scrap paper were called, such as "Where is $1,000,000 for wildlife."

For Missy, the biggest blow of her illness was missing graduation exercises at Rosary College (present-day Dominican University) in Illinois, where she was slated to receive an honorary doctor of laws degree. Fortunately, an alternative was found. "I am delighted that arrangements can be made for this conferring of the degree here in Washington," she wrote to Sister Thomas Aquinas of the college, "and I cannot tell you how much I appreciate this great honor." The picture of Missy in academic robes, accepting the diploma in a June ceremony in the Blue Room as the president and first lady, two severely attired nuns, and a priest in clerical collar looked on, was distributed by the Associated Press. It surely helped dispel any perception among Catholics that FDR was the "anti-God" leader that Father

Coughlin claimed him to be, and added to Missy's efforts to encourage church leaders to muzzle the angry priest.

*Missy accepted an honorary doctorate from Rosary College in 1937, with the Roosevelts looking on.*

She created an "open-door policy" for Catholic clerics, Elliott Roosevelt observing that because of her "A cardinal or other Catholic dignitary was seldom refused a White House appointment." Among the most frequent callers was Archbishop, later Cardinal, Francis Spellman, whom FDR called "my favorite Bishop." The Italian cardinal Eugenio Pacelli called on the president when he and Missy were at Hyde Park in 1936; three years later he became Pope Pius XII and sent a coronation medal to her via Joe Kennedy, whose attendance at the ceremony she had helped to arrange.

With the Supreme Court fight at its height, FDR did not decamp from Washington as he usually did during the scorching days of July, and the White House staff was in a state of extreme jitters. Harold Ickes gave a press conference July 25 in which he was asked his position on the court issue. He said he supported a Constitutional amendment to govern court structure, but in the meantime he favored the president's legislation. Press stories focused only on his support for an amendment, upsetting Missy, "who is very nervous and sensitive these days because she is so close to the president." Ickes spent a day reassuring her and Steve Early he was still in their camp, even sending over a transcript from the press conference. Missy was at the peak of her influence, and Ickes agonized that he would lose her confidence and, with it, the access she gave him to FDR.

By the end of summer, Supreme Court reform was dead, defeated by a coalition of Republicans and disloyal Democrats that Corcoran called "Copperheads," a term that dated back to Abraham Lincoln and disloyal Republicans during the Civil War. FDR would spend the next year exacting revenge on these political snakes, trying to purge them in the 1938 midterm elections. He was notably unsuccessful, even costing himself support in Georgia, where he targeted the unsinkable Senator Walter George.

After the frustrating summer of 1937, Corcoran told Ickes "he didn't think there had been anyone whom [FDR] could really talk to except his son Jimmy and Miss LeHand," and the toll on his health and emotions was evident. Missy confided to Ickes "she didn't see how any man should want eight years of the Presidency, that she didn't see how anyone could stand it." The one bright spot for the White House was that Justice Willis Van Devanter announced his retirement, opening the door for the appointment of a more amenable successor. FDR nominated Alabama senator Hugo Black, who would serve for more than thirty years as a dependable liberal voice on the court, even though he had been elected in 1926 with the support of the Ku Klux Klan. The following year, he filled another vacancy with Felix Frankfurter, with Missy's full support.

In November Missy and Betsey Roosevelt again availed themselves of Joe Kennedy's Palm Beach home while the president went on a stag fishing cruise. She spent a few days at Christmas with her family, during which time the train case Eleanor had just given her and a diamond ring from both Roosevelts were stolen from her car. The ring was recovered two months later at a Boston pawnshop, but Missy filed a claim for the train case with James Roosevelt's insurance company, where her niece Barbara worked.

In the quiet days before the New Year and the White House social season began, Missy assisted FDR with a very important task: writing his funeral arrangements. He dictated his wish to be buried with Eleanor in his mother's rose garden at Springwood, with "a plain white monument" marking their graves.

Earlier in the year, they had begun discussing another way to build his legacy at Hyde Park. It came up one evening while they were working and FDR began ruminating, according to Grace Tully, on "the enormous number of things he had accumulated over the years and the problem of where to house them. . . . That night was born the idea of erecting a library building at Hyde Park."

❁ CHAPTER SIXTEEN

# *Missy Knows*

Missy got a late Christmas gift from *The Saturday Evening Post,* which printed a long and flattering profile of her in its January 8, 1938, issue, written by the political reporter Doris Fleeson. The story was called "Missy—To Do This F.D.R.," taking its title from one of the chits handed her by the president. Fleeson described Missy as a "Jill-of-All-Trades" in the anecdote-rich article, illustrated with pictures of her both at work, looking serious and businesslike, and in an evening gown with a plunging back, "looking very handsome, as evening dress is especially becoming to her."

It ended with a tantalizing list of scenarios interspersed with the sentence "Missy knows." "How did the president bear up during the great war on the depression? . . . When did congressional leaders begin to rebel at rubber-stamping Roosevelt measures? . . . Why have the brain trusters slipped away?" Someone had copies of the article bound into slim blue books with the title stamped in gold, which Missy gave to family members.

But the details of Missy's intimate relationship with the president apparently still raised eyebrows and set tongues to wagging. Syndicated columnist Edith Johnson weighed in with "What Do Women Think of 'Missy'?" Women over forty-five years of age probably won't believe that such a relationship could be purely platonic, she opined, while younger ones would believe it could. She counted herself in the latter camp, adding,

"In all Washington, the most gossipy city in the country, she is above suspicion. Superficially the most modern of modern women, she actually is like the old-fashioned wife and mother, sacrificing herself on the altar of duty and service. For her work has taken the place of husband and children and her office is her home."

*This 1935 Bachrach portrait of Missy shows how she could turn on the glamour.*

Also enjoying some positive press was the newest member of the ambassadorial ranks: Joe Kennedy went to London. Shortly after his arrival, *Life* magazine ran a two-page photo spread showcasing every Kennedy child from handsome, athletic Joe Jr. to freckle-faced Teddy, proclaiming them "the most politically ingratiating family since Theodore Roosevelt's." Kennedy found immediate common ground with Prime Minister Neville Chamberlain, as both were anxious to avoid war with Germany at almost any cost. "Joe is a different human being, completely released mentally," Missy wrote to Bullitt, "and of course the country is saved again for a time!"

Like Kennedy, Bill Bullitt had isolationist views, even after Hitler annexed Austria in March. In a conversation with Harold Ickes, he correctly predicted that Hitler would next claim Czechoslovakia, General Francisco Franco would prevail in the Spanish Civil War, Mussolini would "find Ethiopia a great financial burden," and that the Chamberlain government would retain power in Great Britain. "Bullitt thinks that the civilized world is in one of its great upheavals," Ickes wrote. "He is strongly for the United States keeping out of European embroilments."

Missy spent a good deal of time with Bullitt during his six-week visit to the United States in the spring, but once he returned she begged off on a trip to France, citing the need to pay for a divorce for her niece Barbara. "I want to see you more than I want to do anything on earth, and to spend some time with you at Chantilly sounds like heaven on earth. Please understand, and please let me go over next spring or summer," she wrote. Instead, she and Grace Tully traveled with the president's train to the West Coast, where he departed for a cruise to the Galápagos Islands. The women stayed at Lake Louise in the Canadian Rockies, and Missy boasted of catching a fifteen-pound salmon in Puget Sound. Meanwhile, Ickes, who at age sixty-four had eloped with twenty-five-year-old Jane Dahlman, visited Paris on his honeymoon, where Bullitt hosted the curmudgeon and his pretty redheaded bride at the embassy. "How Ickes accomplished that is beyond me," he wrote FDR.

By late summer James Roosevelt had wilted in the pressure cooker of the White House and checked into the Mayo Clinic for treatment of an ulcer. He had surgery in September—meeting a nurse who would become his second wife—and resigned to work for Metro-Goldwyn-Mayer in California. Betsey, who got full custody of their two daughters, continued to be a favorite of FDR's and a frequent visitor to the White House. Though she was fond of Betsey, Missy eventually disapproved of her hard partying. "She looks awfully tired, but so would anyone who spends time doing the night clubs and cafes of New York," she wrote Bullitt. "She needs a spanking."

The Roosevelts retreated to Hyde Park in late September for a few weeks' rest. During a picnic at Val-Kill Cottage, a major chasm was revealed in Eleanor's relationship with Marion Dickerman and Nancy Cook. Eleanor's alcoholic brother, Hall, was a guest, with his son Danny. Drunkenly horsing around with the boy, Hall accidentally broke Danny's collarbone. While Missy called the emergency room in Poughkeepsie, Hall decided to drive Danny there himself. Marion climbed into the car with them at the request of the frightened boy, and Hall landed the car in a ditch at the end of the driveway. A highway patrol officer witnessed the wreck and took them all to the hospital.

What happened next was as out of character as it was disturbing. Eleanor flew into a rage, called Marion at the hospital and accused her of wrecking the car. Reeling, Marion returned to her room at Val-Kill Cottage, where Missy knocked on the door late that evening, sent by FDR. Again acting as go-between for FDR to patch up things for his wife, she said he knew what had happened and did not want Marion to feel hurt. Eleanor never apologized, and her long friendship and business relationships with Marion and Nancy slowly withered away. Eleanor took over the old Val-Kill factory building and had it remodeled into a home for herself.

FDR, too, was creating a new home for himself at Hyde Park. He and cousin Daisy Suckley had carried on an intense correspondence since the earliest days of his presidency, her letters funneled to him through Missy, who was well aware of their intimate friendship. On drives in his car they had found a spot on Dutchess Hill with a lovely view, and it was there he was building Top Cottage. As usual, Missy was seeing to many of the details, including answering a letter from a young Bronx woman who saw a story about his "dream house"—a label he detested—and asked for a job as a housekeeper. "I am a young girl, a brunette, and I stand 5 ft. 5 ½ inches without shoes, and I wear glasses," she wrote. "The only reference I can give you in this case is my love for your home and cleanliness, and my urge to serve you in any respect. . . . P.S. Please do not let the fact that I am from New York make any difference." Missy wrote a rather frosty response that the president "will not be in need of any additional service of the kind you mention."

Broken friendships and home construction paled in significance that fall as Europe seemed to be hurtling toward war. In late September British prime minister Chamberlain, French premier Édouard Daladier, Hitler, and Mussolini signed a pact that handed over to Germany a part of Czechoslovakia called the Sudetenland. Bullitt returned to Washington in October for meetings with FDR, joining other voices to convince him that the United States needed to immediately step up airplane production in the event that France and Britain were drawn into war. Missy was doubtless present on many of these occasions, and while there is no record of her thoughts, she may have shared during a Children's Hour this bit of black humor sent to her by Bullitt's private secretary, Carmel Offie:

> One night Hitler, Mussolini, and President Roosevelt were dining together. Mussolini remarked, during the course of the dinner: "Gentlemen, I am pleased to inform you that I shall soon be the ruler of the world." Mr. Hitler replied, "You will not. I shall soon be the ruler of the world." Mr. Mussolini folded his arms and replied, "And by whose help?" And Hitler, with that mystic look on his face, and throwing his fist into the air, said: "By the help of God." President Roosevelt, who happened to be munching on a chicken bone at the time, suddenly looked up and said: "I will not!"

No one was chuckling after November 9, 1938, when Nazi storm troopers attacked German and Austrian Jews in what became known as Kristallnacht or the Night of Broken Glass. In reaction to the assassination of a minor German diplomat in Paris by a Jewish man, thousands of shops, homes, and synagogues were destroyed, Jews were attacked and murdered, and tens of thousands were arrested and sent to concentration camps. Tommy Corcoran's legal eagle sidekick Ben Cohen sent a memo to Missy with a report from prominent American Jewish rabbi Stephen S. Wise containing disturbing eyewitness details. He suggested she show it to the president. Cohen also drafted a radio speech for Ickes that criticized Hitler's treatment of the Jews. FDR called Ambassador Hugh Wilson home from Berlin for consultation and issued a statement including the words, "I myself could scarcely believe that such things could occur in a twentieth century civilization." Wilson never went back, and though the United States remained neutral, FDR was clearly on the side of Europe's threatened democracies. In his 1939 State of the Union address, he said, "At the very least, we can and should avoid any action, or any lack of action, which will encourage, assist or build up an aggressor."

The White House inner circle underwent significant changes in the next few months. With James Roosevelt gone and Marvin McIntyre in an Asheville tuberculosis sanitarium, FDR tapped Edwin M. "Pa" Watson into the secretariat. Watson had long been his White House military aide, frequent fishing cruise companion, and steady arm when he executed his "political walk." A large, jovial man whose bonhomie veiled a sharp mind, Watson retired from active duty and joined the staff as a civilian. Harry Hopkins became secretary of commerce, a position that FDR hoped to use to groom him as his successor. Missy was familiar with and fond of both men, and Eleanor and Harry were great friends, Eleanor having made Harry's, daughter, Diana, her ward after his wife died and Harry fell ill. The first lady was fearful that spring that FDR was contemplating a third term, and told Hopkins she was "personally anxious not to have [him] run again."

What was occupying Eleanor's mind for much of that spring, however, was the upcoming visit of King George VI and Queen Elizabeth, the first British monarchs to visit the United States. FDR had proffered the invitation in the fall of 1938, and hoped the attractive young monarchs' visit would chip away at some of the isolationism in the country. Preparations consumed much of official Washington and drove White Housekeeper Henrietta Nesbitt into a frenzy, especially after she received a detailed memo from Ambassador Bullitt about the proper care and feeding of royal guests. His suggestions included hot water bottles in their beds, "a large solid table" for cleaning the king's shoes, "light, but warm blankets with a silk cover," "quantities of hand towels," an ever-ready supply of hot tea, and ham sandwiches whenever the sovereigns returned to their quarters after midnight. Bullitt, who supplied wine and Champagne for all the meals during the state visit, fully appreciated the ridiculousness of his list, sending it to FDR with the observation "I expect you to decorate me at once with the Order of the Royal Bathtub."

The hot water bottles and warm blankets were superfluous, as the king and queen arrived in Washington on Thursday, June 8, during a heat wave. The Roosevelts, in formal dress, met them at Union Station and paraded them through the sweltering streets to the White House, where Missy and a few select staff people waited to greet them. Hundreds of citizens who had lined the streets since dawn fainted in the heat and the soldiers on the White House lawn lay down under the trees, scrambling to their feet just as the cars arrived. Grace Tully observed that the king, in full military uniform, "could not have been more wretched had he been encased in a suit of armor." A select company of fifteen gathered for luncheon, just the president and first lady, Canadian prime minister William Lyon Mackenzie King, three members of the royal entourage, James, Elliott, and Franklin Roosevelt Jr. with their wives—and Missy. The queen's attendant, Lady Katharine Seymour, told a reporter what a surprise Missy was, in her flowered chiffon dress and picture hat. "I was naturally interested in a woman who was performing such an important job for the President," she said. "I had an idea that she would have no time for smart dress and would be quite worn-down. But she was gay and smiling, leisure-mannered and glamorous." That afternoon, Missy and her picture hat joined a throng of 1,400 guests at a garden party at the British embassy, and that evening she was seated across from James Roosevelt at the White House state dinner.

Harold Ickes's young wife, Jane, heavily pregnant and "shrouded in a mandarin garment tentlike enough to cover the acreage," remarked in a letter to the president's daughter on what "genuine, nice, gallant people" the royals were. (Her husband, somewhat less chivalrous, said the royal couple "looked like pygmies beside the towering Roosevelts.") Jane also weighed in on the terrific heat they were enduring. "Anna, I give you my word that it must have been 97 or 98 in that place. If I ever see your father, I have ready for delivery a short but concise dissertation upon why the White House should be air-conditioned NOW." The only event Missy did not attend while the royals were in Washington was a formal dinner Friday night at the British embassy, but most of the cabinet was excluded from that guest list, too. Before the queen departed for the dinner, Harry Hopkins's starry-eyed daughter, Diana, was presented to her, and recalls Elizabeth looking "breathtaking" in her tiara and spangled tulle gown.

After a day at the New York World's Fair, where the queen hugged the Dionne Quintuplets and a souvenir hunter stole the king's hat, the royals spent the weekend at Hyde Park. The president's mother was beside herself—especially after a series of catastrophes involving clumsy butlers, broken china, and shattered glassware that Eleanor gleefully shared in her daily newspaper column—but the big news-making event was a hot dog picnic at the recently completed Top Cottage. Some Americans were outraged that the Roosevelts would serve such homely fare, even on a silver salver, but King George gamely ate a dog and amused himself by making home movies.

Missy leaves no record of her thoughts and impressions of the visit, but Harry Hopkins wrote the president a sweet note about a late night conversation the three of them shared: "And one day two nice people came to visit you—he was a king—and I hope will be a king for a long time and she was a Scotch girl who got to be a Queen. And after dinner that night you and Missy and I talked it all over till 2 a.m." One of Missy's prized possessions was a pair of autographed photographic portraits of the king and queen in custom leather frames that she gave pride of place in her sitting room. As the granddaughter of Irish peasants, she had indeed come far.

*Missy cherished the framed portraits given her by the king and queen of England during their 1939 visit.*

During the summer months that followed, Missy stayed around Washington or traveled with the president. Once again, she had begged off from a trip to France to visit Bill Bullitt, but he made a quick visit home in mid-June to consult his doctor about a shoulder injury. He correctly predicted Germany's next move, telling Ickes that Germany would "move troops up to the Polish border, prepared to do in Poland just what she did in Czechoslovakia." He thought the attack could come as soon as July.

Congress was as ornery as ever. Even in the afterglow of the British state visit, it refused to modify the Neutrality Act and very little else got accomplished, with the exception of amendments to the Social Security Act. The needs of children crippled by polio were ever on FDR's mind, but the amendments passed in early August had a broader focus. A new program was created for children who had heart damage as a result of rheumatic fever. Ultimately, federal-state partnerships were developed in twenty-nine states to serve these young "cardiac cripples," the sort of program that would have greatly helped fifteen-year-old Marguerite LeHand during her own bout of illness.

Another minor victory was keeping William Douglas in his job as chairman of the Securities and Exchange Commission, a good example of the "tag-teaming" FDR and Missy had perfected. Douglas had raised the ire of the president of Bank of America, a major contributor to the Democratic Party, by investigating suspected stock manipulations, and a committee from the New York Stock Exchange was after his head. Missy called him one night and asked him to come to Hyde Park where the committee had an appointment with FDR at noon the following day. "They are coming up here to have him fire you!" she said. Douglas caught a train, arriving two hours ahead of the meeting, and filled in the time by hiking around Hyde Park. Walking through a tunnel, he was almost crushed by a truck, an experience he shared with FDR and the committee when he arrived at Springwood.

"Roosevelt took my story as a cue to filibuster the committee," Douglas recalled, and spent the next half hour in a rambling discourse on "the hazards of travel. . . . He went on and on, lighting one cigarette after another. Then, at twelve-thirty, Missy walked in, saying, 'Sorry, Mr. President, but your next appointment is waiting.'" The committee members, who had never gotten a chance to open their mouths, were hustled out the door, FDR assuring them, "Be sure to come up any time anything bothers you." He gave Douglas a wink. Stopping by

Missy's desk on the way out, Douglas told her "that apparently the committee had changed its mind about having me fired!"

August 1939 brought two personal blows for Missy. Her niece Barbara was injured in a wreck and Missy spent ten days at her hospital bedside. Then her brother Bernard died, "a terrific shock—I flew to Boston but arrived an hour too late. The five days following were killing," she wrote Bullitt. She took a short cruise, bringing Barbara along, but said it "did not help much." By late August she was back in the White House, where "Herr Hitler (or Chamberlain) is keeping me tied to my desk."

Bullitt's secretary, Carmel Offie, had begun writing long letters to Missy, serving as a mouthpiece for his boss. "I have never known the boss to be more sad and longing as he has been the past three weeks," he wrote in early August. Bullitt, he said, wanted to come home. "In a way you are responsible in part for this," he continued, confiding that Bullitt continuously badgered him for letters from Missy in the diplomatic pouch. Was Bullitt really lovelorn, or was he exploiting Missy's affection to fish for a new post in Washington? "If you want to have a word of some kind from her," Offie told him, "we have twenty-four hour telephone service from Washington."

CHAPTER SEVENTEEN

# War

The ringing of Missy's bedside phone jarred her awake sometime after two on the morning of Friday, September 1, 1939. Bullitt's familiar voice was on the line from Paris, but his words were terse rather than playful; he was relaying from American ambassador to Poland Anthony Biddle the news the world had dreaded: the Germans had attacked Poland. He needed to talk to FDR right away. Could she authorize the switchboard operator to wake him?

Thus Missy became the first person in the White House to learn that World War II had begun. The standing instruction to the graveyard shift switchboard operator was not to interrupt the president's sleep without getting his personal secretary's okay. Missy hastily dressed and hurried downstairs to his bedroom. There, they listened, grim-faced, as Bullitt conveyed the news that the German army and air force were butchering the Poles with the first of the attacks to become known as a Blitzkrieg, or "lightning war."

"Well, Bill, it has come at last," the president said. "God help us all." On a dime, the focus of FDR's presidency turned from the New Deal to the war in Europe. His actions in the years to come would define him as the most significant president of the twentieth century.

Roosevelt grabbed a blunt pencil and hastily scratched out a chit: "The President received word at 2:50 a.m. by telephone from Ambass. Biddle through Ambass. Bullitt that Germany has invaded Poland and that four cities are being bombed. The Pres. directed that all Navy ships and army commands be notified by radio at once. In bed 3:05 a.m. Sept. 1 '39 FDR."

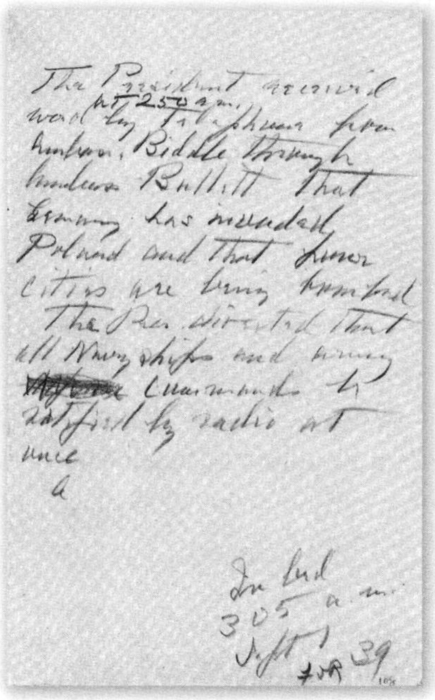

The President received
at 2:50 a.m.
word by telephone from
Ambass. Biddle through
Ambass. Bullitt that
Germany has invaded
Poland and that four
cities are being bombed
The Pres. directed that
all Navy ships and army
commands be
notified by radio at
once

In bed
3:05 a.m.
Sept 1 39
FDR

*FDR's note about Germany's attack on Poland, which launched World War II, was placed by Missy in her scrapbook.*

The chit found its way into Missy's scrapbook. When Grace Tully answered her phone around 7 a.m., the "very tired voice" of Missy was on the line: "Grace, I'm sorry to bother you at this hour but I wonder if you can come down shortly and take over for me. Germany has invaded Poland and the President and I have been up most of the night. I'm going to try to catch a little sleep soon because we are in for some hectic days." Grace arrived within the hour and took over fielding messages from abroad and home. She had no specific recollection of that day, other than that it was "crisp and businesslike . . . the first day of pressure-packed years which continued until after Mr. Roosevelt's death in 1945."

At his press conference later that morning, Roosevelt was asked if he had any reassuring words for Americans about the United States staying out of the war. He replied, "Only this, that I not only sincerely hope so, but I believe we can; and that every effort will be made by the Administration so to do." The Polish army, consisting mostly of cavalry wielding antiquated weapons, was hopelessly outmatched. In an account by Winston Churchill, "In two days the Polish air power was virtually annihilated. Within a week the German armies had bitten deep into Poland. Resistance everywhere was brave but vain, and by the end of a fortnight the Polish Army, nominally of about two million men, ceased to exist as an organized force." As inadequate as the Polish defense was, America's was not much better: the standing army was smaller than Romania's and equipped with uniforms and weapons left over from World War I.

On September 3, Britain and France declared war on Germany. Russia, allied with Germany, began attacking Poland from the east, and set its sights on Finland. Despite his reassuring words, Roosevelt reactivated efforts to repeal the Neutrality Act, which prevented the United States from offering aid to nations at war, be they aggressors or victims.

The intense atmosphere at the White House carried a personal cost for Missy. Still reeling from her brother Bernard's unexpected death in August, she also lost one of her beloved aunts, Emma McCarthy, the first week in September. Missy made a quick trip to Potsdam to pay her respects but didn't stay for the funeral "because of the present world crisis," the local newspaper said. Harold Ickes gives us an idea of the pressure she was under. On September 9 he wrote in his diary, "Missy is really a big woman. She sees the issues that are involved and she is so close to the President that she is in a position to keep him steady at times when he needs advice. The President is the kind of a person who needs help of this sort from someone very close to him." A day later he said Missy was going at the president "hammer and tongs" about Harry Woodring, the secretary of war, widely thought to be the weakest member of his cabinet. Yet FDR hated to fire people, and it would take him another nine months to replace Woodring.

The dire news in Europe did not prevent the White House "family" from gathering for a prolonged dinner to celebrate Missy's forty-third birthday on September 13. Steve Early reminded her she owed him a Pinch bottle of Scotch over a wager she had lost and forgave the debt as a birthday gift. The president didn't go to bed until 2:00 a.m.

The diplomatic pouch from Paris the week after the attack contained a typically droll letter to Missy from Bullitt's secretary, Carmel Offie. He suggested Louise Hackmeister, the sexy chief switchboard operator, come over to do espionage work. "We'll give Hacky a job as seductress of Adolf Hitler to whom we will send her as the perfect Aryan." But then he turned serious. "What they're doing to the Poles is horrible, incredible and terrible," he wrote. "Attila could teach the Germans today absolutely nothing." Missy wrote back a few days later, admitting "I should like to be in Paris for the Fireworks. I know that doesn't sound intelligent, but I really would." Offie said he believed the French and British would lose the war unless the United States would sell them planes and antiaircraft guns. Missy replied, "The President made his speech to Congress yesterday [September 21] and we are now sitting with our fingers crossed hoping the so-called 'peace bloc'"—a group of congressional isolationists—"will not be able to defeat the work on the Neutrality Bill."

Bullitt told Roosevelt flatly that "It is, of course, obvious that if the Neutrality Act remains in its present form, France and England will be defeated rapidly." He began lobbying for a cabinet position, preferably secretary of war, but also offered his services to the campaign to nominate FDR for a third term the following year. Congress amended the Neutrality Act in early November, repealing the arms embargo against victims of aggressors, but requiring combatant nations to pay cash for their purchases upon delivery and convey them in ships flying their own flags. In short, it was a "cash and carry" policy.

*Bill Bullitt and his secretary Carmel Offie, shown at the U.S. Embassy in Paris, kept the White House apprised of the German advance.*

After that, things relaxed a bit. Europe entered the period known as the "phony war," when there was a break in Hitler's aggression. The cornerstone for the presidential library at Hyde Park was laid on November 19, Missy bursting with pride as FDR slathered on the cement with a trowel and dedicated his library-to-be "in this time of strife . . . to the spirit of peace." A few days later Missy and the core staff joined the Roosevelts on the train to Warm Springs, where they enjoyed the Founder's Day dinner on Thanksgiving. (As usual, Eleanor returned to Washington early.) Missy left the White House for a few days at Christmas but didn't go home. There's no record of where she spent her holidays, but at any rate she was back at work on December 26. That night, *Gone with the Wind* was screened for Eleanor and a number of guests in the second-floor hall of the White House, but FDR, Missy, and Grace Tully worked until almost midnight in Missy's apartment. FDR was trying to sleep while the movie was still going on, and "complained vociferously about the amount of time Sherman was taking to win the Battle of Atlanta," according to actress Olivia de Havilland, who played Melanie Wilkes in the film.

That battle ended, but the battle for the White House had begun. In December two men announced their candidacy, Vice President Jack Garner for the Democrats and New York district attorney Thomas E. Dewey for the Republicans. FDR's relationship with Garner was so strained by then that he joked at a cabinet meeting, "I see that the Vice President has thrown his bottle—I mean his hat—into the ring." Similarly, Harold Ickes greeted the thirty-seven-year-old Dewey's announcement with the comment he had "thrown his diaper into the ring."

A more serious contender on the Democratic side was Postmaster General Jim Farley, a backslapping master of politicking, but he had no foreign experience and was Roman Catholic. The first was a drawback with a war brewing, the second a practical consideration: FDR was sure Farley would meet the same fate as Al Smith in 1928. Secretary of State Cordell Hull, another possible candidate, had the foreign experience, but disliked politicking. Harry Hopkins's health had declined precipitously over the previous months, to the point where he seldom left his home or the hospital. He was out of the running.

FDR was maddeningly mum on his own intentions. He accepted a post-presidency position as a contributing editor at *Collier's* magazine at a handsome $75,000 a year, which seemed to indicate he planned to retire. But he neither stated publicly that he would run nor that he would not. At the Gridiron Club dinner in December, newsmen rolled out an eight-foot papier-mâché head of FDR as the Sphinx, complete with cigarette holder. The image was showing up regularly in editorial cartoons.

In January 1940, Missy indicated in a letter to her niece Babe Collins that she expected she would be leaving the White House in a year. "I hope before we leave Washington you and Tom [Babe's husband] can come down again. I've had some things done to my room and I'd like you to see it before I have to tear it up," she wrote. "That will break my heart." Likewise, she sent

Bullitt a greeting on his birthday, "my day of complete joy," that included the words, "at this time next year, heaven knows where we will be! Wherever we are I hope I shall be thinking (as I do today) 'A Happy Birthday to you, darling.' " Bullitt instructed Missy to "Please pat God fifty-eight times on the bald spot for me" in honor of FDR's fifty-eighth birthday on January 30.

Missy wrote the president a poem for his birthday titled "Do You Choose to Run, Mr. R.?," wondering if she needed to "put out to Jim Farley/A friendly sort of feeler?/This thing is awfully hard on me/Relieve my doubts and fears/And tell me, please, who I must see/To renew my lease for four more years!"

A couple of days later, Harold Ickes confided to his diary that Missy had told his wife, Jane, "that the President was very tired and was really looking forward to retiring at the end of the year" but that "She wants the president to run again. In discussing the Democratic candidates for President with FDR, the latter told 'Missy' that 'God will provide a candidate.' Her retort was that God had better get busy pretty soon." In an interview with a local newspaper during a trip home in February, Missy was quoted as saying she hoped FDR ran for reelection because she liked her $5,000 a year job. The comment drew a smirking riposte from an editorial writer: "We could name a lot of other third-termers whose reason is the same. But not another who will admit it." In a subsequent interview, Missy said her words had been twisted and insisted she was just a secretary and never talked to FDR about personal or political matters.

Bullitt returned from Paris in February to report on the situation in Europe and continue lobbying for a cabinet post. Joe Kennedy was also home, still resolutely isolationist and convinced that "everything in France and England would go to hell"—views that were making him extremely unpopular in England, but which echoed those of many Americans. One day at the State Department he interrupted Bullitt during an interview with Doris Fleeson and another reporter and the "altercation became so violent" that the journalists excused themselves and the ambassadors "parted in anger," Ickes wrote in his diary. By then, Bullitt was firmly convinced FDR would not seek a third term. He told Ickes the likely Democratic ticket would be Hull and Farley—and that it would lose.

Bullitt's opinion may have been influenced by an unsettling experience at the White House in February when he was dining with Missy and FDR. Suddenly, the president collapsed at the table. Missy called for the White House physician, Dr. Ross McIntire, who diagnosed "a very slight heart attack." (McIntire was an ear, nose, and throat specialist. Besides polio, FDR's major health complaint was sinus headaches and infections.) The episode, never disclosed to anyone during Roosevelt's lifetime, had to have frightened Missy badly. It would be several years before FDR saw a cardiologist and was diagnosed with congestive heart disease, a fact that was not revealed to the public until years after his death.

Roosevelt may have been dealing with another health concern that, because most of his medical records disappeared after his death, cannot be proven. In January 1940, Dr. McIntire responded to a letter from another doctor questioning him about the prominent mole over the president's left eye. The blemish had grown and darkened noticeably over the years, to the point that it was mentioned fairly regularly in the press. McIntire assured him he was keeping the "pigmented area" under observation and that it was nothing to worry about. But was it? In their book *FDR's Deadly Secret,* Eric Fettmann and Steven Lomazow, MD, argue that the spot was a deadly melanoma that ultimately contributed to FDR's death through metastasis to the brain.

Treatment of such a visible melanoma would have involved surgery and/or radiation, but the disfigurement caused by either of these options would have been obvious to the press and the public. Cancer was considered such a death sentence that FDR would have had no option for reelection had he admitted to the diagnosis. However, it was known by doctors even then that melanoma had a fairly long "shelf life," wherein the patient might live without severe consequences for several years. Fettmann and Lomazow argue that Roosevelt and his doctors "chose to roll the dice with history." Over the next months, the mole slowly shrank, the authors say, due to incremental surgeries and a skin graft. Missy's friend Fulton Oursler, visiting FDR in July, noted "a flap of flesh that had grown over his left eye, and other visible physical deteriorations." By mid-1941 the lesion was barely a shadow.

In truth, FDR felt lousy that spring, skipping office hours and virtually every press conference in March due to what was described by McIntire as stomach flu and colds, while the news from Europe kept getting worse. On April 9, Hitler invaded Denmark and Norway. Denmark collapsed at once, and the battle for Norway was still going on when the presidential entourage left for Warm Springs. Canadian prime minister William Lyon Mackenzie King, whose country had entered the war along with Britain in September 1939, was a guest there in late April, and discussed the war around the table at the Little White House with FDR, Missy, and Basil O'Connor, FDR's former law partner and head of the National Foundation for Infantile Paralysis.

"O'Connor seemed to think that if Germany began to win, the people of the U.S. would become inclined to make [some] sort of trade with Germany," Mackenzie King wrote in his diary. "The President did not hold this view, nor did Miss LeHand. They thought American opinion would be strengthened against Germany; that it would be realized that she would be becoming increasingly a menace to this continent."

Later, on a drive to Dowdell's Knob, the men discussed the election. FDR threw out a few possible candidates, describing Secretary of State Hull as the best of the bunch. He said that he was still undecided about a run, but that "he was mentally tired. That if he could get a year off for a rest, it would be quite different." Before leaving Warm Springs, Mackenzie King chatted with Missy about the president's health, and they shared a "like view" that FDR was "inwardly quite nervous at times and also show[s] real fatigue. Dr. McIntire thought physically he was in good shape and could stand a third term should he attempt it. Personally I do not think he should."

Later that spring, Harry Hopkins confided to his friend Robert Sherwood that he had "grave doubts about" the president's plans for a third term, although he had said in January he was almost sure he would run. The situation in Europe continued to deteriorate. Norway fell, and on May 10 Hitler attacked Holland, Belgium, Luxembourg, and France. Neville Chamberlain resigned as prime minister of Great Britain, succeeded by Winston Churchill.

Hopkins came to dinner at the White House that night. Robert Sherwood wrote, "He was feeling miserable and Roosevelt prevailed on him to stay there overnight. He remained, living in what had been Lincoln's study, for three and a half years. Later, Missy LeHand remarked, 'It was Harry Hopkins who gave George S. Kaufman and Moss Hart the idea for that play of theirs, 'The Man Who Came to Dinner.'" (Actually the play had been produced the previous year.) Harry's ascendancy as an advisor had come at the cost of Tommy Corcoran, who would soon leave the government to start a law practice that specialized in influence peddling.

Churchill summarized the situation that spring:

> Now at last the slowly gathered, long pent-up fury of the storm broke upon us. Four or five millions of men met each other in the first shock of the most merciless of all the wars of which record has been kept. . . . Within three weeks the long-famed French Army was to collapse in rout and ruin, and our only British Army to be hurled into the sea with all its equipment lost. Within six weeks we were to find ourselves alone, almost disarmed, with triumphant Germany and Italy at our throats, with the whole of Europe open to Hitler's power, and Japan glowering on the other side of the globe.

Bullitt kept a steady stream of cables and phone messages flowing to the White House as events unfolded, and Carmel Offie chimed in with long letters to Missy. "We're in the army now!" he boasted on May 11. But the hopeful tone of his letters quickly darkened as it became obvious the French were no match for the Germans. On June 3 German planes attacked the French Air Ministry building during a luncheon for high-ranking military and diplomatic guests, including Bullitt, and a bomb fell through the ceiling. Wrote CBS correspondent Eric Sevareid, "The discipline of social poise has its advantages in warfare: nobody so much as dropped his glass, and the bomb did not go off." Bullitt sent Missy the menu as a souvenir and asked her to inform his daughter, Anne, who was in school in the States, that he was unhurt. As the German tanks rampaged across France toward Paris, he sent her a final message:

> Dearest Lady,
>
> This is a last note out of Paris by the hand of the last member of my staff to leave. The telephone has been smashed by the Germans so that I cannot talk with you. The Germans are close. The Italians have declared war.
>
> The next days may be bad. I have nothing to say except that I am thinking of days that we have had that have been good.
>
> Best, best love and thanks,
>
> Bill

With the French government in disarray, Bullitt on June 12 became the provisional mayor of Paris and helped negotiate its surrender to the Germans without the appalling damage and loss of human life suffered by other cities in Hitler's path. A new French government formed around eighty-four-year-old World War I hero Marshal Henri-Philippe Pétain, and it surrendered to Germany in the same boxcar where the Treaty of Versailles that ended World War I was signed. Bullitt remained in Paris until the end of June, helping American and British citizens escape, before he, too, departed for home.

In the midst of this, FDR on June 20 took a very cagey step, dismissing weak cabinet members and appointing two Republicans to the posts he had dangled before Bullitt. Henry L. Stimson was named secretary of war and Frank Knox secretary of the navy. It was hard evidence that FDR was now committed to a third term, but Missy, who had doubtless been privy to his thinking, wasn't about to get trapped into another gaffe about his plans. A brief item in a Washington column said, "A friend tried to draw out Miss Marguerite LeHand, private secretary to the President, on the third term. Pointing to the White House rose gardens outside her window, he asked, 'Do you expect to see the roses bloom again next year?' Miss LeHand replied, 'Somewhere, yes.'"

Missy's attention wasn't entirely focused on war, politics, and Bullitt. All through the spring and early summer of 1940, she exchanged letters with Pierre Cartier, manager of the famed French jeweler's Fifth Avenue store in New York. He had an earring made to replace one, purchased in Paris, that she had lost, and sent over a selection of gold wristwatches for her to examine. (She had budgeted $200 for the purchase, the equivalent of $3,300 today.) Missy arranged for Cartier to have tea with FDR and made inquiries through the American embassy in Berlin about his soldier son-in-law, who was missing in action and thought to be a POW. He gave her a nice discount on the watch, which was studded with rubies and diamonds.

The Republican National Convention opened in Philadelphia on June 24, and the nominee was a surprise: a politically inexperienced Wall Street lawyer and utility company president from Indiana named Wendell Willkie. Harold Ickes, ever the coiner of a memorable phrase, called him "a simple, barefoot Wall Street lawyer." However, Missy wasn't surprised. Drew Pearson reported in his "Washington Merry-Go-Round" column that she had collected $25 in bets for predicting the nominee, which she donated to the Red Cross.

On July 5, ten days before the Democratic National Convention opened, a picture of Missy appeared on the front page of *The Washington Post* under the headline "Roosevelt's Third-Term Plans Reported Known to Secretary: Secret Reposes with Miss LeHand, Politicians Hear." In fact, he had decided to run in June, but the decision was not revealed in the article, only that Missy knew it.

And Missy wasn't telling.

❁ CHAPTER EIGHTEEN

# Bitter Victory

A tiny box dangles from one of Missy's gold charm bracelets, her initials engraved on the top and the year 1940 on the front. When the clasp is opened, out springs a jack-in-the-box. The charm tells the story of the 1940 Democratic National Convention in fourteen-karat gold.

Fulton Oursler, whose *Liberty* magazine had been highly critical of FDR's handling of his second term, arrived at the White House in July for a short interview. He had recently grown facial hair, which had excited much comment among *Liberty*'s readers; one had sent an envelope containing nothing but a razor blade. When he presented himself at the Oval Office, FDR roared with laughter and shouted, "My God, Missy, come in here and look at Fulton. You wouldn't know him. He's got a moustache and goatee." Oursler recalled Missy kissing him and declaring "it was the nicest feeling moustache she had ever kissed (but they all say that, and I bet she says that to all the senators. At least that is what I told her.)"

Missy's friendship with the Ourslers had cooled along with the editor's regard for her boss, so much so that when Oursler asked if he could speak to her privately after his interview, she didn't reply. Once FDR gave his consent, she said, "I will be glad to see you, Fulton," leaving the men alone. While they talked, FDR received a call from one of his agents at the convention, which Oursler said sent him into "one of the most towering rages that any man let himself get into without committing mayhem. . . . I said to myself, 'It will be a tragedy if this man has four years more in the White House. I am going to vote for Willkie.'"

If the 1936 convention can be compared to a railway system whose efficiency would make even Mussolini proud, the 1940 convention was a train wreck, with FDR in the engineer's seat. The Democratic delegates, feeling they had been backed into a corner, showed FDR only lukewarm support when the nomination process began, refusing to choose him by acclamation. Nevertheless, on July 17 he handily won the nomination on the first ballot, with James Farley a very distant second. Taking a huge gamble, he refused to accept until the convention also gave him the running mate he wanted, Secretary of Agriculture Henry Wallace. He was an odd choice, and not a popular one. Wallace was a dependable liberal and New Dealer, but he had only recently joined the Democratic Party so was not trusted by the rank-and-file members. Although there had been a large field of vice presidential possibilities, in the end the contest was between Wallace and conservative House Speaker William Bankhead of Alabama.

Eleanor Roosevelt flew to Chicago at FDR's behest to urge the delegates to vote for his choice of running mate. Speaking of the heavy responsibility FDR would face, she told the hushed audience, "You cannot treat it as you would an ordinary nomination in an ordinary time." Her choice of words was highly appropriate, as England, under its new prime minister, Winston Churchill, was bracing itself for Germany's inevitable attack on its ports and cities.

As the vice presidential vote was taken on the evening of July 18, FDR played solitaire in his oval study surrounded by close staff. "As the fight became more and more acrimonious," speechwriter Sam Rosenman recalled, "the President asked Missy to give him a note pad and a pencil." He filled five pages with the draft of a statement he would issue if Wallace was not nominated. In it, he declined the nomination for president. Sam took the notes for polishing, and left the room with Missy and FDR's appointments secretary, Pa Watson, who read the statement over Sam's shoulder at a desk in the hall. Missy's reaction was immediate. "'Fine, I'm glad,' she said, and returned to the Oval Room quick, very pleased indeed." Pa wanted to tear the pages up, but Sam followed FDR's orders and labored over the statement, returning to the study to find the staff discussing the matter in whispers while the president resumed his card game. "Missy was all smiles, saying that the President was doing the only thing he could do."

Finally, the tide turned, and the delegates nominated Wallace with a slight majority. In the ovenlike atmosphere of his study, FDR "looked weary and bedraggled," Sam recalled. He retreated to his adjoining bedroom to freshen up and emerged "looking his usual, jaunty, imperturbable self," ready to give his acceptance speech by radio in the White House broadcasting room. "We were all happy and smiling except one; Missy was in tears." Sam, who understood the relationship between boss and secretary better than anyone else, concluded that she "had seen the great toll that the President had paid in strength and health. . . . She knew that the coming struggle would sap the President's strength."

*FDR, Missy, and Bill Bullitt share the backseat of the presidential limousine in July 1940, shortly after Bullitt's return from Nazi-occupied France.*

The following Sunday night, Bill Bullitt arrived in Washington, home safe from Hitler's bombers and U-boats, and joined FDR's train bound for Hyde Park. Photographers shot the president's open car driving away from the station Monday morning, Missy smiling from under a broad-brimmed straw hat trimmed with flowers, sitting between her boss and her love. At Springwood, Bullitt for the first time heard Roosevelt describe what came to be known as Lend-Lease—a means of dodging the cash-and-carry restrictions of the Neutrality Act by assuming the financially strapped British would eventually return any war matériel they got from the United States. "Bill, if my neighbor's house catches fire . . . and I am watering the grass in my back yard, and I don't pass the garden hose over the fence to my neighbor, I am a fool. How do you think the country and the Congress would react if I should put aid to the British in the form of lending them my garden hose?" This was exactly how he would explain it to the American people a few months later, with Britain reeling from the German attacks that began August 7.

Missy had dried her convention night tears and jumped into the effort to reelect FDR with both well-shod feet. In mid-August, she starred in a deft piece of public relations, a four-page photo spread in *Look* magazine. "*Look* Calls on Missy LeHand . . . President Roosevelt's Private Secretary" featured "the first picture-story of him at work in the sanctum next to his bedroom in the White House." Missy, wearing a crisp shirtwaist dress and open-toed pumps with a charm bracelet tinkling on her wrist, was also shown at her own desk, in the Oval Office, on the *Potomac,* and calmly reading in her third-floor sitting room, the photos of the king and queen of England prominently displayed and noted in the caption. The same issue held a photo spread on "Willkie . . . the Republican Roosevelt."

Bullitt was doing his part for the campaign by writing speeches, but his future was uncertain: he could not return to France and had no other appointment in the offing. FDR had told Harold Ickes that Bullitt wanted to be named secretary of state, "'but I can't do that.' In explanation, he said that Bill talked too much, and I got the impression that he also thinks that Bill is too quick on the trigger," Ickes wrote in his diary.

*Missy's suite was shown in the spread in* Look *magazine in August 1940. Note the pictures of the king and queen hanging on the side of her bookcase.*

The president wasn't the only one who was having doubts about Bullitt. It is evident from correspondence between Bullitt and Missy that their romance became strained almost as soon as he got home. Over the years she had begged him to write and call more often, sometimes openly questioning his devotion. Now the tables were turned. In a note in mid-August, Bullitt informed her she had missed their luncheon engagement and hadn't returned three phone calls, but he was "counting on" having dinner with her that week. He had another expectation. FDR had asked him to make an important speech on the war at the American Philosophical Society in Philadelphia. To be given on the steps of Independence Hall, it would be a trial balloon to test the relative strength of interventionists who were ready to declare war, isolationists who wanted to stay out, and a middle-of-the-road group who favored arming Hitler's victims. With German planes raining bombs on Britain, Bullitt wrote in his speech that if that country fell, the United States would be the next target in Hitler's gun sights. "Why are we sleeping, Americans?" he demanded. His speech draft was quickly approved by Under Secretary of State Sumner Welles, FDR's favorite contact at the State Department, and the president himself. Bullitt wrote to Missy, "It will be on Sunday and I am counting on you to come." He asked her to call him at the Shoreham Hotel that night.

Her reply was probably not what he expected. "I was busy last evening and couldn't call you," she wrote the next day. "I think the speech is grand and I wish I could be in Philadelphia to hear it, but I shall be 'on tour' with the P. I shall listen over the radio and applaud all the spots I like, and there are lots of them." She blew off his dinner invitations and closed with a casual, "Best of luck on the big evening—M."

Bullitt's speech drew a warm telegram from Missy that probably reflected her boss's view as well. "HEARD SPEECH ON TRAIN IT WAS GRAND CONGRATULATIONS." It also created a firestorm of controversy in Congress. Isolationists there even called for "warmonger" Bullitt's arrest. FDR never followed up with a foreign affairs speech during the campaign, but he made the controversial decision to trade fifty aging World War I destroyers to Great Britain for long-term leases on Western Hemisphere military bases. (He had also signed bills that greatly stepped up defense appropriations and for the first time created a peacetime draft.) Bullitt's speech was hastily published as a book, *Report to the American People,* and he inscribed a copy "To Marguerite LeHand with love from Bill." He also gave her a gold telephone charm for her bracelet, which Missy thanked him for in a hastily scribbled note—but she pointedly reminded him that "these are very very busy days over here."

Bullitt was not at the White House for Missy's forty-fourth birthday party on September 13. Harry Hopkins wrote her a sweet note, "Dear Missy, You are adorable and I love you very much. Happy Birthday my dear." The party lasted until after midnight, but Roberta Barrows, Steve Early's secretary, recalled in an interview with presidential biographer Doris Kearns Goodwin that Missy was "uncharacteristically quiet . . . as if she were brooding on something."

Missy and Bullitt took their last trip together when they traveled with FDR to Philadelphia a week later to inspect the navy yard—another campaign stop in disguise. The next night, she penned a furious note to Bullitt from Hyde Park, sending it special delivery. "This note will be very brief as I am still very angry after thinking over our conversations on the train," she wrote. "The few people whom I consider my friends are completely accustomed to my breaking dinner or other engagements with the usual courteous explanations which civilized people make to each other in the circumstances. I am not aware that there is any reason for either of us to do more. Each of us is most assuredly entitled to what you call 'an explosion,' but not <u>at</u> each other! As I am still blazing I am asking you to excuse me from dining on Tuesday evening. As ever M." The relationship was over. Except for a terse typewritten note returning some books to him the following spring, Missy would not communicate with Bullitt until after she left the White House. With the break in their correspondence, we lose much of our insight into Missy's thoughts and her emotional life.

Even though she was the one who broke off the romance, Missy had to have been devastated. For seven years she had loved this man, had "lived for his visits," pored over his letters, cherished his gifts of jewelry. She was now middle-aged, her jawline sagging a bit, her hair almost completely silver. Would there ever be another man in her life? To make matters worse, the crown princess of Norway and her three children had moved into the White House after fleeing their country, and FDR appeared to be mesmerized by her. Princess Martha began usurping Missy's place at cocktail hour and in the president's car, hanging on FDR's every word, giggling and flirting. On top of the breakup with Bullitt, Martha added to Missy's misery.

But Bullitt, who was almost fifty, had lost more than a girlfriend. He had also lost his best advocate in the Oval Office. William Douglas, by then a Supreme Court associate justice, might as well have been thinking of Bullitt when he wrote, "Men hungry for power, position and publicity ate out their hearts to get a blessing, an approval, an assignment from FDR. Their happiness turned on his smile, his nod, his handshake." A daring but distasteful plot began hatching in Bullitt's head.

About the time Missy broke up with him, House Speaker William Bankhead had died. Bankhead, father of actress Tallulah, had been Henry Wallace's chief rival for the vice presidential nomination a scant two months before. Demonstrating that all was forgiven—as well as grasping the opportunity to make dozens of brief campaign-style stops at railroad stations from Washington to Alabama—FDR led two trains of mourners to Bankhead's tiny hometown. Under Secretary of State Sumner Welles, married and usually icily patrician, became very drunk on the return trip and propositioned several male black porters. They complained to their supervisors, and the information traveled up the chain of command to railway headquarters in Philadelphia. When Bullitt got wind of the story, he decided to use it to oust Welles and steal his job at the State Department.

Meanwhile, Joe Kennedy was living through the horrors of the Battle of Britain. He wrote to Missy about having "to go to sleep with German planes droning over your head and gunfire all around you . . . and constantly see and listen to people who have lost everything." The Nazi bombing that began in September killed more than forty thousand British civilians and destroyed the homes of millions. Kennedy had sent his family home, felt useless at the embassy, and had stayed on only because he didn't want to appear cowardly. In fact, Kennedy had become quite unpopular in England for his very public lack of faith in that country's ability to withstand Hitler, something that had greatly displeased FDR. Further, he had confided to Henry and Clare Boothe Luce, who owned *Time* and *Life* magazines, that he was thinking of joining them in supporting Willkie, and told friends in London he could "put twenty-five million Catholic votes behind Willkie to throw Roosevelt out." With James Farley disaffected and radio priest Father Coughlin now rabidly isolationist, Kennedy's sway with Catholic voters was something FDR was desperate to harness. He called the ambassador home for consultation in late October, cautioning him to make no statements to the press until they had talked.

As soon as Kennedy landed and reunited with his wife, Rose, they were brought to the White House for a Sunday night scrambled egg supper and an overnight stay. The guest list was designed to put them at ease: Missy was serving as the hostess, and Irish American senator James Byrnes of South Carolina, a close Roosevelt ally and social friend of the Kennedys, was there with his wife. "When we were about half through the dinner, Jim Byrnes, acting as though a wonderful idea had just struck him, said he thought it would be a great idea if I would go on the radio Tuesday night on my own" and endorse Roosevelt, Kennedy wrote in his diary. He wasn't fooled. When they retired to the second-floor study, Kennedy launched into a diatribe, complaining that he had been treated badly. Roosevelt denied any fault, laying all blame on the State Department. Though hardly mollified, Kennedy finally not only agreed to make the speech, but to pay for the radio time, too. Missy leapt to the telephone to set it up.

Kennedy's speech, in which he urged the country to rearm for its own protection and reelect Roosevelt, helped clinch the president's victory. FDR bagged it when he promised, during a subsequent speech in Kennedy's hometown of Boston, that "Your boys are not going to be sent into any foreign wars"—without the usual disclaimer "unless attacked." By then he probably knew involvement in the war was inevitable, but he also knew he couldn't win reelection if he admitted it. When Willkie heard the speech, he knew he was licked. "That hypocritical son of a bitch!" he said.

Missy voted with the Roosevelts in Hyde Park on November 5, and sat at the mahogany table in the dining room at Springwood that night with FDR, freshly sharpened pencils and tally sheets at hand. Three press tickers clacked in the room, and she tore off the election results for him as he calmly totaled the figures. But the early returns looked bad, and at some point FDR, sweating heavily, told Mike Reilly of the Secret Service he didn't want anyone coming into the dining room, including his family. Did he turn Missy out, for the first election night in their years together? Reilly's memoir said FDR asked to be left entirely alone. The report in *Time* said Missy was his "one companion."

Some of FDR's biographers have focused on this hour when he believed he would lose the election, musing over what was going through his mind. What about Missy, whichever side of the dining room doors she was on? Did she secretly hope he would lose, that they could both retire to a quieter life in Hyde Park? Or did she fear the fate of the country and the world without FDR's experienced hand on the wheel of state? It's one of the many secrets she took to her grave. At any rate, by 11 p.m., the tide had turned. Roosevelt had won by almost five million votes in the biggest election turnout in thirty years, carrying thirty-eight states.

Missy told a reporter she had read seven to eight thousand post-election telegrams, adding "with something between a laugh and a sigh . . . 'I can stand another term if the president can.'"

CHAPTER NINETEEN

# Disaster

At the end of 1940, FDR gave a stirring Fireside Chat declaring that the United States must become "the great arsenal of Democracy" for the victims of the Axis powers, Germany, Italy, and Japan. His words hardly met with universal approval. The shrill debate between isolationists and interventionists deeply divided the nation. "Those were bitter, heart-burning days," wrote CBS correspondent Eric Sevareid, assigned to Washington after three years in Europe, "when a vast country was trying to understand itself and the world in which it lived, when the [isolationists] almost took the nation away from its chosen leader."

Missy began every day looking over a selection of newspapers while she had coffee and juice in bed. The newspapers of William Randolph Hearst and the McCormick cousins—Robert R. McCormick in Chicago, Joseph Medill Patterson in New York, and Cissy Patterson in Washington—were resolutely isolationist. Others were urging intervention, as were Henry Luce's magazines *Time* and *Life*. At her office desk, Missy sorted through letters and telegrams, many from personal friends of the president, accusing him of wanting to sacrifice a generation of young men, or demanding that he act more decisively to save Britain. In front of the White House gates, a protester carried a sign reading "Do you want your sons eaten by sharks?" Even members of the cabinet were sharply divided.

In the first two months of 1941, the White House focused on getting the Lend-Lease bill passed. The foes were mighty. Congressional isolationists were egged on by the likes of former ambassador Joe Kennedy and aviation legend Charles Lindbergh, who had emerged as the leading figure in that movement. On the other hand, Wendell Willkie nobly put aside his post-election bitterness and testified before Congress for Lend-Lease, as did Bill Bullitt. The bill passed on March 8, raising Prime Minister Churchill's hopes. But then nothing happened. A strange inertia settled over the White House, and FDR's aides and advisors were puzzled and frustrated by his lassitude.

Harold Ickes kept urging FDR to form an "anti-propaganda" initiative to counteract the isolationism in the country, to no avail. He confided to his diary that if he had known how "inactive and uninspiring" Roosevelt would become, he would not have supported him for a third term. The president spent days in bed with a cold, and the cabinet seldom met. He seemed more interested in visiting Crown Princess Martha of Norway than conducting business, leading some to wonder if he no longer found Missy relaxing company. Certainly a fresh face from a royal family was more diverting than the loyal secretary whose very presence reminded him of the business he was shirking.

For her part, Missy was simply exhausted. While FDR was on a stag fishing cruise in March, she and her niece Babe spent a week in Atlantic City. "I do hope you really want to rest," Missy wrote before they left, "because I shall stay in bed late and go to bed early although I am not promising to go on the wagon or do violent exercise." She said she could bring books from the White House library and hoped they would have "a lot of conversation." Clearly, she wasn't looking for a "gay time" as she had on earlier vacations.

The country was still adrift when they returned from their travels and the president still seemed unable to focus. Journalist John Gunther was squeezed in for a short appointment to share his insights into South America, where many interventionists believed Hitler would get his toehold for an assault on the United States. He found FDR playing with Fala, the Scottish terrier presented to him by his cousin Daisy Suckley a few months before. The photogenic pooch had set off a national mania for items with a Scottie motif, and Missy had added a Scottie charm to her bracelet.

Missy "left the room, pushing Fala along with her," and then the president launched into a forty-six-minute monologue, much of it involving matters of extreme sensitivity, giving Gunther no time to share his own insights into South America. "He had no right to be so talkative; it was indecent and irresponsible," Gunther thought. Finally, FDR dismissed him with a cheery "So long!—I've got to *run* along now!"

Ickes had a long talk with Missy one day about FDR's lack of leadership, and for the first time she was openly critical, telling the interior secretary, "We have a leader who won't lead." After another conversation, he wrote in his diary, "She realizes that something ought to be done to build up public sentiment in the country and remarked caustically that, while we are doing nothing, Senator [Burton] Wheeler and others were going about making speeches and creating an adverse sentiment. . . . It did not strike me that 'Missy' was particularly optimistic about the situation and certainly she was not satisfied with the qualities of the President's leadership, although none can doubt her utter loyalty to him." Weeks later, Missy told Ickes that she still hadn't been able to get through to FDR. Ickes wrote, "If even 'Missy' cannot get to the President in a critical situation, there is not very much chance for any of the rest of us to do it."

The president's circle of close advisors was shrinking—primarily Missy, Harry Hopkins, and Pa Watson—but he still accepted visits from Bill Bullitt. Since learning about Sumner Welles's propositioning the porters on the train returning from Speaker Bankhead's funeral the previous September, Bullitt had been spreading the story around Washington through friends like publisher Cissy Patterson, hoping the gossip would lead to

Welles's dismissal. On April 23, Bullitt took the story directly to the Oval Office, demanding that FDR dismiss Welles as a security risk, saying his homosexual acts could lead to blackmail by an enemy government. FDR was aware of the incident—in fact he had gotten the FBI involved—and told Bullitt he had hired a bodyguard for Welles as a precaution. Both men grew angry, and Roosevelt called for Pa Watson, saying he didn't feel well and to cancel the rest of his appointments that day.

The next evening, Missy and FDR dined alone. No doubt he gave her an earful about her former boyfriend, but after dinner they watched the movie *Citizen Kane*. Harry Hopkins, who had gone to England as an emissary for FDR, had written Missy a note saying "It apparently takes Hearst over the hoops. If you can get it, I think the President would like very much to see it." Orson Welles's cinematic roman à clef about William Randolph Hearst probably gave them some good laughs at the expense of the isolationist publisher.

FDR was furious with Bullitt, but he had good reason to not feel well. On May 4, he traveled with his entourage, including Missy, to Staunton, Virginia, to dedicate a museum at the boyhood home of President Woodrow Wilson. Cutting short the trip, FDR told Dr. Ross McIntire that he felt unusually tired, prompting the White House physician to order a blood exam. "The results must have floored McIntire," wrote Eric Fettmann and Steven Lomazow in *FDR's Deadly Secret*. The president's hemoglobin, "which in a healthy man is between 14 and 17 grams" per deciliter of blood, was just 4.5 grams. "This meant that Roosevelt had lost the equivalent of eight pints of blood. . . . The president of the United States was on the precipice of a medical catastrophe." McIntire blamed the blood loss on hemorrhoids.

If FDR had seemed aimless and lethargic before, he became almost immobile at this point. McIntire told the press he had a slight fever and a stomach upset, insisting it was nothing serious. However, the president stayed in bed for a week, undergoing blood transfusions and iron injections to build his hemoglobin.

Eleanor, who was away during the crisis, described the treatments in a letter to daughter Anna. "I found Pa had really been quite ill," she wrote. For another week, he kept a light schedule, staying away from his office, taking his meals in his bedroom with Missy or Harry. "The situation with Harry, Missy & Pa is funny," Eleanor wrote. "It is a very close corporation just now." For Missy, that "close corporation" meant she was constantly at FDR's side, without even a break for lunch or dinner. Eleanor later confided to Anna that Missy had turned to opiates to help her sleep.

The word from FDR's doctor was that his illness had morphed from a stomach upset to a cold, something speechwriter Robert Sherwood found odd after leaving his room one day and noticing he had not once sneezed or coughed. Missy "smiled and said, 'What he's suffering from most of all is a case of sheer exasperation.'"

*Grace Tully, Steve Early, and Missy laugh around FDR's desk in May 1941. Missy had a health crisis a few weeks later.*

By the end of May he had returned to the office and resumed a heavier schedule, including the annual party for his immediate staff given by Harry Somerville, the dapper, silver-haired manager of the Willard Hotel.

The stately and historic hotel was two blocks from the White House; every president since Franklin Pierce had been a guest, and Mark Twain wrote two books while staying there. Perhaps due to the lingering effects of FDR's anemia, on June 4 the dinner was catered in the Diplomatic Reception Room at the White House. With Eleanor away at Hyde Park, Missy sat in as hostess, gamely presiding over the meal and singing around the piano afterward. Late in the evening she confided to Grace Tully that she did not feel well, but she refused to leave the party until FDR had retired at about 9:30 p.m. Shortly afterward, she screamed and fainted.

As the horrified guests looked on, she struggled for breath, her lips turning blue. Mouth-to-mouth resuscitation revived her, and then Dr. McIntire and Commander George Fox, the president's physical therapist, carried Missy upstairs to her apartment. Her pulse was racing and irregular and when she could gasp out a few words, she complained of severe pain in her neck and chest. McIntire's initial diagnosis of exhaustion from overwork was not surprising, considering the eighteen-hour days she had spent at her desk and at FDR's bedside that spring, but he surely suspected her old heart problem had recurred. He ordered a sedative to help her sleep.

Despite Grace's memory of the night, it's hard to imagine that FDR had rolled off to his stamp collection unaware that Missy had fainted. Indeed, the White House Usher's Log tells a different story. It said FDR did not retire that night until after midnight; by then Missy was no doubt settled and asleep.

Early the next morning, a private duty nurse arrived at the White House and bustled upstairs to Missy's suite. Two more nurses joined her over the next ten days, providing round-the-clock attention. Dr. John Harper, commandant of the U.S. Naval Hospital, came to oversee her care, and soon a parade of medical specialists was rotating through her bedroom.

FDR dropped in on Missy for short visits the day after her attack, but he had other things on his mind, beyond the war, pending Supreme Court appointments and a threatened civil rights march on Washington. His old love, Lucy Mercer Rutherfurd, under the alias "Mrs. Paul Johnson," made her first visit to the White House that day and spent almost two hours in his study. Just turned fifty and beautiful in a matronly sort of way, Lucy was still married to Winthrop Rutherfurd, who was nearing eighty, crotchety and ailing. Her connection with FDR had continued over the decades, primarily through letters and phone calls, but the undercover visit to the White House stepped the relationship up a notch. This renewed intimacy would continue for the rest of his life.

That weekend, FDR and a small entourage, including Princess Martha, took a weekend cruise on the *Potomac,* leaving Missy behind with her nurses. She slept most of the time, subsisting on a diet of milk, water, aspirin, and narcotics.

Over the next three weeks, Missy's condition stubbornly resisted treatment. She repeatedly complained of severe pain in her chest, shoulder, and neck. Her doctors prescribed morphine and other sedatives. Her pulse rattled along irregularly, and she slept only fitfully. Her emotions were on a roller coaster totally at odds with her usual equanimity, and her calm smile was replaced with tears and outbursts. The nurse's log on one date reads "talking quite irrelevantly," on another, "very hysterical." Heavy doses of sedatives were needed to calm her.

Eleanor wrote to daughter Anna, "Missy is very ill again. She's been taking opiates & had a heart attack & and then her mind went as it does, so now we have three nurses & the prospect of some weeks of illness before we get her straightened out." She also mentioned the president had a sore throat. FDR spent another day in bed and canceled his appointments, but scrawled Missy a note: "Missy dear, I'm laid up in bed—bad throat, but will come to see you just as soon as I can get out. Ever so much love, FDR."

For Missy, bedrest, nurses, and visiting specialists weren't enough; Dr. Harper arrived as a White House guest and stayed until mid-June. By then, Missy was feeling well enough to be wheeled out on the grounds, and seemed to be getting better. Then she started running a low-grade fever and the "hysteroid" symptoms recurred. It became obvious she needed to go to a hospital where she could be cared for more effectively.

Doctors Hospital had opened in 1940 at 1815 I Street. Ten stories tall and constructed in the sleek Art Moderne style popular at the time, the private hospital was touted as a "hotel for the sick" with an elegant lobby, stylish furniture, and drapes in its patient rooms, as well as the latest in laboratories, operating rooms, and medical equipment. Missy traveled by ambulance there just as darkness had fallen on the evening of Saturday, June 21, accompanied by Dr. Harper.

What was wrong with Missy? She had been dealing with the effects of residual rheumatic heart disease since age fifteen. Over the years she had suffered from intermittent episodes of atrial fibrillation or rapid, irregular heartbeat that required bedrest and treatment with digitalis. Most probably there were also episodes of heart failure; her three-pack-a-day smoking habit had probably contributed to her problems. Missy's tolerance for exertion had become quite limited, which explains why she had become more vocal about her dislike for exercise, except for dancing. A further complication of rheumatic fever is valve stenosis, a narrowing of the heart's mitral valve. When this happens, blood pools in the lower chamber of the heart and tends to form clots that can travel to the lungs, brain, or other organs. Every episode of a bacterial-based upper respiratory illness—and Missy had them by the score—added to the stenosis. Through the lens of present-day medical understanding, it can be deduced that Missy's catastrophic event on June 4 was a combination of pulmonary embolism—blood clot in the lung—and atrial fibrillation. Besides the clot to her lungs, her heart was probably spewing small clots to her brain, adding to her mental confusion.

Medicine in 1941 had few tools for managing her condition.

The digitalis that had caused her prolonged psychosis in 1927 was the only treatment for her racing heartbeat. Aspirin was in common use for heart issues since the beginning of the twentieth century. These medications, plus morphine for the pain, were all prescribed, and all had minimal effect.

An already serious medical problem began to snowball.

While still at the White House, Missy developed a low-grade fever, which pointed to endocarditis, or mitral valve infection. Penicillin was in its infancy in 1941, and doctors still treated major infections with sulfa drugs, though they were minimally effective for endocarditis. That treatment protocol began for Missy at Doctors Hospital, and over her first few days there apparently was improving. On the morning of June 27, she was sitting up in bed, talking to one of her doctors, and seemed much better. "Talking intelligently and completing sentences," said the medical notes. Suddenly, she "pitched forward and fell on the bed. Following this it was noticed that the patient was paralyzed on the right side of face, right arm and leg" and lost her ability to speak. One of the blood clots had blocked a major artery that supplied blood to the left side of her brain—a disastrous and irreversible event. Missy had suffered a major stroke, and in the days to come, she needed "utmost nursing care."

FDR called in the medical cavalry. The best specialists in the country appeared at her bedside, including a crack cardiologist and the celebrated neurosurgeon from Temple University in Philadelphia, Dr. Temple Fay. Dr. Winfred Overholser, superintendent at St. Elizabeths Hospital for the mentally ill in Washington, was also consulted, which has resulted in some speculation over the years that Missy suffered a nervous breakdown. But he determined that she had a "medical problem with mental symptoms secondary." Throughout the summer, eleven doctors did what they could for Missy, who was totally helpless—incontinent and for a time fed through a tube in her nose. They conducted wide-ranging tests, seeking a source of infection and fever. She had blood cultures, throat cultures, pelvic exams, urological tests, and a spinal tap. The protocol then was to administer sulfa drugs for five days, then stop them. She responded to the drugs, but once they were halted, the fever and pain returned. (Today, mitral valve infections are treated with weeks of strong antibiotics, without break.)

Outside Missy's stylishly appointed hospital room, life moved on at a dizzying pace. The day after she entered Doctors Hospital, Hitler invaded the Soviet Union, violating the 1939 German-Soviet Treaty of Friendship, or Nonaggression Pact. While Hitler's Operation Barbarossa turned his attention from Britain, it caught the Red Army off guard, and the German air attack all but destroyed the Russian air force.

Seeking the social diversions that helped him cope with the demands of his job, FDR on the night of Hitler's attack motored to Princess Martha's mansion for a long dinner. Over the next few weeks, his calendar was crowded with visits from diplomats, cabinet officials, and military leaders. Harold Ickes had suggested to him that he consider an oil embargo against Japan to stall that aggressor nation's military adventures in the Far East. While continuing the delicate high-wire act of neutrality, the president issued an executive order inducting an additional 900,000 men into the armed services.

On the afternoon of June 30, FDR dedicated the Dutch Colonial fieldstone building near his mother's Hyde Park mansion that housed his presidential library. Before a small crowd seated on wooden folding chairs on the green lawn, he conveyed to the National Archives ownership of the building he and Missy had dreamed up together to house all the papers, books, and ephemera of an inveterate collector whose primary collecting obsession was himself. That day almost two thousand people passed through the library doors to see FDR's model ship collection, room of gifted "oddities" that the White House staff had laughed over during the Children's Hour, and a loaned collection of stagecoaches. Lying in her hospital bed, paralyzed and delirious, Missy had no concept of time or activity beyond her own fevered brain, and did not know that the project in which she had taken such pride was moving on without her.

*FDR dedicates his presidential library in Hyde Park, June 30, 1941. Missy was in the hospital, having suffered a massive stroke.*

As the hot summer dragged on, Dr. McIntire closely monitored Missy's condition and reported to the anxious president. Brother Dan LeHand made repeated trips to Washington, spending nights as a guest of the White House. The White House Usher's Log notes a three-hour dinner one night with Dan, FDR, and Grace Tully where they no doubt struggled over what to do. Grace, loyal to her best friend but primarily dedicated to the Boss, stepped up to take over many of Missy's official duties. Eleanor sent gifts of flowers and fruit to Missy's hospital room and visited alone and occasionally with her husband. Her maternal instincts were aroused by a crisis, and the part of her that thought of Missy as a daughter surged forward. The visits were unsettling; she told her secretary, Malvina Thompson, that it was "difficult to realize that it is really Missy, she has changed so much."

Initially Missy's illness had been kept very quiet, but by mid-

July the word was out, and alarming reports began appearing in the press. A story in the Worcester, Massachusetts, *Evening Gazette* described her as "desperately ill from a heart condition" and said messages had "poured into the White House" inquiring about her health. In a one-sentence blurb in its "People" column under the heading "Washington," *Time* described the illness as "neuritis," a common euphemism for a stroke, and said she "planned a month's rest when she got out" of the hospital. The news that Secretary of Agriculture Claude Wickard had gone home to Indiana to check on his ailing hogs and that columnist Joe Alsop had joined naval intelligence preceded the mention of Missy's illness.

By late July, there were glimmers of hope. She was attempting to talk, but was hard to understand. By mid-August, she was more alert and described as "generally better than at any time since admission to the hospital." Her right arm and leg were still useless and she needed a wheelchair for mobility, but she was looking at newspapers and magazines, listening to the radio, and was said to enjoy visitors. When Archbishop Francis Spellman visited the White House to have lunch with FDR, he asked if he could visit her. A White House car took him to Doctors Hospital.

In late August, FDR, who had paid all of Missy's hospital, doctors, and nursing bills, wrote effusive personal letters to all eleven physicians who had been supervising or consulting on her care. He gave the most praise to Dr. Harper, commandant of the naval hospital. "Yours has been a very difficult assignment and you have performed it with unusual ability and untiring devotion," he wrote.

When FDR wrote the letters, he had just returned from a clandestine summit meeting. He departed on August 3 for what was supposedly another fishing trip, with the ever-faithful Dr. McIntire as part of the entourage. "I noted a recovery of his usual gaiety of spirit and put it down to the lift that a vacation at sea always gave him," McIntire wrote. In fact, FDR was engaged in the secret meeting with Winston Churchill that would result in the Atlantic Charter agreement, a historic policy statement about the postwar world. The cloak-and-dagger adventure doubtless appealed to FDR's secretive nature, but he had another, private reason to be happy. In the two days before his departure, he had spent five hours at the White House with Lucy Rutherfurd. However, he visited Missy twice upon his return, and on September 13, FDR and Harry Hopkins shared a White House car to Doctors Hospital, calling on Missy on her forty-fifth birthday.

On the birthday visit, FDR wore a black armband over his summer suit, for he was in mourning for his mother. Sara Roosevelt had died at Hyde Park on September 7. A few days after the funeral, Grace brought her boss a box while he was sorting papers in his office at the new library at Hyde Park. They contained his mother's cherished mementos of his childhood, including his christening gown and first baby shoes. His eyes welled with tears, and he asked for privacy; Grace quickly left the room. No one on the White House staff had ever seen the president weep. Just weeks later, Eleanor was dealt a similar blow when her brother Hall died of complications of his long-term alcoholism. FDR's loss was no doubt the greater one, for he simultaneously lost the two women who loved him unconditionally: his mother was dead; Missy was the merest shadow of the woman he had known.

That summer marked twenty years since poliomyelitis had felled FDR at Campobello. Surely he marked the date and the ironic role reversal for the woman who had been such an encouragement to him throughout his struggle back to prominence. In truth, she was in a far worse state than he had been; polio had stilled his body, but she had lost control of both her body and her mind. The man who had urged the country to "above all, try something" to dig out of the Depression was fast running out of ideas for rescuing his dear friend.

FDR did not share his feelings about Missy's condition with others. This ability to compartmentalize his emotions enraged

Harold Ickes. Writing in his diary after a bitter cabinet meeting in mid-July, Ickes said, "I felt a clear conviction that I had lost my affection for him . . . despite his very pleasant and friendly personality, he is cold as ice inside. He has certain conventional family affections for his children and probably for Missy LeHand and Harry Hopkins, but nothing else. Missy, who has been desperately ill for several weeks, might pass out of his life and he would miss her. The same might be true as to Harry, but I doubt whether he would miss either of them greatly or for a long period."

Ickes was the latest in a string of intimates who had come to the conclusion that they really didn't know FDR or understand what speechwriter Robert Sherwood called "his heavily forested interior." Missy would soon find herself placed into one of FDR's mental compartments from which she could never escape. On October 13, the naval hospital's Dr. A. A. Marsteller examined Missy for the first time in two months and wrote a detailed assessment. He noted that her right side facial paralysis "has cleared up completely" but her right arm and leg had not improved. More troubling was her mental impairment. "She understands the meaning of printed words, but is unable to say them. She has a knowledge of what she wishes to say but is unable to find the word or words to express her thoughts. If asked if she wants something, she will frequently say 'no' if she means 'yes.'" He went on to say that Missy was reading newspapers, recognized people she should know, and could remember events of the previous two or three days, "but seems unable to recall facts over a longer period of time than that," and had no memory of what had happened before the onset of her illness. "There undoubtedly remains considerable mental impairment," he concluded.

What could be done for Missy? Her brother Dan visited the White House the day of Dr. Marsteller's examination, where FDR suggested sending her to the best rehabilitation hospital he knew: Warm Springs.

❁ CHAPTER TWENTY

# The Exiled Queen

FDR made his final visit to Missy's hospital room on October 29, 1941. Three days later she boarded a southbound train, accompanied by Dr. John Harper and a graduate nurse. They were welcomed by Dr. C. E. Irwin, the medical director of the Foundation, who had so often been Missy's genial host at Warm Springs parties.

Missy and her nurse settled not in the tiny cottage she had built as a rental property but at the roomier and better appointed Wilson Cottage, with its exposed wood beam ceilings and heavy pine plank door. A short road connected it to the grounds of the Little White House. Dr. Harper went over her case with Dr. Irwin and his assistant, Dr. James Johnson, and they set up a therapy schedule for her with Alice Plastridge, the Foundation's highly respected chief physical therapist. Missy's paralyzed right foot had begun to drop, and the brace shop fashioned a splint so she could attempt to walk. Another light splint was constructed for her wrist.

In mid-November, Dr. McIntire responded to Dr. Irwin's first report with an enthusiastic letter. "I feel sure that moving Missy to Warm Springs will prove very helpful and beneficial," he wrote. "I can tell you that the President feels mighty good about it. He is hoping that before too long you may be able to get her into the pool." In his reply, Dr. Irwin said Missy was able to walk "by holding onto someone's arm for balance," but she rejected the suggestion of going to the pool. "I believe she is a bit self-conscious and the idea did not appeal to her very much," he wrote. As an alternative, he suggested automobile rides with Miss Plastridge. One of the president's cars was placed at her disposal, and the two began taking long afternoon drives through the Georgia countryside. The outings must have been a poignant reminder of happier days motoring with FDR at the wheel, the car tires scattering fall leaves and terrorizing the local possum population.

*After twenty years of catering to her paralyzed boss, Missy herself was in a wheelchair following her stroke. This may have been taken at Warm Springs in late 1941 or early 1942.*

For all his optimism, FDR had recognized by then that Missy probably would not be able to return to the White House and resume her duties as his private secretary, or work in any capacity anywhere else, although he kept her on the payroll. On November 12, following an hour-long meeting with Basil O'Connor, he signed a new will that provided for her medical care, leaving one half of the annual income of his estate to Eleanor and the other half to "my friend, Marguerite A. Le Hand . . . for medical attention, care and treatment during her lifetime." Any residual from the income, up to $1,000 a year, could be used for living expenses. Other than small cash bequests to servants on his personal payroll, Missy was the only person outside FDR's family who was named as a beneficiary in the will. The president knew the bequest would raise comment, but he told his son James, "I had the damnedest fight with Doc O'Connor over the details of my will, and I simply am not going to go through it again." The conversation took place on the day of his fourth inauguration in 1945, when Missy was dead and Roosevelt was dying. James recalled, "He sighed and added, 'I owed her that much. She served me so well for so long and asked so little in return.'"

FDR had to put his concerns about Missy aside and move on to the threats on national security. Following Harold Ickes's recommendation, FDR had ordered an oil embargo on Japan during the summer of 1941, and by late November tension between the United States and Japanese governments was at the breaking point. Thanksgiving came and went without a presidential visit to Warm Springs, but on Saturday, November 29, the president's train rolled into Georgia for the Founder's Day turkey dinner. As soon as he was helped into his car, FDR and Grace Tully drove to Missy's cottage for a short visit. "The Boss and I were keenly looking forward to spending considerable time with Missy and, having experienced a rather long illness myself in 1933 [tuberculosis], I knew that his visit would pick up her spirits, which were indeed low," Grace recalled.

Meanwhile, the press corps quickly dispersed for the sort of relaxation that usually came between briefings at Warm Springs—golfing, swimming, and plenty of drinking. Grace and FDR drove to the Little White House to settle in for a few days—Grace now got to use Missy's bedroom—but after the holiday dinner that night, Secretary of State Hull called to say "the

Far East picture was darkening and that the talks in Washington were in such brittle state that they might be broken at any time," Grace recalled. The president determined it best to cut his visit short and return to Washington the next day, barely twenty-four hours after his arrival. "I accompanied the President on a short farewell call on Missy, who was almost in tears at losing us so soon and in her understanding of the tremendous pressure then bearing down upon her beloved Boss," Grace wrote. The former assistant—now her successor—was certainly being tactful. Missy must have been devastated as she said good-bye.

On the morning of December 7, the Pacific Fleet at Pearl Harbor, Hawaii, was attacked by Japanese planes. Eight battleships were sunk or severely damaged, hundreds of planes destroyed, and thousands of servicemen killed, wounded, and missing. The usually quiet Sunday at the White House abruptly ended. FDR called an emergency cabinet meeting followed by hours of conferences with congressional leaders. During the early evening, Grace received a call from Missy, asking to speak to FDR. She couldn't put the call through, but took a message at 10:05 p.m. "She would like you to call tonight. I told her you would if the conference broke up at a reasonable hour—otherwise you would call her in the morning." He did not call that night.

Grace took the dictation and typed what could be the most famous line of a Roosevelt speech after "the only thing we have to fear is fear itself." Appearing before a joint session of Congress on December 8, the president began, "Yesterday, December 7, 1941, a date which will live in infamy," asking for a declaration of war. He did not call Missy that day, either, but the attack had made him unusually uncommunicative. "The few days after Pearl Harbor provide the only known interval when FDR was not loquacious to visitors," biographer John Gunther wrote. "He was businesslike and even curt to everybody; appointments were brief, the clock had no mercy, and the President kept time with time."

Sam Rosenman, dropping in on FDR on December 9, found him sitting alone in his study, working on his stamp album. It struck him that "If Missy had been well, she would have been sitting up with him in the study that night. She always did in times of great stress, to see whether there was anyone he wanted to call or talk to, or whether he wanted to make any arrangements for the next day." Sam stayed with him until after midnight.

The following week, Dr. McIntire sent a short letter to Dr. Irwin: "I hope this [war] business is not going to upset Miss LeHand too much, though I hear she is taking it very hard." Irwin replied that he had called on Missy, she was getting around better and, according to Miss Plastridge, "she often completes a sentence entirely." Over the next couple of months, though, Missy made little progress and had many setbacks. She fainted while brushing her teeth one morning in December. Niece Barbara spent Christmas with her in Warm Springs and wrote to Eleanor thanking her for "all the wonderful presents that you and the President sent to her," though there is no indication the president called her. There is no indication, either, that the Roosevelts were informed of a supposed suicide attempt Missy made by swallowing chicken bones. Dr. Irwin's wife, Mabel, told biographer Bernard Asbell that her husband was summoned to Missy's cottage one midnight during the holidays. "I think she tried to kill herself tonight," he told her.

By mid-January Dr. Irwin wrote Dr. McIntire that Missy was not eating, refused to take her vitamins, and "is depressed a great deal of the time and cries a lot." Dr. Harper and a colleague were dispatched to Warm Springs, and shortly thereafter Dr. Johnson was reporting that Missy "is more interested in things, is taking more food and liquids, and is apparently enjoying her treatments." However, Dr. Johnson's February 2 letter gives a measure of Missy's physical decline. He said she "is now 105 pounds, dressed," a loss of twenty-five pounds from her weight when she was admitted to Doctors Hospital in June. For a woman of five-foot-seven, she was skeletal.

Grace came to visit soon after, and a plan to bring Missy back to Washington was hatched. On March 18, Missy arrived at 1600

Pennsylvania Avenue and was waiting in her apartment when FDR was wheeled into her room shortly after 11 a.m. He stayed for just ten minutes. She was able to walk with a brace by then, but her right arm was still paralyzed and her speech almost unintelligible. Once again, nurses were brought in around the clock.

The nurse's log over the next few weeks paints a picture of tedium: massages, baths, long hours alone, and, increasingly, large quantities of alcohol—Scotch and soda, orange blossoms, champagne—followed by nights of vomiting. The president made brief visits, and Grace shared confidential cables with Missy, hoping to pique her interest in the world war in which the United States was now fully engaged. But Missy did not accompany FDR on the *Potomac* or to Hyde Park on the weekends. Princess Martha was now his consort on these pleasure trips, Grace, to a somewhat lesser degree, his "office wife." The president, who had been able to "fix" a broken country and rehabilitate his own body to a remarkable degree, was unable to restore Missy to anything remotely like her pre-stroke self. Knowing his history of emotional detachment, it's no wonder that he saw her less and less.

In *The F.D.R. Memoirs,* Asbell quoted "an informant not wishing in this connection to be named" who said Missy spent her days writing letters to friends about her imaginary love life: "The letters told of this one being in love with her, and that one wanting to marry her. Everyone realized that she could no longer be trusted with important information. These friends and family drew together to get the letters out of sight, to hush up Missy's lapse," he wrote. But was the "informant" correct? Missy's medical records clearly state that she was paralyzed on her dominant right side. It would be two years before she could laboriously pen short letters to friends. In the interim, a nurse or her sister Anna served as her corresponding secretary. This certainly casts doubt on the story.

The tragedy of Missy LeHand came to a head in late April, when her bedclothes caught fire and her hands and chest were badly burned, apparently while she was clumsily striking a match to light a cigarette. (Later, her sister, Anna, wrote to Grace accusing one of the nurses of stealing suitcasesful of Missy's possessions, including the gold cigarette lighter given to her by Vincent Astor. Unlike a box of matches, a lighter is easily handled with one hand.) Brother Dan arrived at the White House on April 25. This was probably the point when he and the White House family decided Missy had to go home to Massachusetts. Mike Reilly, chief of the White House Secret Service detail, called the White House "the biggest firetrap in America, bar none," and FDR's fear of fire was well known. It was clear that Missy would not recover and the added risk of torching the White House was the last straw.

On the night of May 15, FDR and Grace had dinner at the White House and spent four hours working. For part of that time, they had a forty-minute visit with Missy. The next day, FDR picked up Princess Martha at her home in Maryland. He visited Missy for ten minutes after returning to the White House, then joined Princess Martha and Harry Hopkins for dinner. Shortly after 10 p.m., Missy left the White House for the last time.

Missy had climbed high for a young woman of undistinguished background, without a college education or any social connections. She had done it with her own unique combination of brains, street smarts, intuition, tact, patience, and charm. For years, she had rubbed elbows and earned the respect of the elite of the land, from ambassadors and judges to captains of industry and leaders of the military. Cabinet officers had sought her advice and begged for her influence. She had been taken into the bosom of the Roosevelt family, called many of the shots at the White House, and filled a ringside seat at some of the most historic events of the twentieth century. She had shared meals with the king and queen of England and hobnobbed with the stars of Hollywood and Broadway. The president of the United States had regularly and repeatedly sought out her company over that of important men and far more alluring women.

For Missy, it was all over. There would be no more White House dinners, glamour shots in evening gowns, laughter-filled Children's Hours, and flattering articles in national magazines. Broken of body and spirit, she returned to her childhood home on Orchard Street in Somerville to wait for FDR to write or phone or visit. The letters and calls came from time to time, but she never saw him again.

## ❁ CHAPTER TWENTY-ONE

# *Going Home*

Missy went home with a nurse to 101 Orchard Street, where her sister, Anna, and nieces, Barbara and Babe, set up a bedroom for her downstairs. She faithfully continued physical therapy at the Chelsea Naval Hospital, and though she showed some progress—which her White House "family" congratulated her for in glowing letters—she was far from well. When Eleanor Roosevelt made a side trip to her home while visiting wounded sailors at the hospital, she said Missy did not seem much improved. Speech remained her biggest handicap and frustration, although her right hand was so impaired letters had to be written for her by Anna or the nurse. Dawn Ramsey Desley, the little granddaughter of close neighbor and family friend Maydelle Ramsey, sometimes came over and massaged Missy's hand.

She spent time at the beach, sometimes just day trips, other times renting a small house on Cape Cod, and got "as brown as an Indian," according to Anna. A black cocker spaniel, dubbed Roxann, joined the family, and Missy added a tiny gold cocker to her charm bracelet. She went off the federal payroll, but the Roosevelts continued to pay for all her medical care, including her nurse. Dawn Desley recalls the president regularly getting movie tickets for her and even sending a limousine to deliver her to the cinema, friends following in a taxi. Her mind functioned better, and she read herself to sleep at night again.

*Missy enjoyed many days on the beach in Massachusetts after she returned home in 1942. She is shown with Dawn Desley Ramsey, nieces Barbara "Sister" Farwell (seated), and Marguerite "Babe" Collins. She is holding her cocker spaniel Roxann.*

The Roosevelts lavished gifts upon her. For her birthday in 1942, FDR sent a large sterling loving cup, engraved with an elaborate monogram, along with a note: "This is literally a Loving Cup—Take a drink on me & then put a bouquet in it—Love FDR."

When Eleanor returned from a trip to England that year, she sent a silver toast rack that she "thought you might enjoy using on your breakfast tray." Roosevelt cousin Daisy Suckley coauthored a children's book, *The True Story of Fala,* and FDR sent a copy inscribed in his hand, "For Missy from her old friend Fala by FDR." He chided her in a 1943 letter, "A little bird told Fala, who told me, that you are not eating very well. Do please take all the nourishment you can and hold that weight." She was very thin in photographs, her hair now completely white.

Washington friends wrote and sometimes visited: Grace Tully,

Harold Ickes, Sam Rosenman, Harry Hopkins, Mary Eben, and Louise Hackmeister. Whenever someone traveled to Somerville from the White House, FDR sent along a handwritten note, always promising to come see her himself, never quite finding the time. "You know all I am doing from the papers—just one tough day after another—awful hot and awful damp—and a bad nose every night," he wrote in 1943, referring to his ongoing sinus woes and the terrible pressure of being commander in chief.

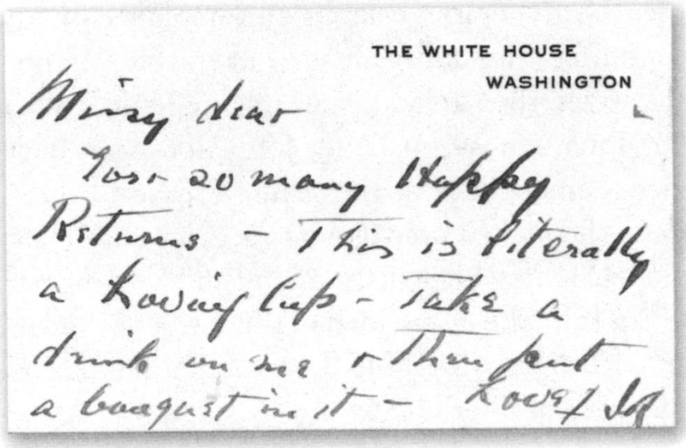
THE WHITE HOUSE
WASHINGTON

Missy dear
Lots & many Happy Returns – This is literally a loving cup – take a drink on me & then put a bouquet in it – Love FDR

*FDR never came to see Missy, but he frequently sent her fond notes, such as this one accompanying an elaborate silver loving cup in 1942.*

Another faithful friend was Bill Bullitt. With her illness, the rancor between them evaporated, and he not only visited but wrote his "Dearest Lady," called her on the phone and sent gifts—a box of crisp fall apples, a globe of the world, a pretty vegetable dish. His secretary, Carmel Offie, still serving his "Chief," sent perfume. Bullitt remained flirtatious: "Washington is queer and strange without you—at least for me." He repeatedly invited her to visit him, assuring her he could provide a separate suite for her and her nurse at his house, and offered to throw a party for her forty-seventh birthday in 1943. She stayed home. Archbishop Francis Spellman sent her a letter that year, telling her he was offering special prayers at the September 13 mass in honor of her birthday.

At the White House, it required several women to take Missy's place. Grace Tully became FDR's private secretary, but she didn't have the breadth of Missy's duties, nor the depth of her personal relationship with the president. Biographer John Gunther, who knew both women, said Grace "was 'better' for him in some ways, because [she was] more detached and business-like." Norwegian Crown Princess Martha was ever-present on social occasions, and FDR drew closer to Daisy Suckley, even giving her a job as an archivist at his presidential library. He reached out to Eleanor, trying to reestablish a semblance of a marriage, but she rebuffed him and widened her travels. Without Missy as a go-between, their relationship was more distant than ever. Daughter Anna, whose husband, John Boettiger, had entered the service, came to live at the White House in the spring of 1944, where she picked up Missy's role as a backup hostess and companion, teaching herself shorthand and keeping her father's cigarette box full. She also joined in the staff conspiracy to bring Lucy Rutherfurd into the White House on numerous occasions, behind her own mother's back.

But none of these women were Missy. One evening Sam and Dorothy Rosenman had dinner with Supreme Court justice Felix Frankfurter. "We talked a good deal about poor Missy LeHand," Frankfurter wrote in his diary, reflecting on the "remarkable judgement, disinterestedness and pertinacity which she combined. Sam agreed with me that Missy's enforced withdrawal is a calamity of world dimensions in view of FDR's responsibility for world affairs. Sam said he always regarded her as one of the five most important people in the U.S. during the Roosevelt Administration, to which I replied that she seemed to me always to be the best most influential factor in the Administration, the President apart." Rosenman later likened her forced retirement to the country losing a battle in the war. Harold Ickes described it as "the greatest loss that the President has suffered since his inauguration."

In the fall of 1943, Missy had a breakthrough, what her sister described as "like a miracle." She was able to walk better and even ride a stationary bicycle, getting around so well that her bed was moved upstairs. She learned to write with her left hand and her speech improved. FDR wrote "It was just grand to hear how well you are doing and that you can say 'Mind your own business!'" to the nurse. Yet she missed her old life, and F.D., terribly. The Christmas holidays were particularly hard, and Anna Rochon wrote a reproachful letter to FDR: "She started crying New Year's Eve about 11:30 and we couldn't stop her and then she had a heart spell and kept calling 'F.D., come, please come, oh F.D.'—it really was the saddest thing I ever hope to see, we were all crying, she was very depressed all through the Holidays and that was the climax. She was expecting you to call on Xmas day and when we sat down to dinner, her eyes filled with tears and she said, 'A Toast to the President's Health' and then again in the middle of dinner—another toast to you."

The letter yielded results. FDR and Grace invited Missy to come spend a week at the White House in March 1944, but they hadn't consulted Eleanor, who canceled the visit, explaining she would be away at the appointed week and wanted to see Missy, too. Her note was kind but brisk, making it clear that Missy no longer had a home at the White House: her rooms were needed for visitors, her possessions had been placed in the attic for safekeeping. Eleanor rescheduled the visit and then canceled again, and Missy refused to consider another date. "It just about killed her to have the trip postponed twice," her sister wrote Bill Bullitt, urging him to let others in Washington know how lonely Missy was and how much she missed her old life. He again asked her to visit him, but Anna replied that even though "Missy thinks the world of you . . . she doesn't think that would look right."

FDR was lonely, too. All four of his sons were in the service, and Harry Hopkins had remarried and moved out of the White House. By the spring of 1944, the sad state of the president's health was obvious to anyone: he was gaunt and thin, his hands shook, he had spells when he seemed mentally absent and would vacantly stare into space. His occasional letters to Missy talked of getting rest at Hyde Park and Hobcaw Barony, the South Carolina retreat of financier Bernard Baruch. The Republican Party, seeing an opportunity to recapture the White House with their candidate, Thomas Dewey, charged that the Democrats were governing with a bunch of "tired old men."

Missy continued to take a keen interest in the war and in politics. On June 8, 1944, she handwrote a note to Grace: "D-day! Invasion! Hurrah!!!" FDR loved it, and sent her a short letter, closing with the hope that "I shall see you soon." Missy's last note to Grace, written on July 17, was about the likely vice presidential nominee at the upcoming Democratic National Convention. "I have been beside myself trying to figure it out," she wrote. Harry S. Truman wasn't on her list.

FDR accepted the nomination for a fourth term from California, where he was poised to depart by ship on inspection tours of Pearl Harbor and the Aleutian Islands of Alaska. Newsreel crews filmed his speech, the president seated and looking extremely haggard. On the evening of July 30, Missy went to the University Theater at Harvard Square with her sister and Maydelle Ramsey. She became disturbed by the president's appearance on a newsreel and asked to go home.

Later that night, Anna heard strange noises from Missy's room. While sifting through a box of pictures and memorabilia from her White House years, she had suffered another stroke. She never regained consciousness, dying the next morning at the Chelsea Naval Hospital, her brother Dan at her side. She was six weeks shy of her forty-eighth birthday.

FDR was on his way to Alaska by then, and his press secretary, Steve Early, issued a statement on his behalf from the White House:

> Memories of more than a score of years of devoted service enhance the sense of personal loss which Miss LeHand's passing

brings. Faithful and painstaking, with a charm of manner inspired by tact and kindness of heart, she was utterly selfless in her devotion to duty. Hers was a quiet efficiency, which made her a real genius in getting things done. Her memory will ever be held in affectionate remembrance and appreciation, not only by all members of our family, but the wide circle of those whose duties brought them into contact with her.

The phrase "She was utterly selfless in her devotion to duty" was chiseled on Missy's grave marker in Mount Auburn Cemetery in Cambridge, a lovely tree-filled park where some of Boston's most distinguished citizens rest. A huge boulder of pink marble—a color Missy loved—marks the family plot.

*Mourners enter the church for Missy's funeral, led by her family, Barbara Farwell, Tom and Marguerite Collins, Anna Rochon, and Dan LeHand. Eleanor Roosevelt follows.*

Her funeral mass was held August 2 at St. John the Evangelist Catholic Church in North Cambridge, celebrated by Bishop Richard J. Cushing. A blanket of white gladioli and red roses, bound with red, white, and blue ribbon, covered the casket, a gift of the White House. Missy's sister, Anna, and brother Dan, nieces, Barbara and Babe, and Babe's husband, Tom, in his navy uniform, were joined by 1,200 others in paying their respects, including Eleanor Roosevelt. Other notables attending were Justice Felix Frankfurter (who would join Missy at Mount Auburn in 1965), Joseph P. Kennedy, former postmaster general James Farley, and James Roosevelt's ex-wife, Betsey.

Bill Bullitt, who had despaired of getting a meaningful war job from FDR, had joined the Free French under General Charles de Gaulle. From Naples, Italy, he sent Grace Tully a telegram asking her to arrange for "appropriate flowers" to be sent on his behalf.

When FDR returned from his travels, he and Grace had a quiet moment together. "I naturally said to him, 'You and I lost a very dear friend,'" Grace told biographer Bernard Asbell. "And he was about to cry and so was I, and he said, 'Yes, poor Missy.' But he never liked to talk about those things because he was—well, being a man, he didn't want to show any emotion. At least I never saw him show any." She had apparently forgotten the tears that welled up in his eyes when his mother died.

Missy's name was mentioned in the White House Usher's Log for the last time on Sunday, November 26, 1944. FDR had been reelected for his fourth term and had just gotten back to the White House from a weekend at Hyde Park. At 12:20 p.m., the log reads, "To East Wing to look over effects of Miss M. A. LeHand." Eleanor was with him, and they spent about an hour examining Missy's furniture, books, and clothing, which included eleven evening dresses. Five of the dresses were blue. It was the president's favorite color; it was Eleanor's favorite color, too.

❁ EPILOGUE

# *Missy's Legacy*

On March 28, 1945, the SS *Marguerite LeHand*, a military cargo ship, was launched at the Pascagoula, Mississippi, shipyard. R. I. Ingalls, whose company had built the ship, made a $1,000 donation to the March of Dimes for the occasion, and FDR and Eleanor sent "warm greetings" and "the hope that a craft which bears so honored a name will make many a safe journey and always find a peaceful harbor." Missy's nieces, Babe and Barbara, were the honorees at the christening ceremony, Babe cracking the bottle of champagne on the bow.

*Missy's niece Babe Collins holds a bouquet of roses for the launching of SS* Marguerite LeHand *in March 1945.*

By then, the war that had consumed the world and claimed millions of lives was winding down. FDR, two months into his fourth term and exhausted after attending the Yalta Conference with Winston Churchill and Joseph Stalin in the Crimea, went to the Little White House to try to recover his strength, accompanied by his cousins Polly Delano and Daisy Suckley. He was secretly joined there by Lucy Mercer Rutherfurd and a Russian artist she had commissioned to paint his portrait. On the morning of April 12, while sitting for the artist, he suffered a cerebral hemorrhage and died later that afternoon. He was sixty-three. The next morning, newspapers across the country added his name to the list of war casualties they published. Missy had not been accorded the same honor, though she was as much a casualty of the war as FDR.

*One of the of the last photos of FDR, taken at the Little White House, shows the physical toll of illness and the war.*

White House maid Lillian Rogers Parks aptly remarked, "The White House used up people like soap!" Marvin McIntyre had died of tuberculosis in 1943 at age sixty-five, and Pa Watson of heart disease and a cerebral hemorrhage on the way home from Yalta at age sixty-two. Of the inner-circle members who survived FDR's presidency, Harry Hopkins succumbed at age fifty-five to complications of his long-term gastrointestinal illness, and Steve Early to a heart attack when he was sixty-one.

The only Children's Hour regular with a long lifespan was Grace Tully. Like Missy, she never married, but she lived to the ripe old age of eighty-three, dying in Washington in 1984. Eighteen years after her death, a large trove of her White House files, including some of Missy's correspondence, was sold in a private transaction for $8 million. The papers, known as the Tully Collection, were donated to the FDR Library in 2010. While this acquisition greatly expanded the collection of LeHand papers at the library, it is quite possible more papers were lost at the time Tully left the White House and over the years as the papers she took were shuffled among her heirs. There are, for example, only a handful of letters between Missy and FDR, which seems very unlikely considering how long she worked for him.

To commemorate the eightieth anniversary of Missy's birth, the Somerville Public Library named its children's library room for her. The dedication ceremony on September 12, 1976, drew a beaming Babe and Barbara, Babe's daughter Barbara Jacques and other LeHand kin, and James Roosevelt. Making a surprise appearance was Representative Thomas P. "Tip" O'Neill of Boston, the neighbor Missy had given such a thrill to when she introduced him to FDR. Three months later he was sworn in as speaker of the U.S. House of Representatives.

In some ways, Missy has faded into obscurity. In other ways, her fate has been worse. Elliott Roosevelt's claim in his 1973 memoir that Missy and his father were lovers and his Eleanor Roosevelt detective series created in the public's eye the role of in-house presidential mistress for Missy. This was further cemented by the movie *Hyde Park on Hudson* in 2012. Using Daisy Suckley's diary description of the 1939 visit of the king and queen of England as his starting point, screenwriter Richard Nelson created a French farce at Hyde Park with Missy and Daisy as the competing mistresses. The portrayal appalled Missy's great-nieces, as well as Roosevelt biographer Geoffrey Ward, who had edited Daisy's diaries and letters.

*Missy's great-nieces, Jane Scarbrough and Barbara Jacques, stand outside the cottage she built in Warm Springs, now owned by the state of Georgia and fallen into disrepair.*

The glowing words about Missy from her contemporaries tend to be ignored in favor of this sort of fictionalized speculation masquerading as history. One of the most astute evaluations in recent years was written by diplomatic historian Frank Costigliola, author of *Roosevelt's Lost Alliances: How Personal Politics Helped Start the Cold War*. In a talk about his book at Hunter College's Roosevelt House in 2012, Costigliola described Missy as "the most remarkable" of FDR's inner circle and "a very, very savvy woman." Her importance has been overlooked by historians, he said, because she was a woman, because of her position as a secretary, and because she left so few official papers.

But the Roosevelt family hasn't overlooked her. Missy died more than seventy years ago, and to this day the Roosevelts maintain her grave. FDR's words to his son James about keeping Missy in his will even after her death are a fitting justification: "I owed her that much. She served me so well for so long and asked so little in return."

# *Afterword and Acknowledgments*

My grandfather Thomas Bruce Yandle was what we in the South call a Yellow Dog Democrat: he would vote for a yellow dog if it was on the Democratic ticket. Like many Southerners who were scarred by the Great Depression, he developed that fierce party loyalty because of FDR. A few weeks after the crash of 1929, Bruce and his wife, my grandmother Mollye Thompson Yandle, had their first baby. Gladys Nan was premature and weighed just three pounds. It's a miracle she lived at all, but her rocky start left my grandparents with $1,200 in medical bills. "Paw Paw" was earning only $25 a week as a newspaper printer. He always had a job during the first years of the Depression, but often the checks his employers wrote were bad, and he had to plead with grocers to give him food for his small family, which soon included my father, Bruce Jr. It was not until they moved to Meriwether County and my grandfather got a job at the *Manchester Mercury* in the mid-1930s that he was again paid regularly with checks that did not bounce.

I learned to love FDR at Paw Paw's knee, but it was when I was an adult fighting cancer that FDR truly inspired me. At age forty-three—about the same age as Missy when she had her stroke—I was diagnosed with breast cancer. Deeply depressed and almost paralyzed with fear, I was watching PBS one night when a documentary about FDR came on. The story of his comeback from polio inspired me to fight my disease, and the words "The only thing we have to fear is fear itself" became my personal motto.

Six years later, I read *The Defining Moment: FDR's Hundred Days and the Triumph of Hope,* by fellow cancer survivor Jonathan Alter, and caught my first glimpse of FDR's enigmatic secretary, Marguerite LeHand. How did she get such an enviable job? I wondered. What cut her life so short? My life was very busy at the time, as I had helped found and was leading a cancer charity in my city. After I retired a few years later, I had more time to read, and I revisited the mystery of Missy. I wanted to read a book that was just about her. Internet searches turned up nothing substantial, so I contacted Robert Clark, then the supervisory archivist at the FDR Library and Museum in Hyde Park. His reply to my query in April 2013 was this: "To our knowledge, there is no single volume biography, dissertation or monograph about Missy LeHand." I decided to write one. The three years that followed have been a journey full of surprises, not the least of which was finding self-described "Missy fans" at every turn.

Originally, I planned to write and self-publish a modest little book that would gather the research of other writers into one narrative. But then I began to realize much of what had been written about Missy was inaccurate. Early on, an Internet search led me to an article "Broken Circle: The Isolation of FDR in World War II," written by University of Connecticut history professor Frank Costigliola. Frank presented Missy as a remarkable and invaluable advisor, rather than as the lovelorn secretary or possible mistress of the president. The article was expanded into his book *Roosevelt's Lost Alliances: How Personal Politics Helped Start the Cold War*. I am indebted to Frank for the light-bulb moment when I read his paper and for urging me to find Missy's family when we talked by phone. "They are the key," he said, and he was right. But it wasn't easy to find them.

My initial research on Missy took me to Warm Springs, Georgia, where the people are as kind, welcoming, and helpful today as they were to FDR and Missy in 1924. I stayed at the Hotel

Warm Springs, run by consummate hostess Gerrie Thompson, sleeping in a Val-Kill Industries bed and using a bathroom that, she told me, had been converted by the press into a makeshift photo lab when FDR's funeral train pulled out of the station in 1945. Mike Shadix, the archivist at the Roosevelt Warm Springs Rehabilitation Campus, generously shared his pictures and files and took me into both the cottage Missy owned and the one in which she lived as a patient after her stroke. The Reverend Bob Patterson, minister of Warm Springs's First Baptist Church and the acknowledged local historian, drove me around town, loaned me books from his considerable FDR library, and even took me to his Rotary Club meeting in Manchester, where I gave a talk about Missy. (Like Bob, I am a Rotarian, and share his passion for Rotary's number one service project, the international eradication of polio.) At the Little White House, ranger Ashley Audley gave me a thorough tour, and another ranger, David Burke, author of a photo book on Warm Springs, shared his picture files. Subsequently, site manager Robin Glass allowed me to enter Missy's bedroom, unchanged since 1945—including the crepelike roll of toilet paper in the bathroom. At the *Manchester Star-Mercury* office, I was turned loose in the newspaper morgue, with its binders full of historic editions of the *Manchester Mercury, Meriwether Vindicator,* and the *Warm Springs Mirror*. What a treat for an old newspaper reporter like me to handle the newspapers my grandfather had typeset!

I owe a tremendous thanks to Mike Shadix, who subsequently procured for me Missy's eye-opening medical file from the Georgia Archives and who put me in touch with her great-nieces, Barbara Jacques and Jane Scarbrough. They generously shared their pictures, letters, scrapbooks, and memorabilia, not to mention Missy's fascinating home movies. (Thank goodness their mothers, Missy's beloved nieces, treasured her papers and memorabilia and kept them together for decades.) It has been my joy and pleasure to get to know these hilarious, straight-talking cousins and their wonderful husbands, Bill and John, during visits to their homes and in Missy meet-ups in New York and Hyde Park. Being around them gives me a notion of what fun Missy must have been at the White House Children's Hour!

This book is dedicated to Jane and Barbara and to a third person, Dr. Steven Lomazow, whose book *FDR's Deadly Secret* is cited several times in my text. Steve, introduced to me by Frank Costigliola, is a practicing neurologist who likes to say he is a historian disguised as a doctor. He is also an inveterate collector of many things FDR, a trustee at the FDR Library, and a great friend. His introductions to many others, including FDR biographer Geoffrey Ward and my marvelous agent, Meg Thompson, helped what I had originally thought would be a little self-published book attract the attention of Michelle Howry, my very gifted editor at Touchstone.

Geoff Ward has been so helpful in so many ways. In one of our first email exchanges, he said, "I've found the field of Roosevelt biographers wonderfully welcoming—which I think says something for the Roosevelts." Like many in the Roosevelt world, he was simply eager for Missy's story to be told. The timing of the Ken Burns film *The Roosevelts: An Intimate History*, for which Geoff wrote the script and did on-camera interviews, in the fall of 2014 was particularly timely, and his enthusiastic endorsement of my project helped attract the interest of Touchstone. Susanna Steisel, the photo researcher at Ken Burns's Florentine Films, was helpful in sharing the enormous photo archive that was used in that project.

Steve Lomazow also introduced me to Dr. Hal S. "Toby" Raper, whose crystal-clear memories of a childhood spent on the Warm Springs Foundation grounds were brought to life during a driving tour. He pointed out where everyone lived, peeling away the decades to show me what things were like in the 1930s. Missy meet-ups with Steve and his wife, Suze Bienaimée, and Toby and his wife, Cathy, were always an adventure and a treat.

Another biographer, David Roll, author of *The Hopkins Touch*, put me in touch with Diana Hopkins Halsted, whose memories of a childhood spent in the White House prompted me to tell her she needs to write a children's book à la *Eloise at the Plaza*!

The Hyde Park Library and Museum was my introduction to the serious world of the history scholar, and I am very grateful to the staff there, especially the aforementioned Supervisory Archivist Robert Clark (now Director of Archives at the Rockefeller Archive Center) and Supervisory Museum Curator Herman Eberhardt. In addition to my own visits, I had the assistance of a talented and enthusiastic young researcher, Holley Snaith, an intern at several Roosevelt properties during the writing of this book, who happily took on some assignments for me. Holley was also in the process of researching the decor of Eleanor Roosevelt's home at Val-Kill and found a copy of the picture of Missy that had hung on ER's bedroom wall. In addition, Holley handled my procurement of copies of the invaluable correspondence between Missy and William Christian Bullitt from Yale University's Sterling Library.

Frank Costigliola, who quoted from Missy's letters to William C. Bullitt in his book, urged me to dig deeper into the Bullitt archive, but he warned me that most of the letters were undated. By the time I got them in the fall of 2014, I was so familiar with Missy's timeline that I was able to plug dates into most of them. The intensity of Missy's love for Bullitt, and the revelation that she, not he, had broken off their affair in the fall of 1940, laid to rest in my mind both the image of lovelorn secretary and presidential mistress. I hope my readers will draw the same conclusion.

My last research trip in June 2015 took me to Somerville, Massachusetts. (In one of the many coincidences that piled up during the writing of this book, I learned that my father-in-law, Leo L. Smith, lived in Somerville for three years when he was in the navy and that my husband's older siblings were born at the Chelsea Naval Hospital, where Missy died.) There I saw the exterior of Missy's old home, beautifully remodeled for a twenty-first-century family, walked into the theater where the Somerville Players performed, and had dinner at an Irish pub on Davis Square. Especially moving for me was my visit to Mount Auburn Cemetery, where passionate and well-informed volunteer Anne Lawthers—another Missy fan—directed me to the LeHand plot where Missy, her sister, Anna, niece Barbara Farwell Atwood and her husband, William—Jane Scarbrough's parents—are buried. She also directed me to the resting place of Marguerite "Babe" Collins and husband, Tom, the parents of Barbara Jacques. A dozen or so years after this peaceful garden cemetery was started, poet Emily Dickinson wrote, "It seems as if Nature had formed the spot with the distinct idea of its being a resting place for her children." No one could put it better than the Belle of Amherst.

My last stop on the "Missy trip" was the main Somerville Public Library, a place absolutely popping with activity. Director of Libraries Glenn Ferdman, reference librarian Kevin Okelly, and children's librarian Cathy Piantigini (who grew up in the house next door to Missy's) were all helpful and interested in the woman for whom the children's room is named.

Bringing Missy to life didn't stop with research. I tried to re-create the experiences of her life by taking long train trips from South Carolina to New York City and Hyde Park, watching movies she and Effdee enjoyed, and reading books of the period, including *Miss Maitland Private Secretary, The Office Wife,* and Bill Bullitt's entertaining *It's Not Done*. Like Missy, I am a Francophile, and on a vacation in Paris I spent a "Missy Day," standing outside the U.S. embassy until I was shooed off by a guard, visiting the House of Guerlain, and strolling along the Rue de Rivoli.

As I completed chapters, I got valuable feedback from Steve Lomazow, Holley Snaith, and Toby Raper, as well as Roger L. Di Silvestro, author of *Theodore Roosevelt in the Badlands,* who patiently taught me how to develop a proposal for a publisher; economists Roger Meiners, Bruce Yandle, and Adam Smith (I am fortunate to be Bruce's daughter and Adam's mom, so I got lots of help interpreting the Depression); diplomatic historian Ken

Bain, who also has an FDR book in the works; history-loving friends Mark L. Hopkins, Charles Welborn (who generously loaned me books from his FDR library), Linda Harral, Sue Tuten, Brandon Grace, and Kelly Durham (a writer of first-rate World War II thrillers); my legal consultant, Jack McIntosh; my mother, Dot Yandle, a talented editor; my dear friend and omnivorous reader Jean Mahaffey; and other members of my family, including my aunt Susan Yandle Middleton (Paw Paw's post-Depression daughter); brothers Bruce and Eric Yandle, and daughter Elizabeth Smith Dowling. Many, many friends, including members of the Foothills Writers Guild, encouraged me along the way by asking, "How's Missy?" I am grateful to Geoff Ward, Bob Clark, and Steve Lomazow for their reading of the full manuscript. They prevented me from publishing several embarrassing mistakes. Any that remain are entirely my fault.

At Simon & Schuster, in addition to my editor Michelle Howry, *The Gatekeeper* benefited from the meticulous copyediting of Fred Chase, overseen by senior production editor Mark LaFlaur. Kyle Kabel is responsible for the lovely design of this book, and, as a printer's granddaughter, I fully appreciate his choice of fonts and embellishments. I know Paw Paw would too! The publishing team at Touchstone and Simon & Schuster, including Carolyn Reidy, Susan Moldow, Tara Parsons, David Falk, Meredith Vilarello, and Shida Carr, helped get the word out on the book. Closer to home, Nichole Mango Smith, the talented mother of my granddaughter, London, developed my websites, kathrynsmithwords.com and margueritelehand.com.

Finally, I have to thank my darling husband, Leo, who has put up with my obsession for more than three years, listened to me gab incessantly about Missy and FDR, accompanied me on "Missy trips," and provided all the support needed for me to write this book. One of the most poignant aspects of Missy's life was that she did not have a partner with whom to fully share her joys and sorrows. There's only one Leo, and I am very grateful he is mine.

# Notes

### *Prologue: The Daring Flight to Chicago*

The most thorough description of the flight is "American Airways Trimotor Transports FDR to Chicago Democratic Convention," written by Baird and Marguerite Wonsey, the son and granddaughter of the pilot. Other eyewitness accounts are from Samuel I. Rosenman in *Working with Roosevelt*, Elliott Roosevelt in *An Untold Story: The Roosevelts of Hyde Park,* and Grace Tully in *F.D.R. My Boss.* Jonathan Alter's *The Defining Moment: FDR's Hundred Days and the Triumph of Hope* gives a colorful account of the action at the Chicago convention. James Roosevelt also describes the scene in *My Parents: A Differing View.*

It's important to note that in having "only" a high school education, Missy had attained a degree held by a minority of Americans. School attendance as reported in the 1920 U.S. Census peaked at age fourteen. By age seventeen, just 34.6 percent of American children were still in school. For that matter, Eleanor Roosevelt did not complete her last year of secondary school or go to college.

The description of Roosevelt's "political walk" comes from Al Vinck, a retired history teacher and volunteer tour guide the author met at Top Cottage in Hyde Park. Dr. Hal S. Raper, whose parents were on the medical staff at Warm Springs, is also a grand demonstrator of the walk, and has constructed his own braces to more thoroughly demonstrate the effect. James Tobin's *The Man He Became* provides an exhaustive analysis of FDR's polio attack and rehabilitation.

Historian Arthur M. Schlesinger Jr. describes Missy's importance in *The Coming of the New Deal*, as does Rosenman in *Working with Roosevelt*. Joseph Persico writes of Lucy Mercer Rutherfurd in *Franklin and Lucy: President Roosevelt, Mrs. Rutherfurd, and the Other Remarkable Women in His Life*.

Articles about Missy cited here include the *Newsweek* piece appearing in the August 12, 1933, issue. She appeared on the cover of *Time* on December 17, 1934 (the cover can be accessed at http://content.time.com/time/coversearch/). "Washington Capitalizes 7 Names in Listing Well-Dressed Women" by Dick Gerry is an undated clipping in the LeHand Family Papers. Doris Fleeson's piece "Missy—to do this—FDR" ran in *The Saturday Evening Post* on January 8, 1938. "LOOK Calls on Missy LeHand" ran August 13, 1940.

Historian Frank Costigliola gives Missy her full due as functional chief of staff in his book *Roosevelt's Lost Alliances: How Personal Politics Helped Start the Cold War.* He also quotes the Drew Pearson column. Both Elliott Roosevelt in his memoir *An Untold Story* and *New York Times* columnist Arthur Krock in a column appearing August 1, 1944, referred to Missy as FDR's "conscience." Finally, the copy of Robert Sherwood's play *Abe Lincoln in Illinois* inscribed to Missy is in the LeHand Family Papers. The play won the Pulitzer Prize for drama in 1939, was presented on Broadway 1938–39, and became a film in 1940.

### *One: When Missy Was Marguerite*

The description of the Irish potato famine comes from John Kelly's *The Graves Are Walking: The Great Famine and the Saga of the Irish People* and Liz Sonneborn's *The Great Irish Famine*. John Mitchell's book was *The Last Conquest of Ireland (Perhaps)*. David Nasaw describes Joseph P. Kennedy's father in *The Patriarch: The Remarkable Life and Turbulent Times of Joseph P. Kennedy.* James Roosevelt relates the story of FDR's mirth about appointing Kennedy in *My Parents*.

The information on Missy's family comes from contemporary St. Lawrence County, New York, newspapers. Hannah LeHand's obituary ran in the *Potsdam Courier & Freeman* on December 12, 1907. Data about the LeHand and Graffin families is taken from U.S. Census records. The year of Missy's birth has been variously reported as 1896, 1897, and 1898. The date on her grave marker is 1896 and coincides with U.S. Census reports and a medical history taken in 1941 when she had her stroke, as well as the birthdate on her 1926 passport in the LeHand Family Papers. The spelling of Missy's surname varies quite a bit, from Lehand to Le Hand to LeHand; her own use is inconsistent, as are census documents. The author decided to standardize it as LeHand, as it appears on her grave marker, though other spellings are used in the context in which they appeared. Information about Daniel LeHand and the Clarkson family comes from "Bayreuth of North Country" in the *Potsdam Courier & Freeman,* April 15, 1954. Missy's obituary appeared in that newspaper on August 2, 1944. The Graffin reunion is described in "Three Generations of the Graffin Family Hold a Happy Reunion" in the *Massena Observer,* August 3, 1911.

Dee Morris and Dora St. Martin give a marvelous historic portrait of Missy's adopted hometown in *Somerville, Massachusetts: A Brief History.* The account of Somerville's disparaging nickname and subsequent gentrification is in Susan Diesenhouse's "Slummerville No More," which ran in the *Boston Globe* on April 6, 2005. Missy's house at 101 Orchard Street is currently valued at $1.4 million by Zillow.com. Read about the What the Fluff? festival at www.unionsquaremain.org.

Missy's great-niece Barbara Jacques provided the information about the family's church. Census reports detailed their living arrangements. Missy's dressed-up accounts of her background come from Fleeson's *Saturday Evening Post* article and *The New Dealers* by the Unofficial Observer. Bernard Asbell's claim about Missy's father was made in his book *The F.D.R. Memoirs.* Barbara Jacques confirmed Asbell's assertion that rooms were rented to Harvard students.

The description of the lively culture scene and Tallulah Bankhead's quote come from Morris and St. Martin. The history of the public library is from an undated pamphlet, "Everything You Wanted to Know About the Somerville Public Library but Were Afraid to Ask," published by the library. (Andrew Carnegie funded the construction of more than two thousand public libraries in the United States.) Missy's elementary school graduation date comes from Annual Report of the City of Somerville, 1912, accessed at http://www.somerville.k12.ma.us/education/components/scrapbook/default.php?sectiondetailid=14716&linkid=nav-menu-container-4-89914.

Missy's rheumatic fever episode is described in the C. E. Irwin Correspondence File, Marguerite LeHand folder, in the Georgia Archives, referred to as the LeHand Medical File. The author interviewed Peter C. English, MD, and used his book *Rheumatic Fever in*

*America and Britain: A Biological, Epidemiological and Medical History* to obtain an understanding of the long-term repercussions this illness had for Missy's health.

Jacques and her cousin Jane Scarbrough, the other LeHand great-niece, filled the author in on their mothers' nicknames. Barbara Muller Curtis's recollections are included in Asbell's *The F.D.R. Memoirs.* Copies of Missy's student newspaper were perused at the Somerville Public Library.

Background on the secretarial profession comes from Agnes Rogers's *Women Are Here to Stay* and a Gregg Shorthand textbook. Geraldine Bonner's *Miss Maitland Private Secretary* is a fun read, even today! Missy shared her checkered employment history with reporters George Sprague and Will Oursler in an interview published as "Miss LeHand Quit Jobs with No Future," *Boston Daily Record,* August 3, 1937. (Will was the son of Missy's good friend Fulton Oursler.) Other accounts of her professional life are "Ladies of the White House Secretariat" by Ruby A. Black, *Democratic Digest,* February 1938; and "Marguerite LeHand with FDR Since 1920" by Bab Lincoln, *Washington Times,* January 18, 1939.

### Two: Scion of the Hudson Valley Roosevelts

Geoffrey Ward's book *Before the Trumpet: Young Franklin Roosevelt, 1882–1905,* Kenneth S. Davis's *FDR: The Beckoning of Destiny,* and Hazel Rowley's *Franklin and Eleanor: An Extraordinary Marriage* provide details about FDR's childhood and upbringing. Eleanor Roosevelt's comment about Sara looking after her son's health is from ER's *This I Remember.* Malcolm MacKay's short book *Impeccable Connections* tells of Richard Whitney and the Porcellian Club. Missy wrote of FDR's collection of pigs in a draft article for *The Saturday Evening Post,* LeHand Papers, Tully Collection, FDRL.

Ward's second book about FDR, *A First-Class Temperament: The Emergence of Franklin Roosevelt,* and the book cowritten with Ken Burns as a companion to their PBS documentary, *The Roosevelts: An Intimate History,* provide details of the Roosevelts' courtship and marriage. FDR's fond description of Eleanor's hair and eyes is from *Mrs. R: The Life of Eleanor Roosevelt* by Alfred Steinberg. Ward, Burns, Rowley, and Blanche Wiesen Cook in her two-volume biography, *Eleanor Roosevelt,* tell the poignant story of ER's childhood. The account of the Roosevelt wedding appeared in *The New York Times,* March 18, 1905.

ER herself admitted the shocking incident of the baby in the basket in her *Autobiography.* This is also the source for the quote of Franklin's wide-ranging campaign for State Senate. The description of Louis McHenry Howe comes from *The New Dealers,* previously cited. Howe told the "true" story of Lizzie Borden to Fulton Oursler, claiming Lizzie's sister was the culprit in the ax murders. Oursler recounted it in *Behold This Dreamer!: An Autobiography.* Frances Perkins's memoir, *The Roosevelt I Knew,* is the source for her quote about FDR's demeanor in the New York Senate. Ward's *A First-Class Temperament* provides the account of FDR's first years in politics.

The U.S. Navy webpage, "Origins of Navy Terminology," http://www.navy.mil/navydata/traditions/html/navyterm.html#joe, is the source of the "cup of Joe" story. Ward's *A First-Class Temperament* provides FDR's derogatory description of Josephus Daniels. Rowley describes ER's calling schedule. Persico's *Franklin and Lucy* is the source of the story of the affair with Lucy Mercer Rutherfurd. Joseph Alsop quoted Alice Roosevelt Longworth in *FDR: A Centenary Remembrance.* Eleanor's devastating comment about how FDR's infidelity affected her is from Ward's *A First-Class Temperament.*

### Three: The Cuff Links Gang

This chapter provides the first instance of historic dollars converted into current ones. The website www.usinflationcalculator.com was used for this purpose throughout the book.

Charles McCarthy's August 23, 1920, letter to Missy is in the LeHand Family Papers. Ward's *A First-Class Temperament* and Ward and Burns's *The Roosevelts* provide good background on the 1920 campaign. An early biography by Ernest K. Lindley, *Franklin D. Roosevelt: A Career in Progressive Democracy,* tells of the visit to the White House to see Wilson. The Mencken quote about Harding is from *Presidential Voices: Speaking Styles from George Washington to George W. Bush* by Allan Metcalf.

Steve Early's life and contributions to FDR's rise are well told in Linda Levin's *The Making of FDR: The Story of Stephen T. Early, America's First Modern Press Secretary.* ER's account of her growing friendship with Howe is in her *Autobiography.* The total number of speeches was compiled by Alter, previously cited. Missy's description of FDR is from her draft article for *The Saturday Evening Post*. Charles McCarthy's gold cuff links are on display at the FDRL.

Missy's account of her first meeting with ER is from "Ladies in Waiting in the White House" by Dorothy Ducas, *Who* magazine, May 1941. The varying descriptions of the ER-Missy relationship come from Ward's *A First-Class Temperament,* Conrad Black's *Franklin Delano Roosevelt: Champion of Freedom,* and Doris Kearns Goodwin's *No Ordinary Time: Franklin and Eleanor Roosevelt: The Home Front in World War II,* among others. Marion Dickerman spoke of Missy's hero worship in Kenneth S. Davis's *Invincible Summer: An Intimate Portrait of the Roosevelts, Based on the Recollections of Marion Dickerman.*

Initial descriptions of FDR's foray into the private sector come from Alfred B. Rollins Jr.'s *Roosevelt and Howe,* James Roosevelt's memoir *Affectionately, F.D.R.: A Son's Story of a Lonely Man,* and Elliott Roosevelt's *An Untold Story,* previously cited. Missy shared her initial reluctance to join FDR's law office with Fleeson in *The Saturday Evening Post* profile. It also told where Missy lived. The subway stops were counted by the author using a historic map at http://www.nycsubway.org/perl/caption.pl?/img/maps/calcagno-1920-elevated.gif.

The account of FDR's workday comes from http://www.roosevelthouse.hunter.cuny.edu/work/franklin-delano-roosevelts-desk/.

Alter, previously cited, tells entertainingly of FDR's get-rich-quick schemes.

Bruce Catton's description of the 1920s is from "The Restless Decade" in *American Heritage* magazine, August 1965. The same issue contains "Memoranda of a Decade," by Malcolm and Robert Cowley, with the fact about scantier women's clothes. The statistic on women smoking is from Rogers's *Women Are Here to Stay.* The Lucky Strike ads were found in a Google search.

The quote about FDR's correspondence is from the Lindley biography, previously cited. Missy described studying her employer to A. J. Woolf in "Roosevelt as His Secretary Sees Him," *New York Times Magazine,* June 10, 1934. (Woolf contributed a lovely pencil sketch of Missy.) Missy's beautiful gold charm bracelets are held by her family. The quote about Missy's laugh is from *The New Dealers,* previously cited. An article was adapted from the book for the front page of *The Washington Post* on March 4, 1934, and was (perhaps) incorrectly typeset to describe her laugh as "thrilling" rather than "trilling." Oursler in *Behold This Dreamer!* mentions Missy's throaty voice. Grace Tully spoke of Missy and FDR's shared sense of humor to Asbell, *The F.D.R. Memoirs*.

The account of the navy scandal is from Ward, *A First-Class Temperament*. Missy told Oursler the story of FDR's forgiveness of the senator. (Oursler's account does not specify if the senator was Keyes or the subcommittee chairman, L. Heisler Ball.) Tobin, previously cited, includes an in-depth account of the visit to the Boy Scout camp where FDR was probably exposed to polio. The first two quotes from Missy's letters to FDR on Campobello were read by the author at the FDRL, Family, Business, Personal/Correspondence file. (The first quoted is dated September 1, 1921, the second is August 1, 1921.) The third letter was quoted by Elliott Roosevelt in *An Untold Story*. The ER–Missy letters of August 17, 1921, and August 23, 1921, are also from the FBP/Correspondence file at the FDRL.

### *Four: Adrift*

The source for the opening of this chapter is the movie *Sunrise at Campobello*. Barbara Jacques said her mother, Marguerite "Babe" Collins, was appalled that a redheaded actress was cast as her brunette aunt. In his memoir *My Parents*, James Roosevelt said, "The play was a good piece of fictionalized fact and at least a tribute to the spirit of our parents."

Tobin, previously cited, gives an excellent account of FDR's illness and is the basis for much of the medical detail in this chapter. Ward's *A First-Class Temperament* is also a valuable source. Missy's letter to FDR is quoted by Elliott Roosevelt in *An Untold Story*. The *New York Times* article is quoted in Ward, *A First-Class Temperament*. The account of the polio epidemic of 1916 is part of David M. Oshinsky's enthralling book about the pursuit of a cure or vaccine, *Polio: An American Story*.

The author is indebted to Dr. Steven Lomazow for his idea that Missy had great insight into FDR's psyche because of her own long recovery from rheumatic fever and her continuing frailty. The reading of numerous accounts of FDR's paralysis and an email exchange with James Tobin convinced the author that the scene in *Sunrise at Campobello* in which FDR hoisted himself backward into his wheelchair from the ground was dramatic license. Tobin said he is "virtually positive" FDR could not do this. (It's hard to imagine how the actor Ralph

Bellamy accomplished it, either.) The trunk elevator at Springwood was pointed out by a National Park Service ranger during a tour the author took there in 2013. Ward's *A First-Class Temperament* is the source of the quote from Anna Roosevelt about her father's loquaciousness.

The description of FDR's fall on his first day back at work is told by Tobin and by Ward in *A First-Class Temperament*. (Basil O'Connor derived his nickname from his first name, Daniel, so that his initials spelled out "Doc." He adopted his middle name as his professional name because there were so many Daniel O'Connors practicing law in New York.) Ward describes life on the *Weona II* and includes Missy as a passenger, as does Elliott Roosevelt in *An Untold Story*. FDR's description of "the great little packet" is from Jean Edward Smith's *FDR*. The "floating tenement" description is from Ward's *A First-Class Temperament,* as is the heated ER–FDR exchange about the boat's expense. The nightgown quote is from Asbell's *F.D.R. Memoirs*.

Smith writes of the rum swizzles (including a recipe), and both James and Elliott Roosevelt describe recreational activities on board in their previously cited memoirs, *Affectionately, F.D.R.* and *An Untold Story*. The snapshots of Missy on the beach in her bathing suit and on deck in her sunglasses are part of the FDRL photo archive. The quote about her sunburn is from Elliott Roosevelt's book *An Untold Story*.

As this book was being finalized, Steve Lomazow procured at auction photos of FDR, Missy, and friends on the beaches of Florida in 1924, along with a signed humorous poem written by FDR. These have been out of the public eye for more than ninety years. He was kind enough to share one of these photos for the book.

The sources of the claims and counterclaims about Missy and FDR's relationship are cited in the text. The conclusion that no one ever caught FDR or Missy in a compromising position is the author's, after reading over a hundred books about FDR in the past three years. Jane Scarbrough made her assertion in an interview with the author. Eleanor's occasional darts at Missy usually came in letters to her friend Lorena Hickok, quoted in Rodger Streitmatter's *Empty Without You: The Intimate Letters of Eleanor Roosevelt and Lorena Hickok*. Missy's telling comment to Frances Perkins about FDR's depression is from Ward's *A First-Class Temperament*.

Concluding paragraphs about FDR's comeback at the 1924 convention are from Ward's *A First-Class Temperament* and James Roosevelt's *My Parents*.

### *Five: Warm Springs*

As a native Georgian, the author has a special fondness for Warm Springs and visited several times during the writing of this book. A fine book about FDR's Warm Springs experience is Theo Lippman's *The Squire of Warm Springs: FDR in Georgia, 1924–1945,* which was consulted extensively for this chapter. Ruth Stevens's folksy memoir with recipes, *Hi-Ya Neighbor: Intimate Glimpses of Franklin D. Roosevelt at Warm Springs, Georgia, 1924–45,* is the source of the description of FDR's arrival in 1924. Previously cited books by Tobin and Ward continue to be sources for this chapter. The telling quote about the sandbar in the ocean is from *A First-Class Temperament*.

Information about the economy of rural Georgia is from Jamil S. Zainaldin's "Great Depression" in *The New Georgia Encyclopedia*. The U.S. Census Bureau statistic about tax collections was cited in the *Manchester Mercury,* January 22, 1926. Jerry Levins, a resident of Warm Springs, told the author about the bootleggers' fight outside her grandfather Bill Slaughter's general store. James Roosevelt revealed his father's taste for moonshine in *Affectionately, F.D.R.*

The story of ER's Confederate relatives is told by Ward and Burns in *The Roosevelts,* previously cited. The travel guide is *So You're Going South!* by Clare E. Laughlin. (It stated a room at the Hotel Warm Springs cost $1.50 per night.) ER's comment about life in the South is from *This I Remember.* The announcement of the Roosevelts' arrival appeared in the *Manchester Mercury,* October 9, 1924. ("Colonel" is an old Southern term of respect.) ER wrote of her campaign trick with the teapot in her *Autobiography.* FDR's letter to ER about riding around with the Loylesses is quoted in Ward's *A First-Class Temperament.* The *Manchester Mercury* account of FDR's speech appeared in the October 30, 1924, issue. Lippman quoted the *Atlanta Journal* article.

Elliott Roosevelt writes of the spirit of Warm Springs in *An Untold Story,* as does Lippman. The history of Dowdell's Knob was found on the website http://www.exploresouthernhistory.com/dowdellsknob.html. (Today, there is a life-size bronze sculpture of FDR seated on a car seat, braces outside his trousers, at Dowdell's Knob. Visitors can sit beside the president, enjoy the glorious view, and take selfies.)

Missy confessed her antipathy for picnics in a letter to William C. Bullitt on April 11, 1939, part of the William Christian Bullitt Papers at Yale University's Sterling Library. (Henceforth, all correspondence between Missy and Bullitt is from this collection, unless otherwise stated.) The story about the Baptist preacher is recounted in Ward, *A First-Class Temperament*. Missy's misspelled name appeared in the *Manchester Mercury,* November 8, 1926.

The information about Missy's rental cottage is from a pamphlet written by Mike Shadix, Roosevelt Warm Springs Rehabilitation Campus archivist, "Roosevelt Warm Springs Historic Cottages." Shadix took the author there in 2013. Hal S. Raper's childhood memories and abiding love for the Foundation were shared in several interviews and a site visit in 2014. Louis Howe's concern about the purchase of the Meriwether Inn resort is from Tobin, previously cited. ER's comment about Missy is quoted in Davis's *Invincible Summer,* previously cited. The contemporary description of the resort purchase appeared in the *Atlanta Georgian,* quoted in the *Manchester Mercury,* July 23, 1926. Egbert Curtis's credentials are from Asbell, *The F.D.R. Memoirs*. Lippman provides information on the first staff.

ER's housing arrangements at Hyde Park are from Davis, *Invincible Summer.* The account of Missy's trip to Europe comes from Asbell, with the itinerary recorded on her passport in the LeHand Family Papers. She described her days in Paris and Norway in a letter to FDR dated July 29, 1926, Roosevelt Family Papers, FDRL. The description of Missy's favorite perfume is from www.guerlain.com. She later told Bullitt's secretary, Carmel Offie, that L'Heure Bleue was her favorite, and letters thanking both him and Bullitt for bottles of it are in the Bullitt Papers. (Henceforth, all correspondence between Missy and Offie is from the Bullitt Papers, unless otherwise indicated.)

Offie sent Missy a hilarious article that appeared in the magazine *Paris-Soir* in August 1938. It portrayed her as the descendant of a Frenchman from Auvergne, said she read three French newspapers every morning, and advised the White House chefs on using French recipes.

Information on the social atmosphere of the Warm Springs Foundation is from Lippman's book and Raper interviews. The April 1, 1927, letter to FDR from Howe about photographing patients is quoted in Rollins, previously cited. The September 2, 1927, letter from George Eastman to FDR is at the Eastman Archive in Rochester, New York. The home movies described in this chapter belong to Missy's great-niece Barbara Jacques. The extent of FDR's relaxation at Warm Springs and his trust of Missy are evident in his willingness to be filmed in a wheelchair; there are only four wheelchair pictures in the FDRL's 130,000-item photo collection, two of them taken by his cousin and close friend Daisy Suckley. A film showing FDR being pushed in his wheelchair in 1944 surfaced in 2013.

Missy used the term "heart attack" in giving her medical history in 1941 (LeHand Medical File). The April 18, 1927, letter to FDR from Howe is in the Howe Papers, FDRL. The explanation of the effect of digitalis is from "Digitalis Delirium" by John T. King, *Transactions of the American Clinical and Climatological Association* 61 (1949): 66–83, accessed at http://www.ncbi.nlm.nih.gov/pmc/articles/PMC2242024/.

The Curtis and Tully interviews were used by Asbell, *The F.D.R. Memoirs.* He quoted ER's June 12, 1941, letter to Anna in *Mother and Daughter: The Letters of Eleanor and Anna Roosevelt.* The LeHand Medical File contradicts the conclusions of previous writers who said Missy was hospitalized and treated at the Foundation. There was no facility for hospitalization in 1927 and no Dr. Pringle on staff. Bernard LeHand's July 10, 1927, letter to FDR is among the LeHand Papers, Tully Collection, FDRL. Missy's June 2, 1928, letter to FDR regarding her cottage and the construction cost and rental fee is in the Roosevelt Warm Springs Rehabilitation Campus archive.

### Six: *Don't You Dare*

A variety of sources were used in this short chapter, opening with Asbell's interview with Egbert Curtis in *The F.D.R. Memoirs.* The description of FDR's walk as "political" was used in the HBO film *Warm Springs* by the actors portraying Roosevelt and Helena Mahoney, his physical therapist. Al Vinck, volunteer tour guide at Top Cottage, also used this language. FDR outlined his plans to walk in a letter to his friend Louis B. Wehle, October 13, 1925, quoted in Wehle's book *Hidden Threads of History: Wilson Through Roosevelt.* Tobin, previously cited, thoroughly describes FDR's rehabilitation efforts—and lack thereof.

ER's letter about the Houston convention is quoted in Ward and Burns, previously cited. Elliott Roosevelt's description appears in *An Untold Story*. The *Manchester Mercury*'s mention of its endorsement of Smith appeared November 9, 1928. Missy related the story of FDR walking across the cottage floor to Tully in *F.D.R. My Boss,* previously cited.

The account of the campaign to get FDR to accept the nomination for governor of New York has been told by every major FDR biographer. This telling draws on accounts in Elliott Roosevelt's *An Untold Story,* Ward's *A First-Class Temperament,* and Lindley, all previously cited. Missy related the "Don't you dare!" scene to Fleeson, previously cited. Howe's wire to FDR is quoted in Schlesinger's *Crisis of the Old Order.* The account of Frances Perkins's election night vigil with Sara Roosevelt is from *The Roosevelt I Knew,* previously cited. Ward and Burns describe the toast with milk in *The Roosevelts.*

The *Manchester Mercury* citations are for the issues of November 9, 1928, and November 16, 1928. Tully picks up the story of her arrival in *F.D.R. My Boss.* Rosenman's *Working with Roosevelt* is the source for his first visit to Warm Springs.

### Seven: The Governor's Girl Friday

The best all-around source on Roosevelt's time as governor is Kenneth S. Davis's *FDR: The New York Years, 1928–1933.* The previously cited memoirs of Rosenman, Tully, and James and Elliott Roosevelt are also helpful. In describing the Governor's Mansion, the author quoted Steinberg, previously cited, and Elliott Roosevelt. The New York State Executive Mansion Resource Kit at www.governor.ny.gov was also used during the research on the book. Missy told Dorothy Ducas of her further illness and growing distaste for exercise in *Who* magazine, previously cited. The conflicting information on the location of Missy's bedroom is from the dueling memoirs of the Roosevelt brothers. (Marion Dickerman in *Invincible Summer* recalls Missy's bedroom being down the hall from the governor's.)

The accounts of the love triangle are from Persico, Cook's *Eleanor Roosevelt,* Vol. 1, Elliott Roosevelt's *An Untold Story,* and Joseph Lash's *Eleanor and Franklin.* Newsman Walter Trohan tells the story of the confused grandchild in *Political Animals: Memoirs of a Sentimental Cynic.*

Missy's daybooks, part of the LeHand Family Papers, offer a tantalizing glimpse into her busy life. She also talked about it in interviews, including "Right Hand Woman for Roosevelt," an undated circa 1932 news clipping in the LeHand Family Papers. The August 12, 1933, *Newsweek* profile, "MISSY: Marguerite Le Hand Is President's Super-Secretary," mentions her New York years. Rosenman's account of their working relationship is from his memoir, supplemented by Cook's

*Eleanor Roosevelt,* Vol. 1. The number of executions was found at http://deathpenaltyusa.org/usa1/state/new_york5.htm. Missy's letters from Warm Springs are from the LeHand Papers, Tully Collection, FDRL. Oursler's *Behold This Dreamer!,* previously cited, provides a lively portrait of Missy in Albany.

The section on the stock market crash benefits greatly from suggestions from the author's economist father, Bruce Yandle, and his colleague Roger Meiners; the articles "The Great Depression: An Overview" by David C. Wheelock, http://www.stlouisfed.org/great-depression/pdf/the-great-depression-wheelock-overview.pdf, and "Comparing the Great Recession and the Great Depression" by Louis Jacobson, http://www.politifact.com/truth-o-meter/article/2013/sep/19/comparing-great-recession-and-great-depression/. Alter's description of the crash was also very useful. Missy's August 25, 1931, letter to Maydelle Ramsey is in the LeHand Family Papers.

Rosenman and Davis are the sources for the train conversation about a run for the presidency. The signed copy of Lindley's biography of FDR is in the LeHand Family Papers. Alter, previously cited, colorfully describes the Jimmy Walker controversy, as does Davis, previously cited. Missy's continuing health problems are mentioned in the LeHand Medical File and in a letter from ER to FDR quoted in Lash's *Eleanor and Franklin.* Missy's April 15, 1932, letter about the drapes at the Little White House is on display at the museum there. Stevens, previously cited, mentions the endorsement by the *Meriwether Vindicator.*

### Eight: Running for President

Oursler, previously cited, is the basis for the introduction to this chapter. Other contemporary sources were the previously cited memoirs of Rosenman, Tully, and Moley, Rexford Tugwell's *The Democratic Roosevelt,* and Edward J. Flynn's *You're the Boss.* More recent books that were helpful include Alter, previously cited, and Michael Golay's *America 1933: The Great Depression, Lorena Hickok, Eleanor Roosevelt, and the Shaping of the New Deal.* Michael R. Beschloss's *Kennedy and Roosevelt: The Uneasy Alliance* and Nasaw's *The Patriarch* provide insight into that fascinating figure. (Incidentally, FDR's advisory group was originally dubbed the Brains Trust, but this was shortened to simply Brain Trust.)

The continuing question of FDR's physical condition is informed by Eric Fettmann and Steven Lomazow's *FDR's Deadly Secret.* The description of the state of the U.S. economy includes insights from "History Repeating" by Roger Lowenstein, *Wall Street Journal,* January 14, 2015. Studs Terkel's oral history of the Great Depression, *Hard Times,* provides riveting descriptions of how Americans were affected. "The Forgotten Man" speech can—and should—be read in its entirety at http://newdeal.feri.org/speeches/1932c.htm.

Missy's pre-convention interview was the previously cited "Right Hand Woman for Roosevelt." The rough draft of the telegram and tally sheet that Missy put in her scrapbook can be found at the FDRL. The account of travel on the *Roosevelt Special* benefits greatly from the anonymous female staffer's unpublished memoir "Traveling with a President," LeHand Family Papers. (The author may have been Roberta Barrows, who later worked for Steve Early at the White House.) Other details were provided in the memoirs of Tugwell and Moley. Kennedy's role comes from the books of Beschloss and Nasaw, and Lorena Hickok's from Golay and Doris Faber's *The Life of Lorena Hickok, E.R.'s Friend,* as well as the anonymous female staffer. The author's brother, Bruce Yandle III, provided research on the World Series game attended by the campaign train passengers.

William C. Bullitt's entrance on the scene is documented in Wehle, previously cited, and Missy's daybook.

The impact of tuberculosis on FDR's circle can't be underestimated. According to Steven Lomazow, in 1944 a major advance in the treatment of TB, streptomycin, was developed by a team of New Jersey scientists. While Cordell Hull was forced to retire in late 1944, and his diagnosis has been questioned, he lived until 1955.

The comic verse and cartoon of Missy driving is in the LeHand Family Papers. Tully writes in her memoir of the close friendship she, Paula, and Missy enjoyed, further evidenced in scenes in which they appear in Missy's home movies. Missy clearly loved both women and remembered them generously in her will.

Mary LeHand's unexpected death is the subject of an undated newspaper article in the LeHand Family Papers, "Mrs. F.D. Roosevelt Here on Sad Errand." Her obituary appeared in the *Potsdam Herald-Reporter,* November 4, 1932. The description of the growing friendship of ER and Hickok is from Streitmatter and Golay, both previously cited. Tully and Flynn describe the scene at Springwood on election night in their respective memoirs. The South Carolina election statistic is from http://uselectionatlas.org/RESULTS/state.php?year=1932&off=0&elect=0&fips=45. The Atlanta newspapermen's election night cannon firing is from Barbara Barksdale Clowse's *Ralph McGill*.

The photo of Missy inscribed by FDR was given to a Somerville neighbor and friend, Dawn Ramsey Desley, and returned to the LeHand Family Papers after Mrs. Desley's death in 2015. The description of Missy as the most famous private secretary in America is from Goodwin, previously cited.

### *Nine: Nothing to Fear*

With FDR's arrival in the White House, his daily schedule became a matter of public record. The chronicles of the Usher's Log and Stenographer's Diary are available on the FDRL website as "Franklin Delano Roosevelt Day by Day" at http://www.fdrlibrary.marist.edu/daybyday/. It informs all the White House chapters in this book. Tully wrote in her memoir about attending the inauguration with Missy. James Roosevelt provides more detail of the event in *My Parents,* plus the observance about his parents' marriage being an armed truce. (Faith Baldwin, the romance writer adored by women in the 1930s, said most marriages are such.)

Alter, previously cited, paints a vivid picture of Inauguration Day, including the lovely quote about the sun breaking through on FDR's head. Geoffrey Ward's editing of *Closest Companion: The Unknown Story of the Intimate Friendship Between Franklin Roosevelt and Margaret Suckley,* brings Daisy's singular voice into the narrative. Documents from the Office of Social Entertainments for the 1933 inauguration at the FDRL and memorabilia in the LeHand Family Papers further define the presence of Missy and her family. Missy's appearance at the inaugural ball comes from photos in Steve Early's scrapbook, Steven Early Papers, FDRL.

Sources for the Warm Springs delegation's trip are the *Manchester Mercury,* November 11, 1932, February 3, 1933, and March 3, 1933; and the December issue of the *Polio Chronicles* newsletter of the Georgia Warm Springs Foundation (now the Roosevelt Warm Springs Rehabilitation Campus). The description of FDR's post-election trip to Warm Springs is from the same newsletter; *New York Times*, November 20, 1932; and Early's scrapbook. Moley, in *After Seven Years: A Political*

*Analysis of the New Deal,* and Tugwell, in *In Search of Roosevelt,* provide details about the assembling of the new administration. Missy's initial salary and the fact that it was half the male secretaries' is from Fleeson's profile. Missy's will and letters to William C. Bullitt indicate the extent to which she financially supported her family.

*So Close to Greatness: A Biography of William C. Bullitt* by Will Brownell and Richard N. Billings covers Bullitt's undercover diplomatic journey. Missy's letter to him about the coded messages is dated May 18, 1934. The description of the winter before FDR's inauguration are informed by Alter, Moley's *The First New Deal,* and Davis's *FDR: The New York Years,* all previously cited. The draft inaugural address with Missy's notation is in the collection of the FDRL.

Sources on the escalating bank crisis are "The Establishment of the FDIC," accessed at https://www.fdic.gov/bank/analytical/firstfifty/chapter3.pdf, Adam Cohen's *Nothing to Fear: FDR's Inner Circle and the Hundred Days That Created Modern America,* and Moley's books *The First New Deal* and *After Seven Years*. Jonathan Daniels's quote comes from his book *Washington Quadrille: The Dance Beside the Documents*. John Gunther in his biography *Roosevelt in Retrospect* gives Missy credit for the suggestion of Cummings, as does Flynn, previously cited. Joseph Lash in *From the Diaries of Felix Frankfurter* mentions her vocal support for Frankfurter's Supreme Court nomination.

Moley mentions Missy maneuvering into an office adjoining FDR's and praises her skills in *The First New Deal*. Alter is the source for the radio address on Sunday, March 5, but this was not a Fireside Chat. The first one was given on March 12.

### *Ten: Queen of the White House Staff*

Many voices contribute to this chapter, beginning with the admirer of Missy's office efficiency, Thomas G. Corcoran. The aforementioned contemporary memoirs of Tully, Moley, and Tugwell are joined here by Lela Stiles's biography of her boss, *The Man Behind Roosevelt: The Story of Louis McHenry Howe,* Henrietta Nesbitt's *White House Diary,* and Lillian Rogers Parks's *The Roosevelts: A Family in Turmoil*. Curtis Roosevelt gives a child's-eye-view in *Too Close to the Sun: Growing Up in the Shadow of My Grandparents, Franklin and Eleanor.* Elliott Roosevelt wrote a less controversial sequel memoir to *An Untold Story* called *A Rendezvous with Destiny,* which covered his parents' White House years.

ER's letter to Hickok is from Streitmatter, previously cited. The version of the first day and the desk bells told here is from Oursler and Tully, previously cited. The letter total is from an FDRL publication, "Action, and Action Now: FDR's First 100 Days." The letter Missy wrote to Bullitt about signing letters is dated February 2, 1935. The author saw numerous Missy letters at the FDRL and in the Bullitt Papers and perused letters on eBay and other online auction sites, including the "Happy Days" handkerchief letter. Although many of these were signed by other staff, the author's friend the Reverend David Bridgforth shared one his father received that did indeed bear Missy's signature with its overhand loop in the "L."

Hickok's role in making ER an activist first lady and the ER mail estimate come from Golay, previously cited. Nesbitt described her job duties and menus in her memoir, while Ernest Hemingway's comment about the White House food came from Smith's *FDR,* previously cited. The dismissive letter from Barbara Farwell to Anna Rochon, November 14, 1933, is in the LeHand Family Papers. Regarding the sorry state of the White House wine cellar, it is important to remember that the domestic wine industry had been almost destroyed by Prohibition and the award-winning wines of California and New York State were decades away.

The chair FDR gave Missy belongs to the LeHand family. Missy's letter to Ramsey MacDonald's secretary Rose Rosenberg, dated May 25, 1933, is part of the LeHand Papers, Tully Collection, FDRL. The invitations Missy received to social events number in the hundreds, if not thousands, and are in the LeHand Family Papers. The jewelry and furs she owned are listed in her August 28, 1935, provisional will at the FDRL. "Washington Capitalizes 7 Names in Listing Well-Dressed Women" was previously cited.

One of the few people the author was able to interview who knew Missy personally is Diana Hopkins Halsted, daughter of Harry Hopkins, who also lived on the third floor of the White House as a child following her mother's death. She gave the location of Missy's room and other fond reminisces of "lovely" Missy in a telephone interview in 2014. Mrs. Halsted recalled sitting in FDR's lap during the Children's Hour and playing with the "fabulous" collection of wind-up toys and gadgets on his desk while the adults enjoyed their cocktails. The section on Hopkins, Lorena Hickok, and the Federal Emergency Relief Administration is from Golay, *1933*.

Faith Baldwin's book *The Office Wife* is a charming novel and provides an amazingly accurate description of Missy's role in FDR's life. The racy movie version, released in 1930, starred Dorothy Mackaill as "a welcome danger to the tired businessman," Lewis Stone as the aging boss, and Joan Blondell as his blond bombshell wife. The author watched it with Missy's great-nieces and we all got a kick out of it.

### *Eleven: The Ambassador to Russia*

The Brownell and Billings biography, previously cited, and Orville Bullitt's *For the President: Personal and Secret: Correspondence Between Franklin D. Roosevelt and William C. Bullitt* are the major sources for this chapter, along with the LeHand–Bullitt correspondence at Yale. James Srodes's *On Dupont Circle: Franklin and Eleanor Roosevelt and the Progressives Who Shaped Our World* offers interesting insights into Bullitt's early career. His critics included Dean Acheson in *Present at the Creation: My Years in the State Department*; Eric Sevareid in *Not So Wild a Dream,* and George Seldes in *Witness to a Century: Encounters with the Noted, the Notorious and Three SOBs.* (Bullitt wasn't one of the SOBs, but was a close fourth.) The author's favorite of Faith Baldwin's "very attractive" men—who always had fatal flaws—is Peter Acton from *Week-end Marriage,* published in 1931.

There are more than eighty letters, notes, and telegrams in the LeHand correspondence file of Bullitt's archive at the Sterling Library at Yale. The dates on the letters quoted in this chapter are as follows: "Your Ladyship," September 21, 1933; "I . . . shall hope to have some sort of embassy in which to entertain you," December 6, 1933; "You really are an angel," January 14, 1934; "I am longing to take a taxi," January 17, 1934; "I am, my dear Mr. Ambassador," March 14, 1934; "Marguerite has been behaving," undated; "five miserable days in bed," April 21, 1934; "I do wish you would tell me," June 4, 1934; "I was really sorry to hear," September 1, 1934; "From all I can gather," September 2, 1934.

ER's snarky note to Hickok about Bullitt and Missy is from Streitmatter, previously cited. The Christmas newspaper interview is from an undated clipping in the LeHand Family Papers, as is the story denying Missy's engagement. The description of Bullitt's bachelor pad embassy is from Costigliola, previously cited.

FDR's joking letter to Missy, dated July 1, 1934, is from the LeHand Papers, Tully Archive, FDRL. ER's August 9, 1934, letter to Missy about her illness is Dobkin Collection #5397, generously shared by Glenn Horowitz Bookseller. The description of ER's ill-fated vacation with Hickok comes from Faber and Cook, both previously cited. Mrs. Rosenman's story about Bullitt and the ballerina is from Ted Morgan's *FDR: A Biography.* An unattributed variation on the story was presented by Black, previously cited, claiming the engagement and visit to Moscow happened in 1936. Brownell and Billings share the story of Evalyn Walsh's visit to Moscow. The description of the Hope Diamond is from http://mineralsciences.si.edu/hope.htm.

## *Twelve: Woman of Influence*

The first volume of Interior Secretary Harold Ickes's *Secret Diary* and Robert E. Sherwood's *Roosevelt and Hopkins: An Intimate History* join the mix of contemporary memoirs, letters, and press accounts that form the basis of this chapter. The description of the White House renovations are from *Time*'s "Presidency" column, December 17, 1934, and letters Missy wrote to Bullitt: one undated from the time of the renovations, the second dated March 9, 1936. The description of Missy's desk comes from the Fleeson profile, previously cited, as well as from photographs in the FDRL collection. The fact that only three *Time* covers featured women in 1934 was found in "Women Through *Time*: Who Gets Covered?," an academic paper written by Sammye Johnson and William C. Christ.

Multiple memos written to Missy from people seeking her favor can be found at the FDRL. Information on Steve Early comes from Levin, previously cited. The inscribed pictures from Early and Louis Howe are among the LeHand Family Papers. Early's memo about FDR's Sunday activities, September 19, 1934, is in the Early Papers, FDRL. The description of Marvin McIntyre is from *The New Dealers,* previously cited. Missy mentioned Howe in several letters to Bullitt. The one in which she wished he would go ahead and die already is dated March 9, 1936. Costigliola, previously cited, is the source for the story about Howe's emergence from the coma.

Missy mentioned pouring tea for the archaeologists in a letter to Bullitt on March 16, 1935. The bill for treatment of "piles" (hemorrhoids) came to Missy via ER, who wrote, "I know F.D.R. will have a fit!" The president wrote on the bottom of the memo, "Pay it. Have had fit." Missy put the memo in her scrapbook, now at the FDRL. The undated letter to Marguerite Collins, probably written in June 1937, is in the LeHand Family Papers.

The description of Missy's day is from Fleeson's profile and the draft article Missy wrote for *The Saturday Evening Post* in 1938. The closest thing to a memoir that she left, it is in the LeHand Papers, Tully Collection, FDRL. Gunther, previously cited, is the source for FDR's evening activities and need for a listening ear.

"Franklin Delano Roosevelt Day by Day" lists passengers on his yacht trips, and Missy was a standard guest. According to the USS *Potomac* Association's History and Mission Statement, the *Sequoia* was a wooden boat with gasoline engines. Due to FDR's fear of fire, it was replaced in 1936 with what had originally been a Coast Guard cutter, christened the *Potomac*. One of the smokestacks was removed to create an elevator shaft for a hand-operated lift much like the one FDR used at Springwood. "FDR's wife, Eleanor, did not participate in overnight cruises because she was not very comfortable at sea," the history states. Missy took her place as hostess.

The letter to Bullitt about fishing was dated June 3, 1935. The dates on the other letters to Bullitt are as follows: "I feel very strongly," April 7, 1935; "*no* help at all," April 10, 1935; "neither hot water," August 6, 1935; and "Wasn't the Supreme Court decision terrific?," June 3, 1935.

The statistic on the improved banking situation is from the Federal Deposit Insurance Corporation, www.fdic.gov. Ward and Burns, previously cited, and the author's tour of the Gettysburg battlefield museum supplied the information on the Civilian Conservation Corps. Unemployment data is from "Employment and Unemployment in the 1930s" by Robert A. Margo, *Journal of Economic Perspectives,* Spring 1993, https://fraser.stlouisfed.org/docs/meltzer/maremp93.pdf. The LeHand Family Papers supplied the information on Dan LeHand's and Barbara Farwell's jobs. Bernard LeHand's job with Somerset is from Nasaw, previously cited.

Sources for the section on the WPA and PWA are Jim Powell's *FDR's Folly: How Roosevelt and His New Deal Prolonged the Great Depression*; Smith's *FDR;* Sherwood's *Roosevelt and Hopkins*; Icke's *Secret Diary,* Vol. 1; and "WPA Was a Model of Public Investment," by Renee Loth, *Boston Globe,* December 2014 (syndicated column, published December 26, 2014, in Charleston, South Carolina, *Post & Courier*).

### *Thirteen: Mixing Work and Play*

Major sources on Tommy Corcoran are David McKean's biography *Tommy the Cork: Washington's Ultimate Insider from Roosevelt to Reagan*; Costigliola, previously cited; and Schlesinger's *The Politics of Upheaval.* Other comments about Corcoran are from William O. Douglas's memoir *Go East, Young Man: The Early Years*; Lash, *From the Diaries of Felix Frankfurter*; and ER's *This I Remember.* FDR was fond of giving men nicknames based on their last names. Besides "Tommy the Cork," he called Harry Hopkins "Harry the Hop" and Sam Rosenman "Sammy the Rose."

Lash's quote regarding ER's prejudice against Catholics is from "God and Mrs. Roosevelt" by Mary Ann Glendon, *First Things (Journal of Religion and Public Life),* May 2010. Alsop's quote is from John Cooney's *The American Pope: The Life and Times of Francis Cardinal Spellman.* According to Smith in *FDR,* Missy visited Father Coughlin at his Detroit church as early as 1935 but refused to talk politics with him.

Missy's letter to Bill Bullitt about the Kennedy mansion is dated August 13, 1935. The description of the dinner party there is from Beschloss, previously cited, and Arthur Krock's *Memoirs: Sixty Years on the Firing Line.* ER's travel plans that night are in "Franklin Delano Roosevelt Day by Day," FDRL.

The description of ER's Gridiron Widows party is from "Masquerade," *Time,* December 17, 1934. Ickes's comments about ER are from his *Secret Diary,* Vol. 1. Oursler's account of dinner at the White House is from his previously cited autobiography. Missy's Christmas letters to the Roosevelts, probably written in 1936, are in the President's Personal File, FDRL. The letters from ER to Missy, all undated, are in the LeHand Papers, Tully Collection, FDRL. Holley Snaith, a Park Service intern at Val-Kill in 2015, identified for the author the photograph of Missy that hung in ER's bedroom there. Missy wrote two wills in the fall of 1935, with the final one signed September 25. Both are in the LeHand Papers, Tully Collection, FDRL. The author thanks Jack McIntosh, Esq., for his help interpreting the will.

Missy's fall activities are informed by Ickes, previously cited, pictures in the LeHand Family Papers, and the October 12, 1935, letter she wrote to Bullitt.

**Fourteen: Polio Redux**

Tip O'Neill tells the story of Missy introducing him to FDR in *Man of the House: The Life and Political Memoirs of Speaker Tip O'Neill*. Chris Matthews elaborates on his discretion in *Tip and the Gipper: When Politics Worked*.

Returning to the subject of polio and Warm Springs, Oshinsky and Theo Lippman, both previously cited, are valuable sources. Another excellent book about the race for the polio vaccine is Jane S. Smith's *Patenting the Sun: Polio and the Salk Vaccine*. Author trips to Warm Springs and viewings of Missy's home movies shot there, as well as chats with Hal S. Raper, archivist Mike Shadix at the Roosevelt Warm Springs Rehabilitation Campus, and local history authority Bob Patterson, pastor of the First Baptist Church of Warm Springs, added texture and depth. The pictorial history *Warm Springs* by David M. Burke Jr. and Odie A. Burke is full of wonderful photographs and information. Coauthor David Burke, a ranger at the Little White House, was also helpful in identifying photos of Missy.

The White House Stenographer's Diary for March 18, 1937, in "Franklin Delano Roosevelt Day by Day," has the entry "Dedicate Elinor [*sic*] Roosevelt W. S. Colored School House." The school was built with a Rosenwald Fund grant, used to construct school buildings for African American children in the South from 1913 to 1948. The now abandoned school bears a stone tablet that reads "The Eleanor Roosevelt School." (Likewise, the Foundation did not accept black patients in those days. Instead, a "separate but equal" treatment facility was established at the Tuskegee Institute in Alabama in 1939 with NFIP money, according to Oshinsky.) Warm Springs continues to remember ER and named a new highway bridge for her on April 12, 2014. ER's mention of FDR's "time with Missy" is in a letter to daughter Anna, from Asbell's *Mother and Daughter*.

The descriptions of the fundraising by the President's Birthday Balls are from Oshinsky and Lippman. The *Potsdam* (New York) *Herald-Reporter* covered the "Ball and Party for Birthday," February 2, 1934. FDR's speech for the first ball's radio hookup is at the FDRL. The photo of the "Hail, Caesar" party is at the FDRL.

The misspelled letter from the farmer's wife is quoted in Lippman. Mike Reilly tells the story about the poetry contest impostor in his memoir, *Reilly of the White House*. The quote from O'Connor is from

Smith's *Patenting the Sun.* The letter from O'Connor to Missy, dated July 20, 1938, is in the LeHand Papers, Tully Collection, FDRL. (Polio hit O'Connor hard when his daughter was partly paralyzed in 1950 at age thirty. She went to Warm Springs for treatment but died of polio complications in 1961.)

The hilarious story of the lost Boy Scouts was told to the author by the Reverend Patterson. Ruth Stevens's *Hi-Ya Neighbor* contains a recipe for Country Captain. (The author was served the dish by Gerrie Thompson at her Hotel Warm Springs in 2014. It is, indeed, delicious.) FDR's jocular telegram to Joe Kennedy, dated March 18, 1937, is in the Joseph P. Kennedy Papers at the John F. Kennedy Library. ER relates the story of the Possum Preserve outing, also captured in a Roosevelt Warm Springs Rehabilitation Campus Archive photo, in her column "My Day," included in Rochelle Chadakoff's *Eleanor Roosevelt's My Day: Her Acclaimed Columns, 1936–1945.* Missy's November 23, 1933, letter to Paula Larrabee is in the LeHand Papers, Tully Collection, FDRL.

The Canadian prime minister's visit is recounted in *A Real Companion and Friend: The Diaries of William Lyon Mackenzie King,* April 23 and 24, 1940, www.collectionscanada.gcca/king. Harry Hopkins's visit is told in Sherwood, previously cited. The author's friend Jack McIntosh contributes the priceless observation about the art of embellishment. Lippman's book contains the funny story about the party at Blue Springs. Founder's Day information is from the *Warm Springs Mirror,* November 24, 1939, and a 1935 Founder's Day program book from the Roosevelt Warm Springs Rehabilitation Campus Archive. ER's comment comes from a letter to Anna, quoted in Asbell's *Mother and Daughter.*

### *Fifteen: Hubris and Hell*

The previously cited memoirs of Rosenman, Moley, Ickes, and Tully inform this chapter, as well as correspondence between Missy and Bullitt, FDR, and her family. Missy's derogatory comment about Howe is from Morgan, previously cited. Smith, in *FDR,* says Howe was "the only person except for Missy who spoke frankly regardless of the consequences." Moley insisted on his own frankness, and ER's is well documented.

Bullitt writes of conditions in Russia to Judge Walton Moore, quoted in Bullitt's *For the President,* previously cited. Missy reassured Bullitt of his pending transfer to France in a letter May 5, 1936. The account of the fight between Moley and FDR and its aftermath is from Schlesinger's *Politics of Upheaval,* Rosenman, and Moley's *After Seven Years.* Rosenman gives Bullitt the credit for the "I hate war" speech. Brownell and Billings, previously cited, tell of Bullitt's assignment to Paris and ER's reaction.

The criticism of FDR is found in Smith, *FDR,* and Schlesinger, *The Politics of Upheaval.* Missy's letter to Bullitt about the "sheep" is undated but from the 1936 election season. Levin, previously cited, relates Missy's fear that the election was lost. The signed tally sheet is in the LeHand Family Papers. Bullitt's telegram is dated November 4, 1936. Missy's undated post-election letter to her niece is in the LeHand Family Papers.

Missy wrote to Bullitt's secretary, Carmel Offie, on November 9, 1936. FDR's unusually emotional letter to Missy about Gus Gennerich, dated December 2, 1936, is in the LeHand Family Papers. Her December 4 response is in the LeHand Papers, Tully Collection, FDRL, as is the December 11, 1936, telegram from actress Marion Davies.

The exchanges between Missy and Bullitt following his posting to Paris are as follows: "You are an angel," January 6, 1937; "Dearest Lady," September 3, 1937; "May I dine quietly," March 8, 1937; "Marguerite would like to know," May 9, 1938. "Dearest Lady" is from the Tully Collection, the others from the Bullitt Papers. Bullitt's embassy experience is from Brownell and Billings (which uses the term "Champagne ambassador"); "His Excellency, Bill Bullitt," *Life,* March 27, 1939; and Sevareid, previously cited. Ralph G. Martin made the assertion about Bullitt's proposal to Cissy Patterson in *Cissy: The Extraordinary Life of Eleanor Medill Patterson.*

Missy's correspondence regarding the Sky Pilot clock is in Marguerite A. LeHand, 1933–43, PPF File, FDRL. ER's letter regarding the birthday party and the script for the skit are in the Early Papers, FDRL. Missy's letter to Bullitt about the "mad month" is dated February 2, 1937. The economic woes are described by Robert M. Burke in "Election of 1940," a chapter in *The Coming to Power: Critical Presidential Elections in American History,* edited by Arthur M. Schlesinger Jr. William Douglas recounts his interview with FDR about James in his previously cited memoir. Details about the strike at the Hershey plant were gleaned during the author's visit to the Hershey History

Museum, Hershey, Pennsylvania, in 2015. FDR's court-packing scheme is the best known overreach of his presidency. Missy's comment about his fighting spirit was made in a letter to Bullitt on July 12, 1937. Nevertheless, his actions exacted a high cost in 1938 when the Republicans netted eighty-one House seats and eight Senate seats in the midterm election.

Missy wrote to Bullitt about her "three endless weeks" in the hospital with the blood clot on May 25, 1937, and to FDR on the same subject in a letter now in the Roosevelt Family Papers, FDRL. The chit from FDR about having dinner is in her scrapbook at the FDRL. The letter to Sister Thomas Aquinas is in the LeHand Family Papers, along with a handsome scrapbook of congratulatory letters from friends upon the conferring of the degree at the White House.

Elliott Roosevelt's comment about Missy's open-door policy for Catholics is in *Rendezvous with Destiny*. Tully writes of visits by various Catholic dignitaries. The letter from Joseph P. Kennedy to Missy, dated March 17, 1939, is in the LeHand Papers, Tully Collection, FDRL.

Ickes writes about the negative reaction to his press conference and his exchanges of confidences with Corcoran and Missy in his *Secret Diary*, Vol. 2. The explanation of "Copperheads" is from McKean, previously cited.

Undated newspaper clippings and letters in the LeHand Family Papers tell the story of Missy's stolen train case. According to Tully, FDR shared his burial wishes with Missy at year's end and their plans for the presidential library were already in progress. Paul Sparrow, director of the FDR Library and Museum, says that without Missy's involvement, the project would probably never have come to fruition because of FDR's well-known penchant for procrastination.

### *Sixteen: Missy Knows*

The Fleeson profile is our most thorough word portrait of Missy during the second term. Bound copies Missy gave as gifts are in the LeHand Family Papers, as is Edith Johnson's undated column. The *Life* article on the Kennedy family appeared April 11, 1938.

Missy's letter to Bullitt in which she mentions Kennedy was dated January 18, 1938. The conversation between Bullitt and Ickes about Hitler, Franco, and Mussolini was recorded in Ickes's *Secret Diary*,

Vol. 2. Missy's letter to Bullitt about visiting Chantilly was dated May 9, 1938. Her letter about fishing in Puget Sound was dated August 15, 1938. Bullitt's response to the Ickes's May-December marriage is from Bullitt's *For the President*. Missy's letter to Bullitt about Betsey Roosevelt was dated March 13, 1939.

The story of the picnic at Val-Kill is from Davis's *Invincible Summer.* The FDR–Daisy Suckley correspondence in Ward's *Closest Companion* contains references to Missy as a conduit for their letters. When Suckley was undergoing surgery in 1939, she left specific instructions for a suitcase containing FDR's letters to be entrusted into no one's hands but Missy's if she didn't survive the operation. The October 1938 exchange with Ann Scaracella, the woman who wished to work at Top Cottage, is from the Disability History Museum, accessed online at www.disabilitymuseum.org.

Bullitt's memo about airplane production is in Bullitt's *For the President*. The humorous letter from Carmel Offie to Missy is dated September 12, 1938. Ben Cohen's memo to Missy about Kristallnacht, dated November 10, 1938, is in the President's Official File 198, Germany, 1935–1938, FDRL. ER's reluctance for her husband to run for a third term is from Sherwood's *Roosevelt and Hopkins.*

Will Swift's *The Roosevelts and the Royals* provides a detailed account of the visit of the king and queen of England in 1939. The list of necessities for the royals is from Bullitt's *For the President*. (Mrs. Nesbitt included the list in her *White House Diary,* but says it was provided by the British government.) The guest list for the welcoming luncheon is in ER's *This I Remember.* Lady Katherine Seymour's comment appeared in an undated news clipping "Glamour Rules Wherever Miss LeHand Is Working," LeHand Family Papers. The seating chart for the state dinner is also in the LeHand Family Papers. Jane Ickes's account of the dinner is from T. H. Watkins's *Righteous Pilgrim: The Life and Times of Harold L. Ickes,* while her husband's comment is from his *Secret Diary,* Vol. 2. The author interviewed Diana Hopkins Halsted about meeting the queen, whose ensemble was described in Sherwood, previously cited. The story of the king's stolen hat is told in Steinberg, previously cited. Harry Hopkins's memory of the late night chat is from Sherwood, previously cited. The handsome autographed photos of the king and queen belong to the LeHand family.

Bullitt's predictions about the war are in Ickes's *Secret Diary,* Vol. 2. The description of the Social Security Act expansion is from Katherine

B. Oettinger's "Title V of the Social Security Act: What It Has Meant to Children," http://www.ssa.gov/policy/authors/OettingerKatherineB.html.

Douglas's story is from his memoir, *Go East, Young Man*.

Missy's letter to Bullitt about Hitler was dated August 25, 1939. Carmel Offie's letter to Missy was dated August 9, 1939.

### *Seventeen: War*

Grace Tully tells the story of the call from Bullitt and the White House policy of first notifying Missy. Background information on the early stage of the war is from Winston Churchill in *The Second World War: The Gathering Storm,* Lynne Olson's *Citizens of London,* and Bullitt's *For the President.* By this point, Ickes had reached Volume 3 of his *Secret Diary,* which gives valuable insight into Missy's thoughts and actions. The comment about Missy being a "big woman" was expurgated from the published edition but remained in Ickes's papers at the Library of Congress. It is quoted from an article by Frank Costigliola, "Broken Circle: The Isolation of Franklin Delano Roosevelt in World War II" in *Diplomatic History* 32, no. 5 (November 2008).

Steve Early's birthday note to Missy is in the LeHand Papers, Tully Collection, FDRL. Carmel Offie's letter about Hacky becoming a seductress is dated September 9, 1939. Missy's reply about being in Paris "for the Fireworks" is dated September 22, 1939.

The deaths in Missy's family are documented in several letters and by the obituary for Mrs. P. J. McCarthy, *Potsdam Herald Recorder,* September 13, 1939. Information about the December 26 showing of *Gone with the Wind* is in "Franklin Delano Roosevelt Day by Day," FDRL. Olivia de Havilland shared her anecdote in an interview in *Garden & Gun* magazine, December 2014/January 2015 issue.

Sources for the 1940 election include Ickes's *Secret Diary,* Vol. 3, *Never Again: A President Runs for a Third Term* by Herbert S. Parmet and Marie B. Hecht, and Burke's essay, previously cited. Missy's letter to her niece and nephew-in-law about vacating her suite was dated January 24, 1940, LeHand Family Papers. Her birthday letter to Bullitt was dated January 25, 1940. Her birthday poem for FDR is also in the LeHand Family Papers. Missy's interview about liking her job and the snarky response are undated newspaper clippings, LeHand Family Papers.

The Brownell and Billings biography of Bullitt informs this chapter. The account of FDR's collapse while dining with Missy and Bullitt is from Bullitt's *For the President.* Fettmann and Lomazow, previously cited, provide an exhaustive analysis of FDR's health problems and their impact on his ability to govern.

The account of the Canadian prime minister's visit to Warm Springs is recorded in Mackenzie King's diary, previously cited. Sherwood, previously cited, gives the details about Hopkins's thoughts and move into the White House in the spring of 1940, as well as Missy's humorous reaction.

Churchill's summary of the situation in Europe that spring is from *The Gathering Storm*. Carmel Offie's letter about Paris was dated May 11, 1940. Sevareid, previously cited, writes of the bombing of the Air Ministry. Bullitt's farewell letter to Missy from Paris was dated June 10, 1940. The account of his role in the surrender of the city to the Germans is from *Americans in Paris: Life and Death Under Nazi Occupation* by Charles Glass, and the Browning and Billings biography.

The correspondence between Missy and Pierre Cartier, spanning March through July 1940, is in the LeHand Papers, Tully Collection, FDRL. Missy's letter to Barbara Farwell is dated September 18, 1940, LeHand Family Papers. The Drew Pearson column about Missy's winning bet on the GOP nominee was published July 5, 1940.

### *Eighteen: Bitter Victory*

Background for the 1940 election comes from Burke, previously cited; Richard Moe's *FDR's Second Act: The Election of 1940 and the Politics of War*; and Goodwin, previously cited. The chapter opens with Oursler's telling of his last visit to the White House during FDR's presidency. Rosenman's account of the nomination of Henry Wallace is from his memoir.

Bullitt's memory of FDR describing Lend-Lease is in Brownell and Billings, who cite Bullitt's postwar writings as the source for his contention. According to Bob Clark, the former supervisory archivist at the FDRL, most historians believe the concept evolved after Roosevelt received a lengthy letter from Churchill in December 1940. The *Look* photo spread on Missy appeared August 13, 1940. The note from Bullitt to Missy asking her to call him at the Shoreham Hotel was dated August 14, 1940, LeHand Papers, Tully Collection, FDRL.

Her response dated August 15 is in the Bullitt Papers, as is the congratulatory telegram sent to him on August 18, 1940. The book written by Bullitt and inscribed to Missy is in the LeHand Family Papers. Missy's angry note breaking off her relationship with Bullitt was dated September 21, 1940 (Bullitt Papers).

Douglas's observation about the hunger for power is from his previously cited memoir. The description of Bullitt's plot against Sumner Welles is from Irwin F. Gellman's *Secret Affairs: Franklin Roosevelt, Cordell Hull, and Sumner Welles*. Other sources are the Brownell and Billings biography, Bullitt's *For the President,* and Srodes's *On Dupont Circle,* previously cited. (The supreme irony here is that Bullitt's secretary, Carmel Offie, was openly and promiscuously gay—and Bullitt knew it. Apparently it didn't concern him that Offie might be a security risk.)

Joseph Kennedy's letter to Missy about conditions in England was dated September 30, 1940, LeHand Papers, Tully Collection, FDRL. The quote about his disillusionment with FDR is from Beschloss, previously cited. The account of his visit to the White House upon his return from England is from Beschloss and Nasaw, previously cited. Wendell Willkie's comment is from Ward and Burns, *The Roosevelts.*

Mike Reilly's version of election night is told in his previously cited memoir. The *Time* version appeared November 11, 1940, titled "The President's Victory." Missy's post-election comment was given to reporter Inez Robb, from an undated clipping in the LeHand Family Papers.

### *Nineteen: Disaster*

Several sources provide background material for the isolationist-interventionist debate of 1941. An excellent recent overview is Lynne Olson's *Those Angry Days: Roosevelt, Lindbergh, and America's Fight over World War II, 1939–41*. Important contemporary sources include the previously cited books of Ickes, Sevareid, Gunther, Tully, and Sherwood.

Previously cited works by Persico, Goodwin, James Roosevelt (*My Parents*), and Walter Trohan explore the attractions Princess Martha and Lucy Rutherfurd held for FDR.

Missy wrote to her niece Babe Collins about their upcoming vacation on March 14, 1941, LeHand Family Papers. The continuation of the Bullitt-Welles contretemps uses the same sources cited in Chapter 18.

Physicians and medical historians are important sources in this chapter. Fettmann and Lomazow make it clear just how ill FDR was in the spring of 1941. ER's response to his life-threatening loss of blood and close relationship with Missy and Harry Hopkins, shared in letters to her daughter, Anna, is from Asbell's *Mother and Daughter*.

The history of the Willard Hotel is from www.washington.intercontinental.com/discover-the-willard/history. Tully's memoir and the schedules in "Franklin Delano Roosevelt Day by Day" helped the author piece together the sequence of events when Missy fell ill and in the days that followed.

FDR's sweet note to Missy when he was confined to his bed with a sore throat is in the LeHand Family Papers. Information on Doctors Hospital was found at http://greatergreaterwashington.org/post/7590/doctors-hospital-a-hotel-for-the-sick/.

The most important documents regarding Missy's heart attack and stroke are the LeHand Medical File from the Georgia Archives, obtained through Mike Shadix, and the nurse's logs from the papers of Dr. Ross McIntire, FDRL. The author is indebted to Dr. Harold G. Morse, South Carolina hospitalist and internist specializing in cardiology, and Dr. Steven Lomazow, a New Jersey neurologist and coauthor of *FDR's Deadly Secret,* for "diagnosing" Missy's problems from a distance of almost seventy-five years. Dr. Morse could not have been more compassionate if he had been talking about a living patient. "FDR gave his life for his country," he said, "and Missy LeHand did, too." In addition, Dr. Lomazow sought the expertise of several of his colleagues, adding to the explanation of mitral valve stenosis, pulmonary embolism, and mitral valve infection. The list of doctors who consulted on Missy's case is from a stack of appreciative letters in the President's Personal File, FDRL, dated August 27, 1941. One of these doctors was James W. Watts, chief of neurosurgery at George Washington University Hospital in Washington. Later that year, Watts performed a lobotomy on Joseph P. Kennedy's twenty-three-year-old daughter Rosemary, and the failed operation put her in an institution for the rest of her life.

Information on the dedication of the FDR Library and Museum is from "One Definite Locality: History of the FDR Presidential Library and Museum," at www.fdrlibrary.marist.edu. Gunther was the observer who described the collection as the "ephemera of an inveterate collector whose primary collecting obsession was himself."

ER's remark about Missy's appearance to Malvina Thompson is from a letter Thompson wrote to Anna Roosevelt Boettiger, September 29, 1941, quoted in Costigliola's *Roosevelt's Lost Alliances.* News of Missy's illness appeared in *Time,* July 14, 1941. Tully told of the archbishop's visit in notes accompanying the rough draft of *F.D.R. My Boss,* Tully Collection, FDRL.

Dr. McIntire's observance about FDR's gaiety is from his memoir, *White House Physician.* Ickes's anger at FDR's apparent disinterest in Missy's illness was in an expurgated entry in his diary, available in its entirety at the Library of Congress. The results of Dr. Marsteller's examination is in the LeHand Medical File.

### *Twenty: The Exiled Queen*

The LeHand Medical File continues to inform this chapter, as it contains letters from Missy's doctors at Warm Springs and replies from Dr. Ross McIntire through the winter of 1942. Mike Shadix at the Roosevelt Warm Springs Rehabilitation Campus took the author to the Wilson Cottage, where Missy stayed during her rehabilitation there.

FDR's letter to Dan LeHand about her termination is dated August 7, 1942, and is in the LeHand Family Papers. (She remained on the government payroll until late that year.) Roosevelt's will is at the FDRL. James Roosevelt shared his father's words about his bequest to Missy in *My Parents.* It's hard to place a value on FDR's estate, as much of it was in property. Springwood was given to the federal government, and family members lived at Val-Kill and Top Cottage for many years after his death. According to the FDRL, the net value of the estate was $1,085,486, or $14.3 million today. His stamp collection alone sold for $228,000, or $2.7 million in current dollars.

Tully told the story of the truncated visit to Warm Springs in her memoir. Her note to FDR about Missy's call on December 7, 1941, is in the PPF, FDRL. Rosenman's thoughts about Missy's absence are from his memoir.

Barbara Farwell's note of thanks to ER for the Christmas gifts, dated January 1, 1942, is in the PPF, FDRL. Asbell's account of the suicide attempt is in *The F.D.R. Memoirs.* The nurse's logs from Dr. McIntire's papers at the FDRL provide details about Missy's final weeks at the White House. Goodwin, previously cited, also covered this period. Anna Rochon's letter to Tully about the larcenous nurse is in the LeHand Papers, Tully Collection, FDRL. "Franklin Delano Roosevelt Day by Day," FDRL, provides records of visits to Missy's room by the president, and her departure on May 15, 1942.

## *Twenty-One: Going Home*

Correspondence is the main source of information for this chapter, along with interviews with Missy's great-nieces, Barbara Jacques and Jane Scarbrough, and Dawn Ramsey Desley, who was a little girl when Missy came home to Somerville.

The gorgeous silver loving cup, along with the sweet note from FDR, is held by the LeHand family, as is the signed copy of Daisy Suckley's book about Fala. The note from ER about the toast rack is undated, LeHand Family Papers. The "little bird" letter from FDR, dated April 6, 1943, is in the LeHand Papers, Tully Collection, FDRL. The letter in which he told Missy how tired and ill he was dates from 1943 and is in the LeHand Family Papers, as is Archbishop (later Cardinal) Spellman's letter of August 8, 1943. The letter from Bullitt in which he says "Washington is queer and strange" is in the LeHand Family Papers, but the remaining letters between him and Missy's household are in the Bullitt Papers at Yale.

The efforts to replace Missy in FDR's life are related in numerous books, including the previously cited works of Costigliola, Goodwin, Gunther, Persico, and Tully. The perilous state of FDR's health at this time is detailed in Fettmann and Lomazow. Jim Bishop paints a poignant picture of the dying president in *FDR's Last Year: April 1944–April 1945*.

Frankfurter recounts the conversation with the Rosenmans in Lash's *From the Diaries of Felix Frankfurter*. Rosenman's comment was also made to Lash, quoted by Costigliola in *Roosevelt's Lost Alliances*. Ickes's August 1, 1944, letter to Anna Rochon is in his papers at the Library of Congress.

Anna Rochon described Missy's breakthrough in an undated letter to Bullitt, circa fall 1943. FDR's letter of congratulations to Missy, which is also undated, is in the LeHand Family Papers. Rochon's reproachful letter to FDR was written in January 1944, LeHand Papers, Tully Archive, FDRL. ER's letter uninviting Missy to the White

House is dated February 8, 1944, ER Correspondence File, FDRL. Rochon's letter to Bullitt describing Missy's extreme disappointment is undated. Missy's last two notes to Tully are in the LeHand Papers, Tully Collection, FDRL. FDR's response to the D-Day letter is dated June 14, 1944, and is in the LeHand Family Papers.

The account of Missy's death is from three sources: Asbell's *The F.D.R. Memoirs,* an interview with Dawn Desley, and a short account written by Mrs. Desley's grandmother, Maydelle Ramsey, which is in the LeHand Family Papers. The news release from the White House was quoted in full by numerous newspapers. News articles and photos from the funeral are in Anna Rochon's scrapbook, LeHand Family Papers. The telegram to Tully from Bullitt asking her to send flowers on his behalf is from the PPF, FDRL. For the author, a visit to Missy's grave at the beautiful and peaceful Mount Auburn Cemetery was a very moving experience. It was the first time she seemed truly dead.

Two weeks after Missy's death, Joseph Kennedy's son Joe Jr. was killed when the experimental bomber he was flying blew up over an English village. It was the end of the fabled Kennedy luck. In 1963, Cardinal Cushing, who had presided over Missy's funeral, led the funeral service of President John F. Kennedy. It was the final link in the chain between Missy and Joe Kennedy.

Tully described her sad moment with FDR after Missy's death in an interview with Asbell, *The F.D.R. Memoirs.* The list of Missy's evening gowns is in an inventory of her possessions being stored at the White House that Basil O'Connor sent to Dan LeHand on May 3, 1945, LeHand Family Papers. Blue was given as FDR's favorite color in Persico, and Eleanor's in the 1941 *Who* magazine article, both previously cited.

### *Epilogue: Missy's Legacy*

The account of the launching of the SS *Marguerite LeHand* is from Asbell, *The F.D.R. Memoirs,* photos in the LeHand Family Papers, the christening plaque (with bottle) at the FDRL, and the letter from R. I. Ingalls, PPF, FDRL.

FDR's death is covered in numerous sources, but Bishop does as good a job as anyone in *FDR's Last Year.* The premise of Fettmann and Lomazow's book, that FDR had a malignant melanoma, cannot be proved because of his missing medical records and the absence of an autopsy at ER's request. His death certificate lists arteriosclerosis as the one contributing factor to his cerebral hemorrhage. (Fettmann and Lomazow point out that 90 percent of melanoma fatalities involve brain metastases, which are "notoriously prone to spontaneous hemorrhage, which is the immediate cause of death of between one-quarter and half of all patients with melanoma.")

Lillian Rogers Parks's remark about the White House staff is from her book, previously cited. The story of the papers that make up the Tully Collection is a fascinating one told by Bob Clark in "The Strange Case of the Tully Archive," available at http://www.fdrlibrary.marist.edu/archives/pdfs/clark_tully.pdf. History owes a debt to Clark, at the time supervising archivist at the FDRL, for the painstaking way in which he sorted and catalogued the long-lost papers.

The author's visit to the busy Somerville Public Library, an interview with Barbara Jacques, and the story "Somerville Library Honors for Famous Missy Le Hand," *Boston Herald American,* September 13, 1976, are the sources for the description of the naming of the Children's Library for Missy.

Interviews with Missy's great-nieces and author Geoffrey Ward resulted in three thumbs-down for *Hyde Park on Hudson.* Jane Scarbrough provided the information that the Roosevelt family continues to maintain the LeHand plot at Mount Auburn.

# *Bibliography*

### *Books and Journals*

*Abstract of the 14th Census of the United States*. Washington: Government Printing Office, 1923.

Acheson, Dean. *Present at the Creation: My Years in the State Department*. New York: W. W. Norton, 1969.

Alsop, Joseph. *FDR: A Centenary Remembrance*. New York: Viking, 1982.

Alter, Jonathan, *The Defining Moment: FDR's Hundred Days and the Triumph of Hope*. New York: Simon & Schuster, 2006.

Asbell, Bernard. *The F.D.R. Memoirs*. Garden City: Doubleday, 1973.

Asbell, Bernard, editor. *Mother and Daughter: The Letters of Eleanor and Anna Roosevelt*. New York: Coward, McCann & Geoghegan, 1982.

Baldwin, Faith. *The Office Wife*. Philadelphia: Triangle, 1929.

Beschloss, Michael R. *Kennedy and Roosevelt: The Uneasy Alliance*. New York: W. W. Norton, 1980.

Bishop, Jim. *FDR's Last Year, April 1944–April 1945*. New York: William Morrow, 1974.

Black, Conrad. *Franklin Delano Roosevelt: Champion of Freedom*. New York: PublicAffairs, 2003.

Bonner, Geraldine. *Miss Maitland Private Secretary*. New York: D. Appleton, 1919.

Brinkley, David. *Washington Goes to War: The Extraordinary Transformation of a City and a Nation*. New York: Alfred A. Knopf, 1988.

Brownell, Will, and Richard N. Billings. *So Close to Greatness: A Biography of William C. Bullitt*. New York: Macmillan, 1987.

Bullitt, Orville H., editor. *For the President Personal and Secret: Correspondence Between Franklin D. Roosevelt and William C. Bullitt*. Boston: Houghton Mifflin, 1972.

Bullitt, William C. *It's Not Done*. New York: Grosset & Dunlap, 1926.

Burke, David M. Jr., and Odie A. Burke. *Warm Springs*. Charleston, S.C.: Arcadia, 2005.

Burke, Robert M. "Election of 1940." In *The Coming to Power: Critical Presidential Elections in American History*, edited by Arthur M. Schlesinger Jr. New York: Chelsea House/McGraw-Hill, 1971.

Burns, James MacGregor. *Roosevelt: The Lion and the Fox*. New York: Harcourt Brace, 1956.

———. *Roosevelt: The Soldier of Freedom, 1940–1945*. New York: Harcourt, Brace, Jovanovich, 1970.

Burns, James MacGregor, and Susan Dunn. *The Three Roosevelts: Patrician Leaders Who Transformed America*. New York: Atlantic Monthly Press, 2001.

Caro, Robert A. *The Years of Lyndon Johnson: The Path to Power*. New York: Alfred A. Knopf, 1982.

Chadakoff, Rochelle, editor. *Eleanor Roosevelt's My Day: Her Acclaimed Columns, 1936–1945*. Seattle: Pharos, 1989.

Churchill, Winston, and the editors of *Life*. *The Second World War*. New York: Time Inc., 1959.

Clowse, Barbara Barksdale. *Ralph McGill*. Macon, Georgia: Mercer University Press, 1998.

Cohen, Adam. *Nothing to Fear: FDR's Inner Circle and the Hundred Days That Created Modern America*. New York: Penguin, 2009.

Cook, Blanche Wiesen. *Eleanor Roosevelt, Vol. 1: 1884–1933*. New York: Viking Penguin, 1992.

———. *Eleanor Roosevelt, Vol.* 2: 1933–1938. New York: Viking Penguin, 1999.

Cooney, John. *The American Pope: The Life and Times of Francis Cardinal Spellman*. New York: Times Books, 1984.

Costigliola, Frank. "Broken Circle: The Isolation of Franklin Delano Roosevelt in World War II." *Diplomatic History* 32, no. 5 (November 2008): 677–718.

———. *Roosevelt's Lost Alliances: How Personal Politics Helped Start the Cold War*. Princeton: Princeton University Press, 2012.

Daniels, Jonathan. *Washington Quadrille: The Dance Beside the Documents*. Garden City: Doubleday, 1968.

Davis, Kenneth S. *FDR: The Beckoning of Destiny, 1882–1928*. New York: G. P. Putnam's Sons, 1971.

———. *FDR: The New York Years, 1928–1933*. New York: Random House, 1985.

———. *Invincible Summer: An Intimate Portrait of the Roosevelts, Based on the Recollections of Marion Dickerman*. New York: Atheneum, 1974.

Douglas, William O. *Go East, Young Man: The Early Years*. New York: Random House, 1974.

English, Peter C. *Rheumatic Fever in America and Britain: A Biological, Epidemiological and Medical History*. New Brunswick: Rutgers University Press, 1999.

Ezickson, A. J., editor. *Roosevelt Album*. New York: Knickerbocker, 1945.

Faber, Doris. *The Life of Lorena Hickock, E.R.'s Friend*. New York: William Morrow, 1980.

Ferrell, Robert H., editor. *FDR's Quiet Confidant: The Autobiography of Frank C. Walker*. Niwot: University Press of Colorado, 1997.

Fettman, Eric, and Steven Lomazow, MD. *FDR's Deadly Secret*. New York: PublicAffairs, 2009.

Fischer, Louis, MD. *Diseases of Infancy and Childhood*. Philadelphia: F. A. Davis, 1910.

Flynn, Edward J. *You're the Boss*. New York: Viking, 1947.

Fried, Albert. *FDR and His Enemies*. New York: St. Martin's, 1999.

Friedel, Frank. *Franklin D. Roosevelt: Launching the New Deal*. Boston: Little, Brown, 1973.

———. *Franklin D. Roosevelt: A Rendezvous with Destiny*. Boston: Little, Brown, 1990.

Galbraith, John Kenneth. *The Great Crash, 1929*. Boston: Houghton Mifflin, 1954.

Gallagher, Hugh Gregory. *Nothing to Fear: FDR in Photographs*. Clearwater, Florida: Vandamere, 2001.

Gellman, Irwin F. *Secret Affairs: Franklin Roosevelt, Cordell Hull, and Sumner Welles*. Baltimore: Johns Hopkins University Press, 1995.

Glass, Charles. *Americans in Paris: Life and Death Under Nazi Occupation*. New York: Penguin, 2010.

Golay, Michael. *America 1933: The Great Depression, Lorena Hickok, Eleanor Roosevelt, and the Shaping of the New Deal*. New York: Free Press, 2013.

Goodwin, Doris Kearns. *The Fitzgeralds and the Kennedys: An American Saga*. New York: Simon & Schuster, 1987.

———. *No Ordinary Time: Franklin and Eleanor Roosevelt: The Home Front in World War II*. New York: Simon & Schuster, 1994.

Gregg, John Robert. *Gregg Shorthand*. New York: Gregg Publishing Company, 1929.

Gunther, John. *Roosevelt in Retrospect*. New York: Harper & Row, 1950.

Ickes, Harold L. *The Secret Diary of Harold Ickes, Vols. I, II, and III*. New York: Simon & Schuster, 1954.

Jackson, Robert H. *That Man: An Insider's Portrait of Franklin D. Roosevelt*. New York: Oxford University Press, 2003.

Kelly, John. *The Graves Are Walking: The Great Famine and the Saga of the Irish People*. New York: Henry Holt, 2012.

Kolpan, Gerald. *Etta*. New York: Ballantine, 2009.

Krock, Arthur. *Memoirs: Sixty Years on the Firing Line*. New York: Funk & Wagnalls, 1968.

Lash, Joseph P. *Eleanor and Franklin*. New York: W. W. Norton, 1971.

Lash, Joseph P., editor. *From the Diaries of Felix Frankfurter*. New York: W. W. Norton, 1975.

Laughlin, Clara E. *So You're Going South!* Boston: Little, Brown, 1940.

Levin, Linda Lotridge. *The Making of FDR: The Story of Stephen T. Early, America's First Modern Press Secretary*. Amherst, New York: Prometheus, 2008.

Lindley, Ernest K. *Franklin D. Roosevelt: A Career in Progressive Democracy*. New York: Blue Ribbon, 1931.

Lippman, Theo Jr. *The Squire of Warm Springs: FDR in Georgia, 1924–45*. New York: Playboy Press, 1977.

MacKay, Malcolm. *Impeccable Connections: The Rise and Fall of Richard Whitney*. New York: Brick Tower, 2013.

Martin, Ralph G. *Cissy: The Extraordinary Life of Eleanor Medill Patterson*. New York: Simon & Schuster, 1979.

Matthews, Chris. *Tip and the Gipper: When Politics Worked*. New York: Simon & Schuster, 2013.

McElvaine, Robert S. *The Depression and the New Deal: A History in Documents*. New York: Oxford University Press, 2000.

McIntire, Ross T. *White House Physician*. New York: G. P. Putnam's Sons, 1946.

McKean, David. *Tommy the Cork: Washington's Ultimate Insider from Roosevelt to Reagan*. South Royalton, Vermont: Steerforth, 2004.

Metcalf, Allan. *Presidential Voices: Speaking Styles from George Washington to George W. Bush*. New York: Houghton Mifflin Harcourt, 2004.

Miller, Nathan. *FDR: An Intimate Biography*. Garden City: Doubleday, 1983.

Mitchell, John. *The Last Conquest of Ireland (Perhaps)*. Glasgow: R. & T. Washbourne, 1858.

Moe, Richard. *Roosevelt's Second Act: The Election of 1940 and the Politics of War*. New York: Oxford University Press, 2013.

Moley, Raymond. *After Seven Years: A Political Analysis of the New Deal*. New York: Harper & Brothers, 1939.

———. *The First New Deal*. New York: Harcourt, Brace & World, 1966.

Morgan, Ted. *FDR: A Biography*. New York: Simon & Schuster, 1985.

Morris, Dee, and Dora St. Martin. *Somerville, Massachusetts: A Brief History*. Charleston, S.C.: History Press, 2008.

Nasaw, David. *The Patriarch: The Remarkable Life and Turbulent Times of Joseph P. Kennedy*. New York: Penguin, 2012.

Nesbitt, Henrietta. *White House Diary*. Garden City: Country Life Press, 1948

Olson, Lynne. *Citizens of London: The Americans Who Stood with Britain in Its Darkest, Finest Hour*. New York: Random House, 2010.

———. *Those Angry Days: Roosevelt, Lindbergh, and America's Fight over World War II, 1939–1941*. New York: Random House, 2013.

O'Neill, Thomas P. *Man of the House: The Life and Political Memoirs of Speaker Tip O'Neill*. New York: Random House, 1987.

Oshinsky, David M. *Polio: An American Story*. New York: Oxford University Press, 2005.

Oursler, Fulton, and Fulton Oursler Jr., editor. *Behold This Dreamer: An Autobiography*. Boston: Little, Brown, 1964.

Parks, Lillian Rogers, and Frances Spatz Leighton. *The Roosevelts: A Family in Turmoil*. Englewood Cliffs: Prentice Hall, 1981.

Perkins, Frances. *The Roosevelt I Knew*. New York: Viking, 1946.

Persico, Joseph E. *Franklin & Lucy: President Roosevelt, Mrs. Rutherfurd and the Other Remarkable Women in His Life*. New York: Random House, 2008.

Phillips-Fein, Kim. *Invisible Hands: The Businessmen's Crusade Against the New Deal*. New York: W. W. Norton, 2009.

Powell, Jim. *FDR's Folly: How Roosevelt and His New Deal Prolonged the Great Depression*. New York: Crown Forum, 2003.

Reilly, Michael F., and William J. Slocum. *Reilly of the White House.* New York: Simon & Schuster, 1947.

Robertson, David. *Sly and Able: A Political Biography of James F. Byrnes.* New York: W. W. Norton, 1994.

Roll, David L. *The Hopkins Touch: Harry Hopkins and the Forging of the Alliance to Defeat Hitler.* New York: Oxford University Press, 2013.

Rollins, Alfred B. Jr. *Roosevelt and Howe.* New York: Alfred A. Knopf, 1962.

Rogers, Agnes. *Women Are Here to Stay: The Durable Sex in Its Infinite Variety Through Half a Century of American Life.* New York: Harper & Brothers, 1949.

Roosevelt, Curtis. *Too Close to the Sun.* New York: PublicAffairs, 2008.

Roosevelt, Eleanor. *The Autobiography of Eleanor Roosevelt.* New York: Harper & Brothers, 1961.

———. *My Day: The Best of Eleanor Roosevelt's Acclaimed Newspaper Columns, 1936–62.* Cambridge: Da Capo, 2001.

———. *This I Remember.* New York: Harper & Brothers, 1949.

Roosevelt, Elliott. Eleanor Roosevelt Mystery series, various.

Roosevelt, Elliott, and James Brough. *A Rendezvous with Destiny: The Roosevelts of the White House.* New York: G. P. Putnam's Sons, 1975.

———. *An Untold Story: The Roosevelts of Hyde Park.* New York: G. P. Putnam's Sons, 1973.

Roosevelt, James, and Sidney Shallett. *Affectionately, F.D.R.: A Son's Story of a Lonely Man.* New York: Harcourt, Brace, 1959.

Roosevelt, James, and Bill Libby. *My Parents: A Differing View.* Chicago: Playboy Press, 1976.

Rosenman, Samuel I. *Working with Roosevelt.* New York: Harper & Bros., 1952.

Rowley, Hazel. *Franklin and Eleanor: An Extraordinary Marriage.* New York: Farrar, Straus & Giroux, 2010.

Saylor, Carolyn. *Doris Fleeson: Incomparably the First Political Journalist of Her Time.* Santa Fe: Sunstone Press, 2010.

Schlesinger, Arthur M. Jr. *The Coming of the New Deal.* Boston: Houghton Mifflin, 1958.

———. *The Crisis of the Old Order.* Boston: Houghton Mifflin, 1957.

———. *The Politics of Upheaval.* Boston: Houghton Mifflin, 1960.

Seldes, George. *Witness to a Century: Encounters with the Noted, the Notorious and Three SOBs.* New York: Ballantine, 1987.

Sevareid, Eric. *Not So Wild a Dream*. New York: Alfred A. Knopf, 1947.

Sherwood, Robert E. *Roosevelt and Hopkins: An Intimate History*. New York: Harper & Brothers, 1948.

Shirer, William L. *Berlin Diary: The Journal of a Foreign Correspondent, 1934–1941*. New York: Alfred A. Knopf, 1942.

Smith, Jane S. *Patenting the Sun: Polio and the Salk Vaccine*. New York: William Morrow, 1990.

Smith, Jean Edward. *FDR*. New York: Random House, 2007.

Sonneborn, Liz. *The Great Irish Famine*. New York: Chelsea House, 2012.

Srodes, James. *On Dupont Circle: Franklin and Eleanor Roosevelt and the Progressives Who Shaped Our World*. Berkeley: Counterpoint, 2012.

Steinberg, Alfred. *Mrs. R: The Life of Eleanor Roosevelt*. New York: G. P. Putnam's Sons, 1958.

Streitmatter, Rodger. *Empty Without You: The Intimate Letters of Eleanor Roosevelt and Lorena Hickok*. New York: Free Press, 1998.

Stevens, Ruth. *Hi-Ya Neighbor: Intimate Glimpses of Franklin D. Roosevelt at Warm Springs, Georgia, 1924–45*. New York: Tupper & Love, 1947.

Stiles, Lela. *The Man Behind Roosevelt: The Story of Louis McHenry Howe*. New York: World, 1954.

Swift, Will. *The Roosevelts and the Royals*. Hoboken: John Wiley & Sons, 2004.

Tobin, James. *The Man He Became: How FDR Defied Polio to Win the Presidency*. New York: Simon & Schuster, 2013.

Trohan, Walter. *Political Animals: Memoirs of a Sentimental Cynic*. Garden City: Doubleday, 1975.

Tugwell, Rexford G. *The Democratic Roosevelt: A Biography of Franklin Delano Roosevelt*. Garden City: Doubleday, 1957.

———. *In Search of Roosevelt*. Cambridge: Harvard University Press, 1972.

Tully, Grace. *F.D.R. My Boss*. New York: Charles Scribner's Sons, 1939.

Unofficial Observer. *The New Dealers*. New York: Literary Guild, 1934.

Walker, Turnley. *Rise Up and Walk*. New York: E. P. Dutton, 1950.

Ward, Geoffrey C. *Before the Trumpet: Young Franklin Roosevelt, 1882–1905*. New York: Harper & Row, 1985.

———. *A First-Class Temperament: The Emergence of Franklin Roosevelt*. New York: Harper & Row, 1989.

Ward, Geoffrey C., editor. *Closest Companion: The Unknown Story of the Intimate Friendship Between Franklin Roosevelt and Margaret Suckley*. Boston: Houghton Mifflin, 1995.

Ward, Geoffrey C., and Ken Burns, *The Roosevelts: An Intimate History*. New York: Alfred A. Knopf, 2014.

Watkins, T. H. *Righteous Pilgrim: The Life and Times of Harold L. Ickes*. New York: Henry Holt, 1990.

Wehle, Louis B. *Hidden Threads of History: Wilson Through Roosevelt*. New York: Macmillan, 1953.

Welles, Sumner. *The Time for Decision*. New York: Harper & Brothers, 1944.

*The White House, An Historic Guide, 19th Edition*. Washington, D.C.: White House Historical Association with the cooperation of the National Geographic Society, 1995.

### Newspapers

*Atlanta Constitution*

*Atlanta Journal*

*Boston Daily Record*

*Boston Evening American*

*Boston Globe*

*Boston Sunday Post*

*Detroit News*

*Manchester* (Georgia) *Mercury*

*Massena* (New York) *Observer*

*New York Times*

*Ogdensburg* (New York) *Advance*

*Ogdensburg* (New York) *Republican Journal*

*Potsdam* (New York) *Courier Freeman*

*Potsdam* (New York) *Herald Recorder*

*Warm Springs* (Georgia) *Mirror*

*Washington Post*

*Worcester* (Massachusetts) *Evening Gazette*

### Magazines

*American Heritage*, August 1965.

*Democratic Digest*, February 1938. Ruby A. Black, "Ladies of the White House Secretariat."

*Ladies' Home Journal,* June 1973. Bernard Asbell, "Missy: The Tragic Story of the Secretary Who Loved President Roosevelt."
*Life,* April 11, 1938. "The Kennedy Kids: America's Gift to Diplomacy."
*Look,* August 13, 1940. "Look Calls on Missy LeHand."
*Newsweek,* various.
*Saturday Evening Post,* January 8, 1938. Doris Fleeson, "Missy to Do This."
*Time,* various.
*Who,* May 1941. Dorothy Ducas, "Ladies in Waiting in the White House."

### *Interviews*

David Burke, ranger, Little White House, June 10, 2013.
Frank Costigliola, historian, June 26, 2013.
Dawn Ramsey Desley, neighbor of Missy's in Somerville, September 30, 2014.
Marion Dunn, former Warm Springs "push boy" and brace shop worker, April 12, 2015.
Peter C. English, MD, medical historian, February 12, 2014.
Nina Roosevelt Gibson, granddaughter of FDR, April 12, 2014.
Diana Hopkins Halsted, daughter of Harry Hopkins, March 3, 2014.
Barbara Jacques and Jane Scarbrough, Missy's great-nieces, numerous interviews, 2013–2015.
Steven Lomazow, MD, medical historian, numerous interviews, 2013–2015.
Harold G. Morse, MD, internist and cardiologist, June 21, 2013.
Rev. Bob Patterson, local historian, Warm Springs, June 12, 2013.
Hal S. "Toby" Raper, son of Warm Springs Foundation physician, April 12, 2014, and September 8, 2014.
David Roll, biographer of Harry Hopkins, February 26, 2014.
Mike Shadix, archivist, Roosevelt Warm Springs Rehabilitation Campus, June 10, 2013.
Geoffrey Ward, FDR biographer, numerous.

### *Tours of Historic Sites*

#### WARM SPRINGS, GEORGIA

Little White House
Rehabilitation Pools
Dowdell's Knob

Hotel Warm Springs
Marguerite LeHand Cottage and other historic cottages, Roosevelt Warm Springs Rehabilitation Campus

HYDE PARK, NEW YORK

FDR Library and Museum
Springwood
Top Cottage
Val-Kill

SOMERVILLE, MASSACHUSETTS, AND ENVIRONS

LeHand home, Somerville
Somerville High School, Somerville
Somerville Public Library, Somerville
Mount Auburn Cemetery, Cambridge

### *Papers at FDR Library*

Family, Business, Personal (FBP)
President's Personal File (PPF)
Roosevelt Family Papers (RFP)
Eleanor Roosevelt Papers
Ross McIntire Papers
Steven Early Papers
Louis McHenry Howe Papers
Grace Tully Collection

### *Other Papers*

Roosevelt Warm Springs Rehabilitation Campus archive
Correspondence and subject file of Dr. C. E. Irwin, Marguerite LeHand Medical File, Georgia Archive
William Christian Bullitt Papers, Manuscripts and Archives, Yale University Library
Joseph P. Kennedy Papers, John F. Kennedy Library
LeHand Family Papers, privately held by Barbara Jacques and Jane Scarbrough
Harold Ickes Papers, Library of Congress
George Eastman Papers, Rochester, New York

### *Documentaries and Videos*

*The American Experience: FDR.*

Roosevelt House, Hunter College, Discussion with Frank Castigliola June 4, 2012, accessed June 22, 2013, on YouTube.

*Presidential Portrait: FDR at Warm Springs.* Film at Little White House museum.

*The Roosevelts: An Intimate History.* A Ken Burns Film.

### *Web Sources*

Association for Education in Journalism and Mass Communications. "Women Through *Time*: Who Gets Covered?" by Sammye Johnson and William G. Christ. San Antonio University, 1987. Accessed July 8, 2013. http://files.eric.ed.gov/fulltext/ED283148.pdf

City of Somerville. *Annual Report of the City of Somerville*, 1912. Accessed June 8, 2015. https://archive.org/details/annualreportof ci1912some.

DeathPenaltyUSA. "U.S.A. Executions 1607–1976 by State." Accessed June 8, 2015. http://deathpenaltyusa.org/usa1/state/new_york5.htm.

Disability History Museum. "Request to Work at Top Cottage as Housekeeper, with Reply." Accessed June 8, 2015. http://www.disabilitymuseum.org/dhm/lib/catcard.html?id=2064.

Explore Southern History. "Dowdell's Knob." Accessed June 8, 2015. http://www.exploresouthernhistory.com/dowdellsknob.html.

Federal Deposit Insurance Corporation. "The Establishment of the FDIC." Accessed June 8, 2015. https://www.fdic.gov/bank/analytical/firstfifty/chapter3.pdf.

Focus Features. "How Richard Nelson Met Daisy." Accessed May 13, 2015. http://www.focusfeatures.com/article/how_richard_nelson_met_daisy?film=hyde_park_on_hudson.

"Franklin Delano Roosevelt Day by Day." Numerous accesses. http://www.fdrlibrary.marist.edu/daybyday/about/.

Franklin Delano Roosevelt Library and Museum. "One Definite Locality: History of the FDR Presidential Library and Museum." Accessed June 25, 2014. http://www.fdrlibrary.marist.edu/library/onedefinitelocality.html.

Guerlain. "L'Heure Bleue." Accessed June 8, 2015. http://www.guerlain.com/us/en-us/fragrance/womens-fragrances/lheure-bleue.

Library and Archives Canada. "A Real Companion and Friend": The Diaries of William Lyon Mackenzie King. Entries of April 23, 1940, and April 24, 1940. Accessed June 21, 2013. http://www.collections canada.gc.ca/king/index-e.html.

New Georgia Encyclopedia. "Great Depression" by Jamil S. Zainaldin. Accessed Nov. 24, 2014. http://www.georgiaencyclopedia.org/articles/history-archaeology/great-depression.

New York Census, 1915. Accessed November 15, 2013. http://www.ancestry.com.

New York Governor. "New York Governor's Executive Mansion." Accessed June 8, 2015. http://www.governor.ny.gov/explore-governors-mansion. (Original source was the New York Governor's Executive Mansion Resource Kit, no longer available.)

New York City Subway. 1920 subway map. Accessed June 8, 2015. http://www.nycsubway.org/perl/caption.pl?/img/maps/calcagno-1920-elevated.gif.

Politifact.com. "Comparing the Great Recession and the Great Depression" by Louis Jacobson. Accessed June 9, 2015. http://www.politifact.com/truth-o-meter/article/2013/sep/19/comparing-great-recession-and-great-depression/.

Roosevelt House. "Franklin Roosevelt's Desk: Working in New York City, 1921–1928. Accessed June 8, 2015. http://www.roosevelthouse.hunter.cuny.edu/work/franklin-delano-roosevelts-desk/.

St. Louis Federal Reserve. "The Great Depression: An Overview," by David C. Wheelock. Accessed June 8, 2015. http://www.stlouisfed.org/great-depression/pdf/the-great-depression-wheelock-overview.pdf.

Social Security Administration. "Title V of the Social Security Act: What It Has Meant to Children" by Katherine B. Oettinger. http://www.ssa.gov/policy/authors/OettingerKatherineB.html.

Somerville Public Schools. "History of Somerville High School." Accessed November 10, 2013. http://www.somerville.k12.ma.us/education/components/scrapbook/default.php?sectiondetailid=14716&linkid=nav-menu-container-4-89914.

"The Strange Case of the Tully Archive" by Bob Clark. Accessed May 29, 2013. http://www.fdrlibrary.marist.edu/archives/pdfs/clark_tully.pdf.

Union Square Main Streets. "What the Fluff?" Accessed June 8, 2015. https://unionsquaremain.org/?s=What+the+Fluff.

U.S. Census, 1860, 1900, 1910, 1920, 1930, 1940. Numerous accesses. www.census.gov.

U.S. Inflation Calculator. Numerous accesses. http://www.usinflation calculator.com/.

U.S. National Library of Medicine. "Digitalis Delirium" by John T. King. Accessed June 8, 2015. http://www.ncbi.nlm.nih.gov/pmc/articles/PMC2242024/.

U.S. Navy. "Origins of Navy Terminology: Cup of Joe." Accessed June 8, 2015. http://www.navy.mil/navydata/traditions/html/navyterm.html#joe.

Virginia Aviation History Project. "American Airways Ford Trimotor Transports FDR to Chicago Democratic Convention" by Baird Wonsey and Marguerite Wonsey. Accessed Nov. 28, 2013. http://vahsonline.publishpath.com/Websites/vahsonline/Images/History%20Project/American%20Airlines%20Fort%20Trimotor%20Transports%20FDR%20to%20Chicago%20Democratic%20Convention.pdf.

# *Photography Credits*

| *Page* | *Credit* |
|---|---|
| 3 | LeHand Family Papers |
| 8 | Franklin Delano Roosevelt Library |
| 15 | Somerville Public Library |
| 17 | Somerville Public Library |
| 18 | LeHand Family Papers |
| 19 | Somerville Public Library |
| 24 | Franklin Delano Roosevelt Library |
| 26 | Franklin Delano Roosevelt Library |
| 29 | Franklin Delano Roosevelt Library |
| 30 | Franklin Delano Roosevelt Library |
| 36 | LeHand Family Papers |
| 44 | Author photo. Source: LeHand Family. |
| 57 | Steven Lomazow Collection |
| 58 | Franklin Delano Roosevelt Library |
| 71 | LeHand Family Papers |
| 73 | LeHand Family Papers |
| 85 | LeHand Family Papers |
| 91 | Eleanor Roosevelt Historic Site, National Park Service, Cook-Dickerman Collection |
| 92 | Franklin Delano Roosevelt Library |
| 101 | Franklin Delano Roosevelt Library |
| 114 | Hulton Archive/Getty Images |
| 125 | Franklin Delano Roosevelt Library |
| 128 | Library of Congress |

131 Author's collection
136 LeHand Family Papers
142 Roosevelt Warm Springs Vocational Rehabilitation Campus, Georgia Vocational Rehabilitation Agency, Warm Springs, Georgia
149 Author's Collection
155 LeHand Family Papers
160 Library of Congress
161 Library of Congress
163 Library of Congress
171 LeHand Family Papers
175 Roosevelt Warm Springs Vocational Rehabilitation Campus, Georgia Vocational Rehabilitation Agency, Warm Springs, Georgia
177 Franklin Delano Roosevelt Library
179 Library of Congress
181 LeHand Family Papers
183 Roosevelt Warm Springs Vocational Rehabilitation Campus, Georgia Vocational Rehabilitation Agency, Warm Springs, Georgia
198 Associated Press
202 Getty Images
209 Author photo. Source: LeHand Family Papers
214 Franklin Delano Roosevelt Library
217 William C. Bullitt Papers, Manuscripts and Archives, Yale University Library
229 Associated Press
231 Author's Collection
241 Franklin Delano Roosevelt Library
247 Franklin Delano Roosevelt Library
252 LeHand Family Papers
260 LeHand Family Papers
261 LeHand Family Papers
265 LeHand Family Papers
267 Somerville Public Library
268 Franklin Delano Roosevelt Library
270 LeHand Family Papers

# Index